Troubleshooting

Basic Writing Skills

Troubleshooting

Basic Writing Skills

THIRD EDITION

William Herman
The City College of The City University of New York

Jeffrey M. Young

HOLT, RINEHART AND WINSTON, INC.
Fort Worth   Chicago   San Francisco   Philadelphia
Montreal   Toronto   London   Sydney   Tokyo

Library of Congress Cataloging-in-Publication Data

Herman, William, 1926–
   Troubleshooting: basic writing skills.

   1. English language—Rhetoric.   2. English language—
Grammar—1950–   . I. Young, Jeffrey M.   II. Title.
PE1408.H468   1986   808′.042   85-14110

ISBN 0-03-002133-2

Printed in the United States of America
         9   016   9 8 7 6 5

Preface

The rules of English composition are often troublesome to students. This book is designed to help students spot their problems and go to work on them. Using the book will not turn the work into fun, but it will make it possible to do the work efficiently and effectively.

As in the first two editions, only the most basic material is covered in grammar, usage, and mechanics; formal terminology is kept to a minimum. Each chapter begins with a brief section which explains the practical importance of the material to be dealt with. The material itself is then broken down into a number of points, each of which is presented separately in simple language and followed by illustrations and practice exercises. Cumulative review exercises are interspersed throughout the chapter, giving the student frequent opportunity to bring together the rules and principles learned in several points. Whenever possible, the student is shown *why* a rule is needed, rather than asked merely to take it on faith. At the end of the chapter, the most essential "how to" concepts are covered in a short boxed section just before an extensive and comprehensive set of chapter review exercises. The important points are restated in summary form at the back of the book, to serve as a study aid.

Exercises of varied types have been included: choose-the-correct-answer, fill-in-the-blanks, write-your-own-sentences. The final exercise of each chapter review provides another twist. Two or three paragraphs of material similar to typical student writing are presented, and the student is asked to rewrite them, correcting the errors.

The third edition contains new, clearer explanations of subjects, verbs, and possessives. Many exercises throughout the book have been revised, especially where the answers were ambiguous in the first two editions. The Answers to Exercises section has been thoroughly checked. In general, the relaxed pace of the book has been retained. The book makes no assumptions about students' knowledge and provides students with numerous varied opportunities for success. We hope that students who use this book will not only learn to write correct sentences but also develop a *feel* for sentences.

Several people have helped in the preparation of the third edition. Among them we would like to thank Charlotte Smith, Holt, Rinehart and Winston; Mark Bauman, Johnson County Community College; Richard Freccero, Brookline Public Schools; Jacqueline Griffin, Essex County College; and Ralph Thompson, Ricks College.

W.H./J.M.Y.

v

To the Student

This book contains a lot of exercises. But it also contains an answer key, so you can check your answers to the exercises. The key, which is at the back of the book, will be most helpful if you use it to check your work *as soon as you finish* each exercise. In this way you will find out right away whether you have understood the material and learned how to apply the rules correctly. If you discover that you have made mistakes, you may be able to figure out for yourself what is wrong—or at least you will be alerted to ask your instructor for help.

Contents

PART I

GRAMMAR REVIEW

PRETEST

Note: This test is designed to identify any problems you may have with basic grammar (subjects and verbs). All the material tested here will be fully explained in Chapters 1 and 2, which follow.

I. Write *S* if the sentence is missing a subject, *V* if the sentence is missing a verb, or *C* if the sentence is correct as it stands.

_____ 1. Carolyn cooking a gourmet dinner tonight.

_____ 2. Doris and her friends to the museum every Thursday.

_____ 3. Used his father's credit card at the gas station.

_____ 4. He is an amateur boxer.

_____ 5. Was ready for action.

_____ 6. A kiss is still a kiss.

_____ 7. Whenever it rains, we stay inside and television.

_____ 8. There were swimming in the lake.

_____ 9. Babies cry.

1

———— 10. He planning to join the club.

———— 11. We walking around the city.

———— 12. We have registered to vote.

———— 13. Are plannning a surprise party.

———— 14. That is no way to treat a person.

———— 15. Is building his own house.

———— 16. My notes need to be retyped.

———— 17. Two types of flowers growing in the garden.

———— 18. Joey in a good mood today.

———— 19. Toto, Tiki, and Jenny meow a lot.

———— 20. The kids ate their dinner and ran upstairs.

II. Underline the complete subject.

1. Jamie is going out for the track team.

2. The Dodgers and the Mets play tonight.

3. Correct grammar is an important aspect of good writing.

4. In the cabana is the rowboat.

5. Jazz is my favorite kind of music.

6. Hans and Lisa bought that car.

7. Organic food is healthful but expensive.

8. Exercising is part of my morning routine.

9. Around the corner fled the stray dog.

10. That hibachi near the garage is broken.

III. Underline the complete verb.

1. My father is retiring from business.

2. We have never been to Europe.

3. She grew more and more tired.

4. I never promised you a rose garden.

5. You should be sure to check the oil.

6. Holding down a job is never easy for Luke.

7. I have tried my hardest to succeed.

8. Woodworking requires skill and patience.

9. We spent our paychecks yesterday.

10. I always visit my parents on holidays.

1

Subjects

IMPORTANT TERMS INTRODUCED IN THIS CHAPTER

subject the person or thing about which the rest of the sentence makes an assertion.

simple subject the noun or pronoun that the sentence is primarily about.

complete subject the simple subject PLUS any words that modify or describe it.

noun a word that names a person, place, thing, or idea.

pronoun a word that takes the place of a noun.

compound subject the combination (with *and* or *or*) of two or more subjects that share the same verb.

A sentence is a group of words that expresses a complete thought. The thought may tell something, ask a question, express a request or command, or express a strong emotion or feeling. *Every sentence must contain a subject*—except requests or commands, where the subject is not in the sentence but is only understood (in the request, "Turn off the lights," the subject is really *you*—the person addressed; but the word *you* is not *in* the sentence). The subject is the person or thing about which the rest of the sentence makes an assertion. In other words, any sentence must *be about* someone or something, and therefore *every sentence must have a subject*.

POINT 1   **Identify the subject of the sentence by asking *who or what* is doing something (or being something).**

Rain falls.

In this sentence, the subject is *rain*. We find the subject by asking, "Who or what falls?" The answer to that question, *rain,* is the subject.

Mario works hard.

Who or what is doing something? Or who or what works? *Mario* works. *Mario* is the subject of the sentence.

The girl sings in the choir.

Who or what sings? The *girl* sings. What, then, is the subject of this sentence?

● Subjects may be either *singular* or *plural.* A singular subject refers to *one* person or thing; a plural subject refers to *more than one.* Plural subjects usually end in *-s.* Some exceptions include *men, women,* and *children.*

Singular		**Plural**	
	boy		boys
	girl	*more*	girls
one	car	*than*	cars
	dog	*one*	dogs
	pencil		pencils

In the previous sentences, the subjects were singular (*rain, Mario, girl*). You can find plural subjects in a sentence by asking the same "who or what" question.

The sandwiches were delicious.

Who or what were delicious? The answer to that question, *sandwiches,* is the subject, and it is plural.

My sisters are named Lynn and Karen.

Who or what are named? *Sisters* is the plural subject of this sentence.

Buses run every hour on the hour.

Who or what run? *Buses* is the plural subject of this sentence.

Exercise: Point 1

Determine the subject in each of the following sentences by answering the "who or what" question.

1. The plumber works.

   Who or what works? The subject is _____ *plumber* _____

2. Doug acts in the play.

   Who or what acts? The subject is _____

3. The tree fell in the storm.

   Who or what fell? The subject is _____

4. The motorcycle roared.

   Who or what roared? The subject is _____

5. Lucy eats an apple a day.

   Who or what eats? The subject is _____

6. Our family celebrates Christmas.

   Who or what celebrates? The subject is _____

7. Those speakers sound great.

   Who or what sounds? The subject is _____

8. My brother plays basketball on weekends.

   Who or what plays? The subject is _____

9. Fans cheer in the stands.

   Who or what cheers? The subject is _____

10. The store was robbed last night.

    Who or what was robbed? The subject is _____

Another Exercise: Point 1

For each of the following sentences, write *S* if the subject is singular or *P* if it is plural. Underline the simple subject.

__*S*__   1. <u>Sally</u> ran after the bus.

_____   2. My friend built a new beach house.

_____   3. Ducks swim in that pond.

_____   4. The airplane needs to be refueled.

_____   5. Our daughter gave us a surprise party.

_____   6. Sam writes extremely well.

_____   7. The clouds obscured the sun.

_____ 8. Jason sings in the choir.

_____ 9. Ms. Peterson bought a moped.

_____ 10. The snowstorm lasted for hours.

POINT 2   A subject may be a noun.

A _noun_ is a word used to name a _person, place,_ or _thing._

Persons	**Places**	**Things**
Ruth	Nebraska	cat
Luis	Main Street	tooth
Mrs. Maxwell	Belgium	house
man	Russia	car
teacher	Lake Erie	love

Most of the subjects we have seen are nouns. However, not every noun in a sentence is a subject. Remember, we determine a subject by asking who or what performs the action. Each of the following sentences contains more than one noun, but each sentence has only one subject.

> Jim works in a store.

First determine the subject. Who or what works? Jim works. So _Jim_ is the subject. Are there any other nouns in this sentence? That is, are any words used to name a person, place, or thing? _Store_ is a thing; therefore it is a noun.

> Janet mailed the letter.

Which words are nouns? How can you determine the subject of this sentence?

Exercise: Point 2

Underline all the nouns in each of the following sentences. Then circle the subject of the sentence.

1. (California) joined the Union in 1850.

2. Henry runs a mile every day.

3. Flowers grow best in sunlight.

4. Exercise strengthens the body.

5. That boy joined our club.

6. My watch comes from Japan.

7. The senators voted on the bill.

8. Sally wrote a letter to her member of Congress.

9. Starvation worries people all over the world.

10. Bills are a part of life.

Review Exercise: Points 1 and 2

Fill in the blank with an appropriate subject.

1. _____*Vermont*_____ is a state in New England

2. _____ taught me everything I know.

3. _____ discovered America.

4. _____ fought against America in World War II.

5. _____ sailed around the world.

6. _____ is a former president.

7. _____ appeared on television.

8. My _____ is my mother's brother.

9. _____ make good pets.

10. _____ was my favorite teacher.

POINT 3   A subject may be a *pronoun*.

A pronoun is a word that takes the place of a noun. It takes the position that a noun can take in a sentence. For example, the sentence

> **The detective** solves the case.

can be changed to

> **He** solves the case.

Detective is a noun; *he* is a pronoun. Like nouns, pronouns **may be** singular or plural. The following pronouns may be used as subjects:

Singular Pronouns
I—when the subject is the speaker himself or herself

> **I ride** the bus daily.

you—when the subject is the person spoken to

> **You owe** me ten dollars.

he—when the subject is masculine and singular

> **He drives** a Ford.

she—when the subject is feminine and singular

> **She wants** to buy a stereo.

it—when the subject is a thing or an action, neither masculine nor feminine, and singular

> **It is** a good way to exercise.

Plural Pronouns

we—when the subject is a group which includes the speaker

> **We sang** Chrismas carols.

you—when the subject is the persons spoken to

> **You** all **finished** the assignment.

they—when the subject is a group of persons or things not including the speaker

> **They voted** in the last election.

Exercise: Point 3

Rewrite the following sentences, changing the noun subjects to pronoun subjects.

1. Harvey is a shrewd businessman.

   He is a shrewd businessman.

2. My wife has just completed college.

   _____

3. Nude sunbathing does not bother me.

   _____

4. John and I are going to write a song.

   _____

5. Large corporations make a lot of money.

   _____

6. Mrs. Grant is buried in Grant's Tomb.

   _____

7. Learning to write well takes time.

_____

8. Wally surely knows how to water-ski.

_____

9. All my relatives sent me birthday cards.

_____

10. Buster Brown and his dog, Tige, understood each other.

_____

POINT 4   A subject may be an *-ing* word.

    Fishing is my hobby.

To determine the subject of this sentence, ask who or what is my hobby. The answer to that question, *fishing*, is the subject.
    Do not be confused by a sentence such as

    I enjoy fishing.

To determine the subject of this sentence, ask who or what enjoys. The answer, *I*, is the subject.

    Parachuting may be dangerous.

Who or what may be dangerous? *Parachuting* is the subject of the sentence.

    Tim likes to go parachuting.

Who or what likes? *Tim* is the subject.

Exercise: Point 4

Underline the subject in each of the following sentences.

1. <u>Singing</u> is her chief talent.

2. Driving drives me crazy.

3. Jogging is good exercise.

4. I am losing my patience.

5. I don't like cleaning my apartment.

6. You are finding it difficult to concentrate.

7. Sewing was never her favorite activity.

8. Advertising is a good way to get votes.

9. They always go skiing in January.

10. Cooking is her favorite hobby.

POINT 5   A subject may consist of more than one word.

So far, most of the subjects have been just one word: *rain, Mario, plumber, cars, I, we, jogging, biking,* and so on. This noun or pronoun that the sentence is primarily about is called the *simple subject*. When the subject of a sentence contains more than one word, all those words make up the *complete subject*. The simple subject is part of the complete subject.

In the following examples, the simple subject is underlined, and the complete subject is circled.

The <u>man</u> sitting in the bleachers is eating a hot dog.

The fresh <u>vegetables</u> from my garden are tasty.

Note that the *complete subject* contains (1) the simple subject and (2) any words that modify or describe the simple subject.

A *compound subject* consists of two or more subjects that share the same verb.

Pat and Louise work together.

Pat and Louise is the compound subject.

Mowing the lawn and raking the leaves are two of my least favorite activities.

Mowing the lawn and raking the leaves is the compound subject.

Exercise: Point 5

Underline the complete subject in each of the following sentences.

1. <u>Collecting stamps</u> is my hobby.

2. His sister is an expert pianist.

3. Looking for an apartment is hard work.

4. Herb and Everett are starting a dynamic new business.

5. Choosing a spouse can be confusing.

6. Using common sense is important.

7. Bowling on Wednesdays keeps me sane.

8. Clara's radio needs to be repaired.

9. Jack and Jill went up the hill.

10. A green light means that we may go.

Review Exercise: Points 1–5

Fill in the blank with an appropriate subject.

1. _____*Jogging*_____ is a good way to get exercise.

2. _____ go great with a barbecue.

3. _____ use a lot of gasoline.

4. _____ is more fun than watching television.

5. _____ is a great singer.

6. _____ is exciting but dangerous.

7. _____ comes once a year.

8. _____ makes me remember the good old days.

9. _____ always beat us in tennis.

10. _____ fought against the Allies.

Another Review Exercise: Points 1–5

Choose a subject from Column A and match it with a group of words from Column B. Write the complete sentence in the space provided. Make sure the subject answers the "who or what" question.

Column A	**Column B**
Practical jokes	are twin brothers.
Ms. Murphy	can get you into trouble.
Collecting coins	can give you tired feet.
Robert and Richard	is running for mayor.
Shopping for shoes	is my hobby.

1. _____*Practical jokes can get you into trouble.*_____

2. _____

3. _____

4. _____

5. _____

POINT 6   A subject may appear anywhere in the sentence.

So far, all the subjects have been at the beginning of the sentence. However, subjects sometimes appear elsewhere. They are still easy to find if you ask the same "who or what" question.

> There were alligators in the swamp.

Who or what were in the swamp? *Alligators* were in the swamp. *Alligators* is the subject of this sentence.

> Here are two different problems.

Problems is the subject.

> All night long, James listened to records.

Who or what listened? *James* listened; therefore *James* is the subject.
Note: There and *here* are never subjects.

Exercise: Point 6

Underline the simple subject in each of the following sentences.

1. Around the corner went the <u>motorcycle</u>.

2. In the box seats was the commissioner of baseball.

3. There was a long line at the ticket booth.

4. Here is one way to solve the problem.

5. There is work to be done.

6. Down the ladder came a fire fighter with a baby in his arms.

7. There was no way out.

8. Through the train walked the conductor.

9. In town this week is a great new show.

10. There was a sale in the department store today.

POINT 7   The simple subject is never within a phrase that begins with such words as on, in, of, before, behind, near.

A phrase of this sort can be *part of* a complete subject, but it cannot be the whole subject.

> The man on the corner is playing a clarinet.

Who or what is playing? The answer to that question reveals the subject; clearly, it is the *man*, and not the corner, that is musical.

The jar on the shelf is filled with Japanese black soybeans.

Who or what is filled? The *jar*, not the shelf.

The book in the library was written by Herman Melville.

Book, not library, is the subject.

Once you spot and eliminate any confusing phrases of this sort, it is easy to recognize the subject.

The roof ~~of the house~~ collapsed.
Three members ~~of the group~~ were arrested.

The words listed in Point 7 are called *prepositions*. Other common prepositions include the following:

about	below	from	past	upon
above	beside	inside	through	with
across	between	into	to	within
after	beyond	off	toward	without
around	by	out	under	
at	during	over	until	

Exercise: Point 7

Determine the simple subject in each of the following sentences by asking the "who or what" question.

1. A program of popular music was scheduled.

   Who or what was scheduled? The subject is _____*program*_____.

2. The woman on the bus wore a jacket and tie.

   Who or what wore? The subject is _____.

3. That man with a gun is dangerous.

   Who or what is dangerous? The subject is _____.

4. Those weeds in the garden should be pulled.

   Who or what should be pulled? The subject is _____.

5. That problem on the blackboard is difficult.

   Who or what is difficult? The subject is _____.

6. Dreaming of days gone by is hopeless.

   Who or what is hopeless? The subject is _____.

7. The fishermen on the wharf are talking.

   Who or what are talking? The subject is _____.

8. Teachers in nursery schools must be patient.

   Who or what must be patient? The subject is _____.

9. The calm before the storm is threatening.

   Who or what is threatening? The subject is _____.

10. Those beers in the cooler are ready.

    Who or what are ready? The subject is _____.

Review Exercise: Points 1–7

Underline the complete subject in each of the following sentences.

1. <u>Melvin</u> wants to study law.

2. Obeying the speed limit helps conserve fuel.

3. He and I will do it together.

4. The switch in the glove compartment opens the trunk.

5. Eating low-calorie foods is one way to lose weight.

6. On the beach is a lighthouse.

7. The stores on Third Street are closed today.

8. There must be something wrong with you.

9. The man in the bullpen will soon come in to pitch.

10. Around the corner is the mailbox.

HOW TO USE SUBJECTS CORRECTLY

> 1. To identify the subject, ask yourself *who or what* performs the action.
> 2. Remember that a subject may be a noun, a pronoun, an *-ing* word, or a group of words.
> 3. A subject may appear anywhere in the sentence.

Chapter Review

I. Write *S* if the example has a subject or *X* if it does not. Underline the simple subjects that you find.

_____ 1. Was writing letters to me daily.

_____ 2. Listening to my stereo relaxes me in the evening.

_____ 3. That dog with the floppy ears is mine.

_____ 4. Fighting with his sister.

_____ 5. A collection of rare books is a real treasure.

_____ 6. Ms. Strauss is coming to visit me.

_____ 7. Were doing their best.

_____ 8. In the closet is a pillow.

_____ 9. Bob Dylan was a cultural hero of the 1960s.

_____ 10. Spring cleaning is a necessary chore.

II. Underline the complete subject in each of the following sentences.

1. A fear of dogs is common to many people.

2. Phyllis travels to Japan with her husband.

3. Going on a picnic is a great way to spend an afternoon.

4. One part of my idea involves you.

5. Home repair might become a lost art.

6. Juggling requires good eyesight and coordination.

7. There are three gas stations at that corner.

8. Of all my friends, Chris is the nicest.

9. Blowing my nose unclogs my ears.

10. That leak in the radiator should be fixed.

11. Choosing courses wisely is a student's responsibility.

12. She is the one for me.

13. The filter of an air conditioner should be cleaned regularly.

14. Going to the dentist was a painful experience for me.

15. We all believe his explanation.

16. Repaving the road takes time.

17. Who wrote the textbook?

18. Lost in space, the astronaut tried to radio Earth.

19. He got a job in the new shopping mall.

20. Over the river, the exploding fireworks shed light.

III. Fill in the blank with an appropriate subject.

1. Her _____ was parked illegally.

2. In the cupboard is a _____.

3. _____ helps keep the bugs away.

4. _____ is the country just south of the United States.

5. _____ are coming to see us.

6. My _____ is learning how to play tennis.

7. The rear-view _____ has to be adjusted.

8. _____ is one way to stay in shape.

9. Rainy _____ keeps people indoors.

10. _____ taste great when they are barbecued.

11. The _____ were shattered during the storm.

12. Three _____ were arrested for drunken driving.

13. _____ come out only at night.

14. _____ is president of the United States.

15. In the sink was a _____ of dirty dishes.

16. _____ can give me a headache.

17. _____ never want to see you again.

18. _____ is my idea of fun.

19. _____ are beautiful house plants.

20. Through the city marched _____.

2

Verbs

In any sentence, something must happen; that is, something must be done or felt by the subject of the sentence. A verb is a word that is used to express action; it tells us what is happening. In order to be complete, every sentence must contain a verb. Effective use of the various types and forms of verbs leads to effective communication.

POINT 1   A *verb* is a word (or group of words) used to express action.

Arthur fixed the flat tire.

What action is taking place in this sentence? What happened? The subject of this sentence, *Arthur*, took part in the action of fixing a flat tire. What did the subject do? He *fixed*. *Fixed* is the verb in this sentence.

I work in a public school.

What action is taking place? What does the subject, *I*, do? I *work*. Therefore *work* is the verb in this sentence.

The girl ate her dinner.

What did the subject, *girl*, do? She *ate*. *Ate*, therefore, is the verb in this sentence.

Ted will do the job quickly.

What is the action? The subject, *Ted, will do*. *Will do* is the verb.

Exercise: Point 1

In each of the following sentences, draw one line under the subject and two lines under the verb.

1. <u>Paul</u> <u>mailed</u> the letter.

2. The police officer directs the traffic.

3. I took that exam yesterday.

4. The dog chased the cat around the yard.

5. Arthur operated the ice-cream maker.

6. The cow slept in the shade.

7. A good investment pays for itself.

8. A good fan cools a hot room.

9. The firefighter rescued the child from the burning building.

10. She wrote the lyrics to that song.

POINT 2   **The *tense* of a verb shows the time when the action happened—past, present, or future. Many verbs can be changed from the present tense to the past tense by adding *-d* or *-ed* to the end.**

1. *Present tense*—the action takes place now.

> I walk.
> I vote.
> I scream.
> I jump.

2. *Past tense*—the action expressed by the verb has already taken place (at some time in the past).

> I walked.
> I voted.
> I screamed.
> I jumped.

Note that each of these verbs was changed into the past tense by adding *-d* (when the word already ends in *e*, such as *vote*) or *-ed* to its end. Verbs of this kind are called *regular verbs*.

There are, however, many verbs in English which do not follow the same pattern. These are called *irregular verbs* and will be dealt with in Point 5.

3. Either the present or the past tense can be used to express continuous or frequently repeated action, as well as a single action.

> I walk to class every morning.
> Jim worked here for six months.

Exercise: Point 2

Change the following verbs from the present tense into the past tense by adding *-d* or *-ed* to the end.

1. smile _____ *smiled* _____

2. laugh _____

3. agree _____

4. fix _____

5. bounce _____

6. love _____

7. explode _____

8. adopt _____

9. rent _____

10. call _____

Review Exercise: Points 1 and 2

Write *Pr* if the verb is in the present tense or *Pa* if the verb is in the past tense. Underline the verb in each sentence.

Pr   1. Russ <u>smokes</u> a pack of cigarettes a day.

_____   2. The poet imagined a better world.

_____   3. He confessed his part in the practical joke.

_____   4. The candle sheds a soft light.

_____   5. The neighbors play bridge every Thursday.

_____   6. I wandered through the public garden.

_____   7. I joined the fraternity as a sophomore.

_____   8. I cook her breakfast every morning.

_____   9. Jack watered his bonsai.

_____   10. Our doctor treats his patients kindly.

Another Review Exercise: Points 1 and 2

Fill in the blank with an appropriate verb. In some of the sentences, only one tense (past or present) makes sense. In other sentences, either tense will work. Make sure the verb you choose shows action

1. Yesterday Sam _____ *called* _____ his mother on the telephone.

2. I _____ for the candidate from Maine.

3. She _____ if she would ever return.

4. We _____ to the mall twice a week.

5. Theresa _____ tomatoes in her garden.

6. To avoid an accident, the driver _____ to one side.

7. I _____ to send her a card on her birthday.

8. In a thunderstorm lightning often _____ a tree.

9. Peanuts and beer _____ well together.

10. The baby _____ all night long.

POINT 3   A *linking verb* is used to link the subject to a descriptive word in the sentence or to another noun.

All the verbs we have seen so far in this chapter have been action words. Such verbs as *jump*, *call*, *scream*, and *walk* express a specific action. Another kind of verb, the linking verb, functions differently.

> Wendy is very beautiful.

The linking verb *is* links the subject, *Wendy*, to a word that describes her. The descriptive word in this case is *beautiful*. Note that the verb *is* does not show a particular *action*. It simply serves a "linking" or "connecting" purpose.

> Wendy is a skydiver.

Here the linking verb *is* links the subject to another noun, *skydiver*.

> I grew weary of the journey.

The linking verb *grew* links the subject, *I*, with a descriptive word, *weary*. These words that describe the subjects are called *adjectives*.

> *Note:* A linking verb is often some form of the verb *to be (am, is, are, was, were)*. Other verbs such as *seem*, *look*, *sound*, *grow*, *appear*, and *become* may also sometimes be linking verbs.

Exercise: Point 3

Underline the linking verb in each of the following sentences.

1. Michael is going.

2. You seem to read my mind.

3. This cigarette tastes stale.

4. The union members are ready to strike.

5. They were standing and applauding the runner.

6. The actor appeared to have forgotten his lines.

7. She looked angry as she spoke.

8. The steak was rare and juicy.

9. The sky grew dark before the thunderstorm.

10. He sounded furious.

POINT 4   Verbs ending in *-ing* require another verb (often some form of the verb *to be*) before them.

> I going to the store.

The verb in this sentence, *going,* is incomplete because it does not tell us when the action takes place. In order to make it complete, another verb must precede it. We may add a verb in either the present or the past tense. The sentence should read

> I am going to the store.

(*am going* is the complete verb) or

> I was going to the store.

(*was going* is the complete verb).

> The little boy jumping and laughing.

Once again, the sentence has no complete verb. We need to add another verb before the *-ing* word.

> The little boy kept jumping and laughing.

Notice that it is not necessary to add another verb before every *-ing* word in the sentence. The verb *kept* before the *-ing* word *jumping* is sufficient to complete the verb form *laughing.*

The following chart shows the present and past tenses of the verb *to be*. It is important to memorize these tenses, as it is impossible to use *-ing* words without a working knowledge of this verb.

Present Tense		Past Tense	
I	am	I	was
you	are	you	were
he, she, it	is	he, she, it	was
we		we	
you	are	you	were
they		they	

Note: You have probably noticed that these *-ing* words are of the same sort as the *-ing* words that we used as subjects in Chapter 1. Many kinds of words have more than one use in a sentence. The trick lies in learning the right way to handle them for each use.

More information on how verbs *help* other verbs in sentences will be provided in Point 7.

Exercise: Point 4

In each of the following sentences, underline the *-ing* word and circle the helping verb.

1. Brian(is)washing his car.

2. The player began circling the bases.

3. Dogs were barking all night long.

4. Kevin is weeding the garden.

5. I am preparing for the worst.

6. Mr. Potts is running for a post on the city council.

7. They keep trying to resolve their problems.

8. Americans are choosing a new president.

9. Lucy was singing in the nightclub.

10. We are attempting to improve our performance.

Another Exercise: Point 4

Fill in the blank with the proper form of the verb *to be*.

1. We _____ *are* _____ going on a camping trip. (present tense)

2. I _____ waiting for that bus for an hour. (past tense)

3. You _____ trying too hard. (present tense)

4. Janice _____ balancing her checkbook.

5. We _____ vacationing in Canada. (past tense)

6. They _____ remodeling their basement. (present tense)

7. The children _____ making all kinds of noise. (past tense)

8. I _____ studying for an English exam. (present tense)

9. Bobby _____ swatting flies. (present tense)

10. The mayor _____ shaking everybody's hand. (past tense)

Review Exercise: Points 1–4

Underline the complete verb in each of the following sentences.

1. Ted <u>was cleaning</u> his room.

2. She seemed elated about the news.

3. He drives like a maniac.

4. I am vacuuming the carpet.

5. The baby grows more interesting every day.

6. Debra cut slices of her birthday cake.

7. We are developing new habits.

8. The day turned cold and bleak.

9. They started issuing free passes to the amusement park.

10. He remembered his father's advice.

POINT 5   Some verbs are *irregular*. They do not follow a set pattern when they change tenses.

In Point 4 of this chapter, we saw how the verb *to be* changed its form in unusual ways. *To be* is an irregular verb.

All verbs have principal parts. That is, a verb has different forms to suit its different uses. See how the principal parts of the verb *to begin* work:

Present	Past	Past Participle
begin	began	have begun

Present—begin: It is happening now.

I begin my homework.

Past—began: It happened already.

I began it an hour ago.

Past Participle—have begun: Note that this form of the verb always has a helping verb (some form of the verb *to have*) before it.

I have begun it already.

Become familiar with the way the verb *to have* works, as it will be important when you need to use the past participle.

Irregular Verb (to have)

Present Tense		Past Tense	
I you we you they	have	I you we you they	had
he, she, it	has	he, she, it	

Study the following examples:

Present	Past	Past Participle
give	*gave*	*have given*
I give.	I gave.	I have given.
You give.	You gave.	You have given.
He gives.	He gave.	He has given.
She gives.	She gave.	She has given.
It gives.	It gave.	It has given.
We give.	We gave.	We have given.
They give.	They gave.	They have given.

Here is a list of the most common irregular verbs with their principal parts:

Present	Past	Past Participle
be	was	have been
blow	blew	have blown
break	broke	have broken
bring	brought	have brought
catch	caught	have caught
choose	chose	have chosen
come	came	have come
deal	dealt	have dealt
dive	dived (dove)	have dived
do	did	have done
draw	drew	have drawn
drink	drank	have drunk
drive	drove	have driven
eat	ate	have eaten
fall	fell	have fallen
fly	flew	have flown
forget	forgot	have forgotten
freeze	froze	have frozen
give	gave	have given
go	went	have gone
grow	grew	have grown
know	knew	have known
lay	laid	have laid
lead	led	have led
lie	lay	have lain
lose	lost	have lost
raise	raised	have raised
ring	rang	have rung
rise	rose	have risen
see	saw	have seen
send	sent	have sent

Present	Past	Past Participle
set	set	have set
shake	shook	have shaken
sing	sang	have sung
sink	sank	have sunk
sit	sat	have sat
speak	spoke	have spoken
steal	stole	have stolen
swim	swam	have swum
take	took	have taken
wear	wore	have worn
write	wrote	have written

Note: You will be able to recognize when most of these are correct just from the way they sound. But you should review this list carefully and learn any principal parts you do not know.

Give special attention to the following pair of verbs. These are commonly confused.

lie (to recline)

Now I will **lie** down and take a nap. (present tense)
About an hour ago I **lay** down to take a nap. (past tense)
I am **lying** down to take a nap.
I **have lain** down in that bed before.

lay (to put, to place)

I **lay** the book on the table. (present tense)
Yesterday I **laid** the book on the table. (past tense)
I am **laying** my gun down forever.
I **have laid** my gun down forever.

A Quick Exercise: Right or Wrong?

1. I have laid my music down on the harpsichord.

2. The dollar bill was just lying there.

3. I like to just lay around in bed.

4. My driver's license lay under the table all day.

5. Lying in the sun on the beach is my favorite activity.

Exercise: Point 5

Fill in each blank with the correct form of the verb that appears in parentheses below the blank.

1. There must have _____*been*_____ a full moon out tonight.
   (be)

2. I thought I had _____ that clock when I dropped it.
   (break)

3. Yesterday, for the third time, I _____ the Daily Double.
   (lose)

4. I could have _____ another mile if you had not stopped
   (swim)
   me.

5. My, how you children have _____ !
   (grow)

6. The treasure from the ship must have _____ to the
   (sink)
   bottom of the ocean floor.

7. Have you _____ me the proper number of cards?
   (deal)

8. I would never have _____ there if I knew it was your
   (lie)
   spot.

9. Did you hear about the goose who _____ the golden
   (lay)
   egg?

10. The band must have _____ a dozen different songs.
    (sing)

Another Exercise: Point 5

Write your own sentences, using the verb forms given in parentheses.

1. (have brought) _____

2 (have flown) _____

3. (lay) _____

4. (have led) _____

5. (lie) _____

6. (have eaten) _____

7. (ate) _____

8. (sank) _____

9. (lying) _____

10. (have laid) _____

11. (have lain) _____

12. (laid) _____

13. (swam) _____

14. (have drunk) _____

15. (did) _____

POINT 6   **The *to* form of a verb (known as an infinitive) is incomplete and needs another verb before it.**

He **to run** in the race. (incomplete)
He **hopes to run** in the race. (complete)
She **to start** yesterday. (incomplete)
She **was expecting to start** yesterday. (complete)

Exercise: Point 6

Underline all the verbs in each sentence. Mark *C* if the sentence contains verb forms that are complete, *I* if it contains forms that are incomplete.

___*C*___   1. The boys plan to come tomorrow.

_____   2. The boy to shake the apples from the tree.

_____   3. She meant to take a tour of New Orleans.

_____   4. My younger sister is longing to have a horse of her own.

_____   5. The leaves to fall in September.

_____   6. They are hoping to go on a picnic tomorrow.

_____   7. My mother to go back to college next year.

_____   8. The lake to freeze if the temperature drops.

_____   9. Larry's brother tried to join the navy at sixteen.

_____   10. Do you expect to see Dolores on your vacation?

POINT 7   **Be sure to identify the *complete* verb in a sentence.**

In Point 4, we saw that *-ing* words need a form of the verb *to be* to help them, or make them complete. In addition to that combination, there are many other forms verbs may take. For example, the verb *walk:*

walk	had been walking	would walk
walks	has walked	should walk
am walking	have walked	could walk
is walking	had walked	must walk
was walking	shall walk	can walk
have been walking	will walk	might have walked

> I **am walking** to school.
> She **has walked** to school.
> They **have walked** to school.
> We **had walked** to school.
> You **should walk** to school.
> He **might have walked** to school.

These are only a few of the forms in which the verb *walk* may appear. *Helping (auxiliary)* verbs help the main verb make its statement. When a helping verb and a main verb act together to express a single action or state of being, that group of verbs is called a *verb phrase (or complete verb)*. In each of the preceding examples, the *complete verb* appears in darker type. Sometimes words such as *only, just, not ever, never, always,* and *not* may appear in the middle of a complete verb. They are *not*, however, part of the complete verb.

> They **have** never **walked** to school.
> You **should** always **walk** to school.

Exercise: Point 7

Underline the complete verb in each of the following sentences.

1. She <u>should have been elected</u> class treasurer.

2. He has always wanted an outfit like that one.

3. They should never have lost that game.

4. Richard was appointed chairperson of the committee.

5. You should have learned from your mistakes.

6. Monica is learning to build cabinets.

7. He has just purchased a condominium.

8. Gretchen had never experienced that before.

9. We had been hoping for better news.

10. It would not have alarmed me.

Review Exercise: Points 1–7

In each of the following sentences, draw one line under the subject and two lines under the complete verb.

1. <u>Joe</u> <u><u>would have been</u></u> the perfect candidate for the job.

2. Moe, Larry, and Curly are acting wildly.

3. The pollution seems to be getting worse.

4. The caterpillars have eaten the leaves.

5. We are prepared to do anything necessary.

6. I am looking for true love.

7. The professor should not have assigned so much homework.

8. You will have to plug it in.

9. Joining the club will be good for your spirits.

10. She was recalling her childhood.

POINT 8   A sentence may contain two or more verbs.

The sentences we have seen so far have contained one verb. It is true that some of the verbs have consisted of more than one word (*have walked, am preparing,* and so on), but we have not seen sentences which contain two or more complete verbs. Consider this sentence:

Joe **ran** for public office and **won**.

In this sentence, *ran* is a verb, and so is *won*. This sentence contains two verbs.

I **have applied** to three colleges and **have been accepted** by two of them.

Again we see a sentence with two complete verbs.

The boys **were pitching, hitting,** and **running** in the competition.

Here is a sentence with three verbs. Note that it is not necessary to repeat the word *were* before each *-ing* word.

Exercise: Point 8

Underline all the verbs in the following sentences.

1. Mandy <u>washed</u> the dishes and then <u>dried</u> them.

2. Tourists were swimming in the ocean and tanning themselves on the beach.

3. We stripped the wallpaper and painted the walls.

4. The fans were cheering and waving banners.

5. Renata took the course and learned to speak Spanish.

6. He was moaning and groaning all night long.

7. In the summer, I sneeze a lot and get itchy eyes.

8. I called her and told her the news.

9. They were angry and did not hesitate to tell us so.

10. We have always worked hard, and now it is paying off.

HOW TO USE VERBS CORRECTLY

1. Find the verb by asking what action takes place in the sentence.
2. Make sure the tense—past, present, or future—is accurate.
3. Remember that incomplete verbs need another verb before them.

Chapter Review

I. Write *C* if the example has a *complete verb* or *I* if it has an *incomplete verb*.

_____ 1. We expecting a snowstorm tonight.

_____ 2. You should ask your boss for a raise.

_____ 3. I was watching television when the lights went out.

_____ 4. She apparently going to win the contest.

_____ 5. I driven across the country twice.

_____ 6. You must have heard the news bulletin.

_____ 7. Alan and Della laughing in the library.

_____ 8. We used to own a lava lamp.

_____ 9. He eager to buy a lottery ticket.

_____ 10. The earth revolves around the sun.

II. Underline the complete verb in each of the following sentences.

1. I should never have brought that dog home.

2. Toni was talking with her professor.

3. I was raising the flag.

4. The bandits hid in the warehouse.

5. Raoul was spreading the good news.

6. Golf had never been so enjoyable.

7. We preserve our own vegetables every year.

8. The children want to play.

9. Herb has been appointed chairperson of the committee.

10. We have always spent our summers in Cape Cod.

11. Phoebe had never before cooked spaghetti.

12. Alex is going to the dump tomorrow.

13. Mel appears to be making progress.

14. Shirley is worrying.

15. He was whining like a baby.

16. Margaret is an editor at a big publishing company.

17. He arrived late too often and lost his job.

18. She looked in the mirror and saw that her hair was turning gray.

19. The city lights look beautiful tonight.

20. We have begun saving money and planning for the future.

III. Fill in the blanks with appropriate verbs.

1. He _____ installing the storm windows.

2. I should _____ bought it when it was on sale.

3. Leslie _____ lovely in that dress.

4. Yesterday, I _____ and had a great time.

5. We _____ and _____ until

class was over.

6. My mother _____ when I _____ .

7. I _____ that magazine and _____ it every month.

8. She is _____ until midnight tonight.

9. You should _____ and _____ whenever you get the chance.

10. I _____ ready, willing, and able.

11. The job _____ interesting, but I _____ not to take it.

12. I _____ _____ taken you there if you _____ asked me.

13. Carrie is _____ and _____ in the play.

14. Stuart _____ hard, but he is _____ the course.

15. The teacher _____ the entire class session _____ that poem.

16. We _____ around, looking for a theater.

17. The fireworks display _____ a sight to behold.

18. I have _____ the best possible job.

19. Donna is _____ scales on the piano.

20. You _____ never _____ to get away with this.

Mastery Test

Note: This test is designed to tell you how well you have mastered the information presented in Chapters 1 and 2. It would be useful to compare your success on this test with your success on the Pretest to see how much you have improved.

I. Write *S* if the sentence is missing a subject, *V* if the sentence is missing a verb, or *C* if the sentence is complete and correct as it stands.

_____ 1. You should trained harder for that event.

_____ 2. Were rehearsing for opening night.

_____ 3. We arranging to pick up the piano.

_____ 4. I see you.

_____ 5. Must be ready to explode.

_____ 6. He very dapper in that three-piece suit.

_____ 7. Was undecided about my future.

_____ 8. Choosing a career is a big decision.

_____ 9. Oil and coal energy sources.

_____ 10. Is about the Vietnam era.

_____ 11. Extreme heat seems to drive people crazy.

_____ 12. Always hopes for the best.

_____ 13. It is true.

_____ 14. I should never have invited you.

_____ 15. Thinking aloud often quite productive.

_____ 16. Will we never find a solution?

_____ 17. He shaken the dust from the mop.

_____ 18. Looking for bargains is my grandmother's hobby.

_____ 19. There are singing in the woods.

_____ 20. She was nominated, but she declined.

II. Underline the complete subject.

1. With the aid of a telescope, the class saw Jupiter.

2. Betty and her friend arrived late.

3. "Lover Baby" is what I call my wife.

4. Breakdancing and moonwalking are my specialties.

5. Into the stratosphere shot the space shuttle.

6. The murmur of the ocean is music to my ears.

7. By changing your mind, you ruined our plans.

8. My dog is better than your dog.

9. A volcano is a mountain that expels ashes and lava.

10. Every sentence must have a subject.

III. Underline the complete verb.

1. Our plans include a trip to Niagara Falls.

2. I might have known better than to trust him.

3. Citronella candles keep the bugs away.

4. Last night they told us of their plans.

5. You are home!

6. This case smells of foul play.

7. He went out and had a good time.

8. Sculpture has always been my hobby.

9. We have been wondering where you were.

10. I have just spent my week's salary.

PART II
WRITING BETTER SENTENCES

3

Subject-Verb Agreement

In any sentence, the subject and the verb must agree. If the subject is singular, the verb must be singular. If the subject is plural, the verb must be plural.

Singular refers to *one*.

> The rooster crows.
> The train stops.

In each of these sentences, the subject is singular. Only one rooster is involved: only one train is mentioned.

Plural refers to *more than one*.

> The roosters crow.
> The trains stop.

Here the number of roosters or trains is indefinite. That is, we may be talking about two roosters or fifty roosters. In any case, it is clear that more than one rooster is involved. The subject, *roosters*, therefore, is plural.

POINT 1 **Use singular verbs with singular subjects and plural verbs with plural subjects.**

Singular

> The **man jumps** over the fence.
> The **detective solves** the case.

In each of these examples, the subject is *singular* (*one* man; *one* detective). The verb must therefore be singular (*jumps; solves*). The subject and the verb *agree*.

41

Plural

The **men jump** over the fence.
The **detectives solve** the case.

Now the subjects are plural (there is *more than one* man and *more than one* detective). The verb must therefore be plural (*jump; solve*). The subject and the verb *agree*.

Exercise: Point 1

Write *S* for a singular subject or *P* for a plural subject. Then finish the sentence. Finally, underline the verb in your sentence.

_____*S*_____ 1. The detective _____ *solves the case.* _____

_____ 2. Trees _____

_____ 3. The professor _____

_____ 4. A book _____

_____ 5. Children _____

_____ 6. Motorcycles _____

_____ 7. My nephew _____

_____ 8. Accidents _____

_____ 9. Karen _____

_____ 10. The apartments _____

POINT 2   **When it is used as a subject, a pronoun must agree with the verb.**

Remember: The following subject pronouns are singular:

I, you, he, she, it

The following subject pronouns are plural:

We, you, they

Be certain to use a singular verb with a singular subject pronoun and a plural verb with a plural subject pronoun.

Note that except in the case of *was*, the pronoun *I* always takes a plural verb.

I *was* happy to hear from you.
I *jump* that fence every day.

Exercise: Point 2

Change each subject given in the parentheses into a pronoun and complete the sentence. Then underline the verb in your sentence.

1. (Mr. Small) _____ *He is a businessman.* _____
2. (My sister) _____
3. (All of us) _____
4. (Cats) _____
5. (The desk) _____
6. (Paul and I) _____
7. (The police officer) _____
8. (Jogging) _____
9. (Denver) _____
10. (The two women) _____

POINT 3   **When a subject is compound (includes two or more elements), make sure it agrees with the verb.**

Compound subjects joined by *and* take plural verbs.

> Los Angeles and San Francisco **are** in California.

The subject includes the names of two cities and is therefore plural. For this reason the plural verb, *are*, is used.

> Liza Minnelli, Michael York, and Joel Grey **starred** in *Cabaret*.
> My parents, my brother, and my sister **send** me birthday cards every year.
> Lucy and I **are** going to the show.

- One way to see whether a plural verb should be used is to try substituting the pronouns *we* or *they* (which are plural) for the subject.

> **They** send me birthday cards every year.
> **We** are going to the show.

However, when a compound subject expresses a singular idea, it takes a singular verb.

> My friend and colleague **is** a good man.

Here the two parts of the subject, (1) *friend*, and (2) *colleague*, both refer to the same person. Since only *one person* is being described, a singular verb, *is*, is used.

Bacon and eggs **is** my favorite breakfast.

Bacon and *eggs* refer to the same meal.

Note: Compound subjects sometimes include the word *and*. Always determine whether the subject is singular or plural before choosing a verb.

Compound subjects joined by *or* or *nor* take singular verbs when both subjects are singular. The use of *or* or *nor* suggests that only *one* of the singular subjects is involved at a time in the action; therefore, use a singular verb.

Either Doug or Abby **cooks** lasagna every weekend.

Cooks is a singular verb.

Neither the Toyota nor the Nissan **is** running properly.

Is is singular.

When a singular subject is joined to a plural subject by *or* or *nor*, the verb agrees with the subject closer to the verb.

Either the players or the coach **is** responsible for the team's shoddy performance.

Neither my brother nor my three sisters **care** what I do.

Coach is singular, and so is *is*.

Sisters and *care* are plural.

Exercise: Point 3

Each sentence begins with a compound subject. Add a verb and complete the sentence.

1. The players and coaches *sign autographs before the game.*

2. My father or his friends _____

3. Mary and Joseph _____

4. A gentleman and a scholar _____

5. Either my aunt or my uncle _____

6. Cars, boats, and trains _____

7. Spring and summer _____

8. Salary and benefits _____

9. The owner and manager _____

10. Pieces of wood and glue _____

Review Exercise: Points 1–3

Write *S* for a singular subject, *P* for a plural subject, *CS* for a compound subject with a singular meaning, or *CP* for a compound subject with a plural meaning. Add a verb and complete the sentence.

CP   1. Jim and I _____ *are best friends.* _____

_____   2. Beer _____

_____   3. Neither my dog nor my cats _____

_____   4. Traffic jams _____

_____   5. Jack and his gerbil _____

_____   6. Either staples or paper clips _____

_____   7. Violins and cellos _____

_____   8. The owner and captain _____

_____   9. Millionaires _____

_____   10. Stu, Alice, and I _____

POINT 4   Some indefinite pronouns are singular and take singular verbs.

The following indefinite pronouns are singular:

> Words ending in -*one* or -*body* (*anyone, anybody, everyone, everybody, someone, no one*)
> *either, neither*
> *another, anything, each, everything, much, nothing, one, other, something*

When one of these pronouns is the subject of a sentence, use a singular verb.

> **One** of us **owns** a car.

One is the subject. Don't be confused by the use of *of us*. What you are really saying is, "I own a car," or "She owns a car," or "He owns a car." Only *one person* owns a car; therefore the subject is singular and must take a singular verb, *owns*.

> **Nobody wants** to go to the party.

Not one single person wants to go.

> **Everyone** who was invited **is** here.

Every single person is here.

> **No one helps** prepare the dinner, but **everyone wants** to eat.
> Either color **is** fine.

There are two colors, but the speaker is going to choose only one of them.

> Either one **suits** me perfectly.
> Neither of us **is** ready to go.
> Neither player **wants** to bat.

Like *either* and *neither,* the word *each* concerns one thing or person at a time. *Both* concerns two things or persons together.

> Each of us **has** a daughter.
> Each of the employees **is** responsible for the upkeep of the area.

Exercise: Point 4

Complete the sentences and circle the verb. Use the present tense.

1. One of them _____ *(carries) a large suitcase.* _____

2. Anyone _____

3. Everyone _____

4. Nothing _____

5. Anybody _____

6. Everything _____

7. Somebody _____

8. Nobody _____

9. No one _____

10. Neither _____

Another Exercise: Point 4

Circle the correct verb given in the parentheses.

1. Neither of us (care, (cares)) to attend.

2. Either of you (get, gets) the starring role.

3. Anything (serves, serve) the purpose.

4. Neither one of them (deserve, deserves) the award.

5. Neither pair of pants (fit, fits) correctly.

6. Either flavor (taste, tastes) delicious.

7. Either seat (are, is) fine with me.

8. Each of the tools (work, works).

9. Neither of those candles (has, have) a wick.

10. No one (do, does) the work properly.

Review Exercise: Points 1–4

Circle the correct word given in the parentheses.

1. The green car (race, (races)) through the street.

2. Neither of my friends (call, calls) me anymore.

3. No one (bother, bothers) me anymore.

4. Neither of those batteries (work, works).

5. Sears, Roebuck, & Co. (are, is) a big mail-order house.

6. Beautiful women and weightlifters (is, are) on the beach.

7. Phil and his wife (buy, buys) lottery tickets every month.

8. One of you (die, dies)!

9. Never again will they (hitchhike, hitchhikes).

10. The boxer and his manager (knows, know) their business.

Another Review Exercise: Points 1–4

Write *S* for a singular subject, *P* for a plural subject, *CS* for a compound subject with a singular meaning, or *CP* for a compound subject with a plural meaning. Complete the sentence, using the present tense, and underline the verb.

____*S*____ 1. Anyone _____*is welcome in my house.*_____

_____ 2. Fishing _____

_____ 3. Everyone _____

_____ 4. Buildings and grounds _____

_____ 5. You and I _____

_____ 6. Either of those recipes _____

_____ 7. Somebody _____

———— 8. Neither of those responses ————————————

———— 9. They ————————————————

———— 10. Anne, Susan, and I ——————————————

POINT 5   Some indefinite pronouns are plural and take plural verbs.

The indefinite pronouns *both, few, many, others,* and *several* are plural. When these pronouns act as subjects, use a plural verb.

Many of us **enjoy** watching the tennis matches.

Enjoy is a plural verb.

Others **find** them boring.

Find is plural.

Both of us **want** to see the show.
Both you and I **are** going to vote in the next election.

Note: Some indefinite pronouns (*all, any, more, most, and some*) can be either singular or plural, depending on the meaning of the sentence.

Singular—Most of our time **is** spent here.
Plural—Most of the fans **are** gone.

Exercise: Point 5

Circle the correct word in the parentheses.

1. (Each, Both) of us are packed and ready to go.

2. Many of us (need, needs) a vacation.

3. Several phones (is, are) ringing.

4. (Each, Both) of the canisters is empty.

5. Each of the citizens (vote, votes) once.

6. Few people (wish, wishes) upon stars.

7. Others (want, wants) to change jobs.

8. Both of them (visit, visits) often.

9. (Each, Both) of us minds his own business.

10. Both Alex and Marty (work, works) for the phone company.

POINT 6 **Singular subjects followed by phrases that describe the subject take singular verbs; plural subjects take plural verbs.**

>   The car with the two flat tires **is** mine.

Car is the singular subject of the sentence. The phrase *with the two flat tires,* which describes the subject, does not influence the choice of a singular or plural verb form. Do not write this sentence as

>   The car with the two flat tires **are** mine.

Flat tires, although plural, is not the subject of this sentence.

>   The education of adults **is** important.

Education, the subject of the sentence, is singular and takes the singular verb form, *is.*

Note: The verb must agree with the subject stripped of its modifiers. Subjects are sometimes followed by phrases beginning with *with, as well as, together with, including,* and so on. These phrases are not part of the subject and do not influence the choice of a singular or plural verb form.

>   The cabdriver as well as his passengers **was** startled by the sight of the horse in the street.

Here the subject, *cabdriver,* is singular, and therefore takes the singular verb *was.*

>   The actors, including the star of the show, **were** appreciative of the applause.

Actors is plural.

Exercise: Point 6

Circle the correct verb in the parentheses.

1. The bus as well as the car (was, were) damaged in the accident.

2. The presentation of the trophies (follow, follows) the game.

3. The theories of my professor (is, are) controversial.

4. John, along with thirty friends, (was, were) in attendance.

5. The moon as well as some stars (is, are) visible tonight.

6. The children together with their mother (watch, watches) the movie.

7. The seasons of the year (is, are) all distinct.

8. The street singer with a crowd around him (perform, performs) beautifully.

9. A pile of rocks (have, has) to be moved.

10. Sadie, in addition to her friends, (is, are) protesting the school board's decision.

Review Exercise: Points 5 and 6

Complete the following sentences.

1. Both food and drink _____ *are necessities of life.* _____

2. Each time _____

3. Both notebooks and rulers _____

4. Both men as well as their wives _____

5. The captain, along with the other players, _____

6. Everyone _____

7. Both shoes and sneakers _____

8. Each of the Beatles _____

9. Part I together with Part II _____

10. The musicians, including the drummer, _____

Review Exercise: Points 1–6

Circle the correct word in the parentheses.

1. Both you and I together with Al (want, wants) ice cream.

2. Neither of the sandwiches (have, has) onions.

3. Rakes and mowers (is, are) used by gardeners.

4. Each of the boys (need, needs) a haircut.

5. I will be glad to see anyone who (wish, wishes) to come.

6. Neither of the boys (was, were) allowed to enter the race.

7. Chris, Maureen, and all their children (visit, visits) us weekly.

8. Those cars, including the white Ford, (is, are) parked illegally.

9. Both women (was, were) hired.

10. A wild and woolly dog (run, runs) around our apartment.

Another Review Exercise: Points 1–6

Complete these sentences.

1. Neither of the appointments ___*was convenient for me.*___

2. Coffee, as well as tea, _____

3. Both coffee and tea _____

4. Either one of the movies _____

5. You and I _____

6. Each daughter of mine _____

7. Nobody who is anybody _____

8. Strolling through the park _____

9. My girlfriend _____

10. The area including First and Second Streets _____

POINT 7   **A *collective noun* (group word) takes a singular verb when the group is being referred to as a single unit; it takes a plural verb when the members of the group are being considered as a set of individuals.**

> The jury **is** deliberating in the back room.

The subject, *jury,* refers to the group as a whole.

> The jury **are** arguing among themselves.

Here *jury* refers to the individual members of the group, all of whom are arguing.

> The Hackensack Meadowlands **is** the site of a sports complex.
> The rolling meadowlands **were** green in the springtime.

Some collective nouns are *group, crowd, team, band, family, audience, number, dozen, lot,* and *kind.* You can think of other words that are used to describe groups of persons or things.

Exercise: Point 7

Circle the correct verb in the parentheses.

1. A lot (was, (were)) trying out for the team.

2. My family (is, are) the most important thing in the world to me.

3. The band (was, were) louder than we expected.

4. A lot (was, were) accomplished at the last meeting.

5. The audience (was, were) booing and throwing tomatoes.

6. A number of items (is, are) missing.

7. A class (is, are) cancelled almost every week.

8. One team (is, are) Pat and Mike.

9. Today our committee (reach, reaches) a decision.

10. A dozen (are, is) prepared to strike

POINT 8 **When the verb comes before the subject of the sentence, it is especially important to identify the subject and make the verb agree with it.**

Common sentences of this sort are those which begin with *there is* or *there are.*

There **is** a better way to get there from here.

The subject of this sentence, *way,* is singular; therefore we use the singular verb form, *is.*

There **are** times when your dog seems to be the best friend you have.

Times, the subject, is plural, calling for a plural verb, *are.*

Beyond that field **sits** an abandoned house.

House is singular and so is *sits.*

Just ahead **waits** the enemy.

Enemy, which can be a group word, is singular in this case. The verb, **waits,** must also be singular.

Here **is** what I mean.

What I mean, the subject, is singular and requires a singular verb, *is.*

Exercise: Point 8

Circle the correct verb in the parentheses, and underline the subject.

1. There (is, are) a way to stop the leaking faucet.

2. There (is, are) veterans of the war here tonight.

3. Inside the shack (is, are) a stray dog.

4. Over there (is, are) the governor of our state.

5. Behind that door (wait, waits) danger.

6. There (is, are) more than one way to skin a cat.

7. Under that rock (is, are) over a hundred ants.

8. In our system, there (is, are) two senators from each state.

9. Right behind me (is, are) everyone who supports me.

10. Beside the table (was, were) a high chair.

POINT 9   **Words or names that are plural in form but singular in meaning take a singular verb.**

- Be careful: A word ending in *-s* or *-es* is not necessarily plural!

  Social studies **is** one course I will take this semester.

Social studies is the name of one course, and therefore singular.

  The *New York Times* **has** a large circulation.
  The sports news **is** on television at 6:15.

Exercise: Point 9

All of the subjects in these sentences end in *s* or *es*, but only some of them are plural. Mark *S* for a singular subject or *P* for a plural subject. Then complete the sentence.

_____*P*_____ 1. The Dodgers _____*lead the league.*_____

_____ 2. The *Daily News* _____

_____ 3. Animals _____

_____ 4. Benchley's *Jaws* _____

_____ 5. The five senses _____

_____ 6. Mathematics _____

_____ 7. Shouts _____

_____ 8. Games _____

_____ 9. Economics _____

_____ 10. Business _____

Review Exercise: Points 7–9

Fill in the blank with the correct form of the verb given in the parentheses. Look again at the chart on pages 27–28 if necessary.

1. There _____*are*_____ are twenty students in this class.
   (to be)

2. The *London Times* _____ an excellent newspaper.
   (to be)

3. Up the hill _____ Jack and Jill.
   (to run)

4. There _____ danger involved in that plan.
   (to be)

5. _____ you any spare change?
   (to have)

6. The public _____ the right to be informed.
   (to have)

7. Yesterday there _____ a terrible snowstorm.
   (to be)

8. *The Pickwick Papers* _____ a novel by Charles Dickens.
   (to be)

9. The Yankees _____ a baseball team.
   (to be)

10. There _____ a good audience tonight.
    (to be)

Another Review Exercise: Points 7–9

Complete these sentences.

1. The House of Representatives *is part of the government.*

2. My family _____

3. Many _____

4. There is _____

5. Here are _____

6. Liberal arts _____

7. Beside the field _____

8. Our English class _____

9. The members of our class _____

10. A heap of trash _____

HOW TO MAKE SURE THAT SUBJECTS AND THEIR VERBS AGREE

> 1. Remember that it is the singular or plural *meaning* of a subject, not its form, which determines whether it takes a singular or a plural verb.
> 2. When the verb comes before the subject, be especially careful to identify the subject before deciding on the form of the verb.

Chapter Review

I. Circle the correct verb in the parentheses.

1. Almost everybody (has, have) some difficulty with writing.

2. Neither the chipmunk nor the squirrels (is, are) bothering us.

3. Both of us (is, are) voting in the next election.

4. Milo, Phoebe, and I (was, were) offering our help.

5. Neither of you (jump, jumps) to conclusions.

6. Some say the Indians (have, has) been treated unfairly.

7. There (was, were) only two choices on the menu.

8. Rudy as well as his cat (like, likes) milk.

9. He (are, is) my boss and friend.

10. Sunbathing (is, are) my favorite form of exercise.

11. Either of us (have, has) to pay the fine.

12. The twins and their parents (travel, travels) together.

13. Nobody (believe, believes) your alibi.

14. American and Russia (is, are) the most powerful nations.

15. "Safe" and "out" (is, are) two calls in baseball.

16. Neither of them (dance, dances) to disco music.

17. Each (serve, serves) a different purpose.

18. The hammer as well as the saw (make, makes) work easier.

19. Jacques (was, were) working for his uncle last year.

20. Our team (play, plays) hard every night.

21. Neither of the boys (has, have) to shave.

22. The Johnsons, including their son Frank, (ski, skis).

23. The Seven Wonders of the World (is, are) extraordinary.

24. The Empire State Building and Macy's (is, are) in New York.

25. Time (fly, flies) when you're enjoying yourself.

26. Either Cathy or the Millers (cook, cooks) dinner on Fridays.

27. Each of the brothers (has, have) been on a quiz show.

28. My wife and I (was, were) late for the movie.

29. There (was, were) no way out of the tunnel.

30. You (is, are) nobody until somebody (love, loves) you.

II. Fill in the blank with an appropriate form of the verb.

1. The enemy _____ captured late last night.
                   (to be)

2. I _____ the men are safe now.
      (to suppose)

3. Nothing _____ those two.
          (to excite)

4. It _____ as testimony to a great person.
      (to stand)

5. One of us always _____ the right answer.
              (to guess)

6. The Smiths _____ in the next apartment.
         (to live)

7. Amos and Andy _____ a great comedy team.
          (to be)

8. Someone _____ to take me to the station.
       (to have)

9. I _____ disappointed with their performance.
      (to be)

10. They _____ the best of times.
          (to be)

III. Fill in the blank with the appropriate form (singular or plural) of a subject.

1. The_____ is not working today.

2. _____ are expecting their first child.

3. _____ signed up for the event.

4. _____ of us cares much for caviar.

5. _____ and _____ are examples of foul weather.

6. _____ , together with Mr. Powers, are going sailing.

7. _____ , _____ , and _____

   want more food.

8. _____ went shopping for a used car.

9. There are never enough _____ in the day.

10. _____ is a good way to pass the time.

IV. Write *C* if the sentence is correct or *X* if it contains an error in agreement.
Correct each incorrect sentence on the line below it.

_____ 1. Marge, as well as Amy, do not wish to register.

_____

_____ 2. Each assignment need to be done carefully.

_____

_____ 3. One of you have to sit on my lap.

_____

_____ 4. Babies are innocent and adults is not.

_____

_____ 5. Neither of us are in the mood.

_____

———————   6. Weddings is fun.

_____

———————   7. Alfonso buy records and listens to them in his room.

_____

———————   8. Both of them wishes they were going.

_____

———————   9. Grammar and spelling is being tested.

_____

———————   10. Anyone who winks at me embarrass me.

_____

V. Complete these sentences.

1. Each of the teams in the NFL _____

2. Either of those latex paints _____

3. Swimming in salt water _____

4. Charles Dickens _____

5. There are _____

6. Here is _____

7. Rain and sleet _____

8. The group, including fifty women, _____

9. Skydiving _____

10. Charlotte and Mark _____

VI. Rewrite this entire passage in the following space, changing the subject from *a carpenter* to *carpenters*. Keep in mind that verbs and other words that refer to the subject will have to be changed from singular to plural.

A carpenter uses many different tools in his work. When he is faced with a job that is particularly difficult, he has to use his patience as well as his skill. Without patience, a hammer, a saw, or a screwdriver will do a carpenter no good. He has to be able to understand the problem, and find the best way to solve it. Sometimes, the quickest solution is not the best one. His customer, or client, has to be pleased with his work, or he loses his chance to be hired for another job. There is a great pressure on the carpenter to succeed. By no means is his job an easy one.

Carpenters use many different tools in their work.

_____

_____

_____

_____

_____

_____

_____

_____

_____

_____

VII. Rewrite this passage in the following space, changing the subject from *a person* to *people*.

A person who grows up in the South gets used to warm weather. There is never a major snowstorm there, although hurricanes are not unusual. A northerner, on the other hand, has to learn to live with harsh weather for several months of each year. A person who travels from one region of the country to another is almost always surprised at the change of climate. Although a southerner thinks that warm weather is nice all year round, a northerner may enjoy the change of seasons.

_____

_____

_____

_____

_____

_____

_____

_____

_____

_____

_____

_____

_____

_____

VIII. Rewrite this passage in the following space, making subjects and verbs agree.

In John Steinbeck's *Of Mice and Men* two men travels around California looking for work. George, the shorter and smarter of the two, want to find a steady job so he can saves enough money to buy his own farm. His friend, Lennie, always ask George to tell him about what it will be like when they have their own place. George promise that when they have their farm, Lennie will be the only one who ever take care of the rabbits. However, Lennie get the men in trouble, and George is forced to shoot him. He wish he did not have to do it, as losing his friend make him very unhappy. Steinbeck's novel force the reader to consider the qualities of a true friendship.

_____

_____

_____

_____

_____

_____

_____

4

Fragments

A *fragment* is something broken away from the whole. If you're not careful drying a dish and drop it, you're left with fragments, or broken pieces. In the same way, if you're not careful writing sentences, you might end up with a lot of fragments. And since a sentence is supposed to express a complete thought, it is important that you don't break it up into meaningless parts that leave your reader confused.

A complete sentence should include a subject and a verb. When one or the other is missing, we are left with a sentence fragment. In conversation, we use fragments all the time. Sometimes, for special emphasis, a writer may use a fragment. But for college writing, you should write complete sentences.

POINT 1   Make sure every sentence has a subject and a verb.

>   **Joe works** at a bank.

The verb, *works*, tells what kind of action the subject, *Joe*, takes. He *works*.

>   The **baton twirlers look** cold in this November weather.

Look is a linking verb. It connects the subject, *baton twirlers*, with the descriptive word *cold*.

Exercise: Point 1

In each of the following complete sentences, draw one line under the subject and two lines under the verb.

1. Heating <u>costs</u> <u>are</u> on the upswing.

2. We choose the freshest fruit we can find.

3. There is a pickle in the refrigerator.

4. Many people read best-selling novels during the summer.

5. That train is late as always.

6. Babies require a great deal of attention.

7. A good meal improves my disposition.

8. You are a sight for sore eyes.

9. Gardening is therapeutic for some.

10. These are the best years of your life.

Another Exercise: Point 1

Mark *C* for a complete sentence. Mark *F* for a fragment. Make the fragments into complete sentences by adding a subject, a verb, or both, and a period at the end. Finally, draw one line under the subject and two lines under the verb.

C   1. Doris is working late tonight.

_____ 2. Near the center of town

_____ 3. Ate at a famous restaurant

_____ 4. He won the Grand Prix last year

_____ 5. I swept that floor already

_____ 6. At my grandparents' house

_____ 7. There is a phone call for you

_____ 8. With only fifty cents

———————   9. The University of Georgia

_____

———————   10. She plans to hitchhike to California

_____

POINT 2   **Watch out for -*ing* words. No word ending in -*ing* can ever be the complete verb of a sentence.**

Don't mistake an -*ing* word for the complete verb of a sentence. Are these sentences or fragments?

> Sitting on the bench feeding the pigeons.
> Wondering about his future.
> The woman running down the street.
> Was calling his friends, rounding them up, and handing out the tickets for the game.

None of the preceding is a complete sentence. Each, however, can be made into a complete sentence by adding a subject or a verb, or *sometimes* both.

> **The man was** sitting on the bench feeding the pigeons. (Add subject and verb.)
> **My father is** wondering about his future. (Add subject and verb.)
> The woman **was** running down the street. (Add verb.)
> **Harry** was calling his friends, rounding them up, and handing out tickets for the game. (Add subject.)

Now each of these is a complete sentence because it has a subject and a complete verb.

Don't be fooled by length. A fragment need not be short. There is a lot of action in the last example—calling, rounding up, handing out—but the subject is missing. You need to say who is doing all that action.

Exercise: Point 2

Make each fragment into a complete sentence and rewrite the entire sentence in the space provided. Add a subject or a verb, or both if necessary. Put a period at the end of the complete sentence.

1. the customer asking a question

    The customer was asking a question.

2. birds singing in the trees

_____

3. the man trying to escape

_____

4. always working on his house

_____

5. the woman beginning a new career

_____

6. practicing the piano

_____

7. the attendant checking the tire pressure

_____

8. the convict trying to evade the police

_____

9. smiling at me from across the room

_____

10. Mel making his career plans

_____

Review Exercise: Points 1 and 2

Place a *C* before a complete sentence or an *F* before a fragment. Make each fragment into a complete sentence, and put a period at the end.

___*F*___ 1. Racing wildly through the park

The motorcyclist was racing wildly through the park.

_____ 2. Was falling in love

_____

_____ 3. She called

_____

_____ 4. Rockefeller, Carnegie, and Getty

_____

_____ 5. Rarely displayed any emotion

_____

_____   6. The hail dropping like stones from the sky

_____

_____   7. Are you shouting or am I deaf

_____

_____   8. The punishment that he deserved

_____

_____   9. The burglar left the apartment in a shambles

_____

_____   10. Choosing a new major

_____

_____

POINT 3   **A group of words containing a subject and a verb is called a clause.**

In the English language, there are two types of clauses:
1. *Independent:* has a subject and a verb
      can stand alone as a complete sentence
2. *Dependent:* has a subject and a verb
      cannot stand alone because it begins with a word or word group such as *because, since, though, although, if, as if, where, unless, as soon as, whereas, in order that, when, whenever, while, before, after, as, until, so that, as long as, such as, provided that, during.*

This is an independent clause:

   He ran to the store.

But if we put any of the preceding words in front of it, it becomes a dependent clause:

   Because he ran to the store
   Since he ran to the store
   Before he ran to the store
   When he ran to the store
   If he ran to the store
   After he ran to the store

A dependent clause standing alone is a fragment. Turn it into a complete sentence by adding an independent clause.

   He was late for work because he ran to the store.
   He got there before it closed, since he ran to the store.
   He put on his tennis shoes before he ran to the store.

He lost his keys when he ran to the store.
Why did he get there late, if he ran to the store?
He sat down to catch his breath after he ran to the store.

By itself, a dependent clause doesn't make sense because it is a fragment of a thought, even if you put a period at the end.

Until I joined the "Y."

Dependent clause alone = fragment.

Until I joined the "Y," I never exercised regularly.

Independent clause added to dependent clause = complete sentence.
Elements that can stand alone usually can be identified by reading them aloud.

Exercise: Point 3

Mark *I* for an independent clause and *D* for a dependent clause.

___D___ 1. Because Sam speaks Spanish.

_____ 2. Unless you change your attitude.

_____ 3. She wants to go, too.

_____ 4. If you must miss your appointment.

_____ 5. Until we get to the beach.

_____ 6. As long as you're here.

_____ 7. When I arrive at your place.

_____ 8. Such as lamps and drapes.

_____ 9. Since we have to repay the loan.

_____ 10. When you know the answer.

Another Exercise: Point 3

Mark *I* for an independent clause and *D* for a dependent clause. If the clause is independent, and therefore a complete sentence, capitalize the first letter and put a period at the end. If the clause is dependent, and therefore a fragment, add an independent clause to make it a complete sentence and put a period at the end.

___I___ 1. _____ We went to the movies.

_____ 2. _____ while we are waiting

_____ 3. _____ Abby and I are married

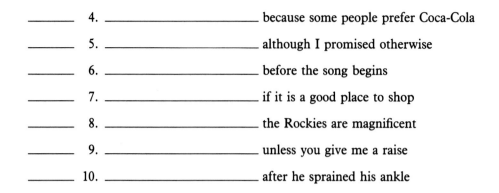

———— 4. ———————————— because some people prefer Coca-Cola

———— 5. ———————————— although I promised otherwise

———— 6. ———————————— before the song begins

———— 7. ———————————— if it is a good place to shop

———— 8. ———————————— the Rockies are magnificent

———— 9. ———————————— unless you give me a raise

———— 10. ———————————— after he sprained his ankle

POINT 4   When a dependent clause comes at the beginning of a sentence, it is followed by a comma.

A dependent clause may come at the beginning of a sentence or at the end. When it comes at the beginning, always separate it from the independent clause with a comma.

> When he spoke, the audience was silent.
> Before they arrived, I set the table.
> Since you asked, I will tell you.

However, if the independent clause comes first, you may or may not need a comma. It depends on whether or not the meaning is clear. Use a comma only if it is necessary to make the meaning clear.

> The audience was silent when he spoke.
> I set the table before they arrived.
> I will tell you, since you asked.

Exercise: Point 4

Place a comma in each sentence if it is necessary.

1. Because it is raining, we cannot go outside.

2. While you wait you may read a magazine.

3. My life has changed since I met her.

4. If you want to go you will have to buy a ticket.

5. If you go swimming wear a swimcap.

6. Unless you change your ways you will lose your job.

7. When he left the room was dark.

8. After this inning the game will be over.

9. I want to try even if it is difficult.

10. After I swept the floor I dusted.

Review Exercise: Points 1–4

Turn each of these dependent clauses into a complete sentence by adding an independent clause before or after it. Be sure to place a comma where it is required and a period at the end of each sentence.

1. even though he is tired

   He hopes to go tonight even though he is tired.

2. since I fell for you

3. if I decide to go along with your wishes

4. although he has been teaching for twenty years

5. until they discover a cure for the common cold

6. while he was standing at the meat counter in the supermarket

7. unless he changes his vile ways

8. after the sun goes down

_____

_____

9. as the world turns

_____

_____

10. before we packed the car

_____

_____

▎POINT 5   Every sentence must have at least one independent clause.

Don't let a dependent clause stand alone. That's a fragment. Add an independent clause to make it into a complete sentence.

An independent clause is the main idea, a complete thought. It can be a complete sentence in itself. A dependent clause serves only to further the meaning.

While we watched television, the stew burned.

The main idea is that the stew burned. The dependent clause merely gives additional information. In this case, it tells when.

Exercise: Point 5

Underline the independent clause in each of the following sentences.

1. Even though there is enough time, I feel rushed.

2. Unless you work harder, you will receive a poor grade.

3. As long as you use suntan lotion, you will not get burned.

4. The show begins when the curtain rises.

5. My paper was better after I revised it.

6. If I am nominated, I will not run.

7. I didn't like olives until I had them on pizza.

8. I am happy when I am reading.

9. As soon as the match ends, the winner will be crowned.

10. Lock the door before you leave.

Another Exercise: Point 5

Turn each of these fragments into a complete sentence by adding an independent clause before or after it. Be sure to place a comma where it is required and a period at the end of each sentence.

1. since we painted the house

   Since we painted the house, we've gotten lots of compliments.

2. as soon as I finish the assignment

3. before calling to say thank you

4. until the tide comes in

5. whenever you need a friend

6. even though we have known each other for years

7. while working the night shift

8. because there is no other choice

9. although there was little hope for recovery

_____

_____

10. whenever I'm feeling depressed

_____

_____

POINT 6   Avoid other common types of fragments, such as the "list" type.

Our family loves celebrating holidays. For example, Christmas and Thanksgiving.

For example, Christmas and Thanksgiving is a fragment in that it does not express a complete thought. It is a piece of the previous sentence that has been broken apart from the original.

Our family loves celebrating holidays such as Christmas and Thanksgiving.

Here the fragment has been pieced back together with the sentence to make one complete and correct sentence.

I like sports. Like baseball, football, and golf.

Fragment.

I like such sports as baseball, football, and golf.

Correct.

Review Exercise: Points 1–6

In the space provided, make the following fragments into complete and correct sentences.

1. including my friend Roger

    Several people, including my friend Roger, are going.

2. as soon as the mail arrives

    _____

3. to attempt to break the world record

    _____

4. for example, baseball and football

_____

5. even though we used to be friends

_____

6. after she finished the manuscript

_____

7. including my parents and me

_____

8. such as the dictionary and the thesaurus

_____

9. while I was weeding the garden

_____

10. to find his way home

_____

POINT 7 **Command sentences do not contain obvious subjects, but they are still complete and correct.**

In the sentence "Come here," the subject is understood although it is not specifically mentioned. The subject of this sentence is _you._

Note the following examples of command sentences which contain _understood subjects._

Hello.
Watch out!
Get out of here.

All these sentences are complete and correct.

Exercise: Point 7

In the space provided write _C_ if the example is a complete and correct sentence or _F_ if it is a fragment.

_____*C*_____ 1. Don't drink the water.

_____ 2. Go somewhere else, please.

_____   3. Go.

_____   4. To my house tonight.

_____   5. Save your money.

_____   6. Start boiling the potatoes.

_____   7. Forget everything I told you.

_____   8. Before it is too late.

_____   9. As soon as she arrives.

_____   10. Shout "Surprise!" as soon as she arrives.

HOW TO AVOID FRAGMENTS

1. Make sure every sentence has a subject and a verb.
2. Don't mistake an -ing word for the complete verb.
3. Make sure every sentence has at least one independent clause.

Chapter Review

I. Mark *C* for a complete sentence or *F* for a fragment. Add a period to each complete sentence.

_____   1. After cleaning out the gutters

_____   2. They lost the battle

_____   3. He spending his money unwisely

_____   4. As the candidate raised his fist

_____   5. Come over for dinner

_____   6. Never say die

_____   7. Expecting to hear from you soon

_____   8. Finishing the marathon

_____   9. Michael and his beautiful wife

_____   10. Even though it is early

II. Mark *C* for a complete sentence or *F* for a fragment. Add a period to each complete sentence.

_____   1. Until the morning comes

_____   2. Provided that you pass the exam

_____   3. Sports cars are fun

_____   4. Chasing its own tail

_____   5. Last but not least

_____   6. I was amazed at the performance

_____   7. If they get their act together

_____   8. Bring it tomorrow

_____   9. Such as the Twins and the Red Sox

_____   10. My sister combing her hair

III. Underline the independent clause in each of these sentences.

   1. We played baseball until it grew dark.

   2. Even though it was foggy, we made a smooth landing.

   3. Because he hurt himself, he could not play.

   4. I should quit smoking because it's unhealthy.

   5. Although she has a quick temper, Mary kept calm.

   6. While I'm here, I should call my aunt.

   7. After you run, take a shower.

   8. We bought their album after we saw them in concert.

   9. I brought my guitar since I knew you would be here.

  10. When you come to the third stop light, turn left.

IV. Fill in the blank and complete the sentence with an appropriate independent clause. Add commas where necessary.

   1. Because I want to know you better _____

   2. Even though I am broke _____

   3. Unless you change your mind _____

   4. When the time comes _____

   5. As long as you are away _____

   6. _____ after we go for a swim.

   7. _____ while you chop the onions.

   8. _____ so that you can find your way.

9. _____ whenever I visit my grandparents.

10. _____ although she was pretty.

V. Mark *C* for a complete sentence or *F* for a fragment. Add a period to each complete sentence.

_____   1. Call me if you need me

_____   2. If you desire a change of pace

_____   3. Opening a charge account

_____   4. When I heard the news

_____   5. After everything has been said and done

_____   6. For a good reason

_____   7. As soon as the rain stops

_____   8. I know

_____   9. It's okay with me

_____   10. Later on in the show

VI. Mark *C* for a complete sentence or *F* for a fragment. Rewrite the fragments to make them complete sentences. Capitalize each sentence and put a period at the end.

_____   1. the traffic was heavy

_____

_____   2. a gorgeous autumn afternoon

_____

_____   3. to make the dean's list

_____

_____   4. to find a bigger apartment

_____

_____   5. after chasing my dog around the block

_____

_____   6. with all the noise and confusion of a busy airport

_____

_____   7. at the last possible moment

_____

_____   8. laughing and crying at the same time

_____

_____   9. before I change my mind

_____

_____   10. like root beer and ginger ale

_____

VII. Each of the following examples contains one fragment and one independent clause. Combine the fragment with the independent clause to make one complete sentence. Remember to use commas where they are needed.

1. As long as you're not lazy. I won't complain.

_____

2. We're celebrating tonight. Because I gave up cigarettes.

_____

3. If you want to play. Change your clothes.

_____

4. Having moved to the country. He leads a quieter life.

_____

5. After all. We have known each other for a year.

_____

6. We hated summer. Until we bought an air conditioner.

_____

7. Since you left me. I am so lonely.

_____

8. You have to fix the leak. Before you can go sailing.

_____

9. As soon as we arrived in Miami. We ran out to the beach.

_____

10. We are raising a family. Because we love children.

_____

VIII. Each of the following examples contains at least one fragment. Combine the fragment (or fragments) with the independent clause to make one complete sentence.

1. I worked hard. So that I could get a promotion.

_____

2. Although she enjoys painting. She doesn't take art courses.

_____

3. We went to the circus. Saw lions. Saw clowns.

_____

4. Tell me the truth. If you know it.

_____

5. There may have been improvements. Since he was elected senator.

_____

6. I love facing danger. Wherever I can find it.

_____

7. I am too tired. To go for a walk.

_____

8. He was arrested. Because he was speeding.

_____

9. You will find the underwear. In the drawer. Where I keep my socks.

_____

10. Judging the distance. Holding her breath. She jumped.

_____

IX. The following passages contain many fragments. Rewrite each passage in complete sentences. Some of the fragments can be combined with independent clauses. For others you will need to add a subject, a verb, or a new independent clause.

Today, more and more people are becoming interested in discovering their roots. Because of the popularity of a book by Alex Haley, called _Roots_. It tells the story of

Haley's search for his ancestors. In Africa and other places. Before he wrote *Roots*, Haley worked on another book. *The Autobiography of Malcolm X*. After *Roots* was published. It became a best-seller. Then they made a movie for television based on it. Now, people of all backgrounds are interested in tracing their ancestry. A good book. A great man.

_____

_____

_____

_____

_____

_____

_____

_____

_____

_____

_____

_____

Ten years ago there were not as many shopping malls. As there are today. In a mall, many stores are gathered together. Under one roof. Shoppers appreciate the convenience a mall can offer. Because they can make one stop and accomplish all their shopping. In one place. On Saturday, malls are usually very crowded. People walking, talking, eating, and buying all over the place. Malls are air-conditioned. So that shoppers can browse comfortably. You can buy a birthday card, a mattress, and a baseball mitt all under one roof. Or pizza. A great way to shop.

_____

_____

_____

_____

When we moved from an apartment to a house. We discovered that we had more belongings than we thought. So much stuff had to be packed. In boxes. In suitcases. And even in large garbage bags. We rented a truck. From the local gas station. So we could avoid spending the extra money to hire a mover. We certainly put in a full day's work. That day. Although the process was long and hard. It was worth it.

5

Run-ons

A sentence expresses a complete thought. You saw in Chapter 4 how fragments can interfere with the meaning of a sentence. Run-on sentences can cause similar problems of unclear meaning.

Whereas a fragment occurs when a sentence is broken apart, a run-on develops when one sentence runs into another one.

This happens in one of two ways:

1. You finish one independent clause and go on to write another without putting any punctuation between.

> The train stops here it is always late.

2. You put just a comma between the two independent clauses.

> The train stops here, it is always late.

Remember: An independent clause has a subject and a complete verb, and it does not begin with any of the words that begin a dependent clause. You may want to look back at the list of such words in Chapter 4, Point 3.

In the preceding run-ons, each of the independent clauses can stand alone as a sentence:

> The train stops here.
> It is always late.

The three exercises that follow will give you practice in recognizing run-ons.

Exercise: Recognition

Each of the following is an example of a run-on sentence. Draw a line between the independent clauses. Cross out incorrect commas.

1. I like rock music/I don't like jazz.

2. The invitation was beautiful it was hand-lettered.

3. The tide is high it is a good time to swim.

4. Ben is a trucker, he is from Georgia.

5. It was a good film, I saw it twice.

6. Babies are cute they cry a lot.

7. He is my friend he understands me.

8. The trip was postponed we had no sleeping bags.

9. The firefighters were called, they handled the blaze.

10. I raked the beach, there is no seaweed left.

Another Exercise: Recognition

Mark *C* for a complete sentence or *RO* for a run-on sentence.

RO   1. They were neighbors, they were good friends.

_____ 2. There is a leash law, no one obeys it.

_____ 3. Change that tire it is flat.

_____ 4. A bad grade bothers me, don't think it doesn't.

_____ 5. She is packing cartons, they will take them away.

_____ 6. Ann has wanted to buy the ring since she saw it in the store window.

_____ 7. The boys went fishing the girls went hiking.

_____ 8. I love to eat that's why I am fat.

_____ 9. There was a lovely sunset, we watched it.

_____ 10. Give me a chance I can do better.

A Third Exercise: Recognition

Mark *C* for a complete sentence or *RO* for a run-on sentence.

RO   1. What should we do, I don't know.

_____ 2. He was a star athlete he won trophies.

_____ 3. We walked around the block.

_____ 4. If you ask me, I will tell you.

_____ 5. The snowplows came through, they cleared the street.

_____ 6. She entered the marathon she placed third.

_____ 7. The governor made a statement, it was surprising.

_____ 8. Ed drives too fast he will get in an accident.

_____ 9. She couldn't light the candle the wick was gone.

_____ 10. Brian made a mistake he corrected it later.

Now that you can recognize run-on sentences, it is important to know how to correct them. _There are four ways to correct a run-on sentence._ Each method is described in one of the following points.

POINT 1   Connect two independent clauses with a comma plus one of these connecting words: and, but, for, or, nor, yet, so.

● _Remember:_ A comma by itself is not sufficient.

Students write papers, **and** teachers correct them.

This is now a complete and correct sentence. The two independent clauses are connected by a comma _and_ the connecting word _and_.

The men cooked dinner, **so** the women mixed the drinks.
The train stops here, **but** it is always late.

Exercise: Point 1

Change each of the following run-on sentences into a complete and correct sentence by placing a comma plus a connecting word where necessary. Rewrite the new, correct sentence in the space provided.

1. It was my mother's birthday, I called her on the phone.
   It was my mother's birthday, so I called her on the phone.

2. Going out to dinner is fun it is expensive.

   _____

3. I won't do it, you can't make me.

   _____

4. We can usually see for miles, today it is too cloudy.

_____

5. I want that job, I don't think I have enough experience.

_____

6. We found some shells on the beach they were beautiful.

_____

7. I never knew his name, I'll never forget him.

_____

8. Tell me your problem I can help you.

_____

9. Our daughter is in the third grade, she is very bright.

_____

10. I've never tried blueberry ice cream I bet I will like it.

_____

Another Exercise: Point 1

What is one way to correct a run-on sentence? By connecting two independent clauses with a comma *plus* one of these connecting words (fill in the blanks):

_____ , _____ , _____ ,

_____ , _____ , _____ ,

_____ .

POINT 2   Separate two independent clauses with a semicolon.

Students write papers; teachers correct them.

The semicolon separates the two independent clauses and makes the sentence complete and correct.

The men cooked dinner; the women mixed the drinks.
The train stops here; it is always late.

In addition, connecting words such as *however, therefore, consequently, nevertheless, likewise, besides, also, then,* and *furthermore* may be used after the semicolon.

These words are stronger and more emphatic than the words *and*, *but*, and the other words listed in Point 1.

Because these are strong words, it is often a good idea to put a comma after them. The word *then* is an exception; it does not generally take a comma.

Students write papers; **then** teachers correct them.
The men cooked dinner; **therefore,** the women mixed the drinks.
The train stops here; **however,** it is always late.

Exercise: Point 2

Correct each of the following run-on sentences by placing a semicolon between the independent clauses. Add commas where they are needed. Rewrite the complete and correct sentence in the space provided.

1. I received the most votes therefore I was elected.

   I received the most votes; therefore, I was elected.

2. The ship sails from Worth Wharf it leaves at 2:00 P.M.

   _____

3. We lost however we still lead the league.

   _____

4. The play was a tragedy, we left the theater weeping.

   _____

5. You want your freedom nevertheless you will have to get a job.

   _____

6. I am running for office, furthermore I intend to win.

   _____

7. She must be out of town otherwise she would be here.

   _____

8. First buy your ticket then get in line.

   _____

9. Those shoes are comfortable I'll take two pairs.

   _____

10. There was no heat consequently we froze all night.

   _____

Review Exercise: Points 1 and 2

Fill in the blank with either a comma and a connecting word or a semicolon and a connecting word, making the sentence complete and correct. Place a comma after the connecting word if it is needed. Use five of each type.

1. We rented a floor buffer, _____ it did not work.

2. Joe ran all the way home _____ he was tired.

3. I cooked a hamburger for dinner _____ I forgot to buy a roll.

4. The horse I bet on came in second _____ I lost money.

5. The window was shattered _____ we had to get a new one.

6. The candle burned for hours _____ we did not have to use the lamp.

7. Apple pie is delicious _____ it is fattening.

8. The show came on too late _____ she wasn't really interested in seeing it.

9. Summers are hot and humid _____ winters are cold and dry.

10. He was wealthy _____ he could buy anything he wanted.

Another Review Exercise: Points 1 and 2

Fill in the blanks. Tell two ways to correct a run-on sentence.

1. Connect two _____ clauses with a _____

plus one of these connecting words: _____ , _____ ,

_____ , _____ , _____ ,

_____ , _____ .

2. Separate two _____ clauses with a _____ .

POINT 3   Make two independent clauses into two sentences by using a period, a question mark, or an exclamation point.

Students write papers. Teachers correct them.

Since an independent clause is already a sentence, we can easily make the two clauses into two sentences by placing a period between them.

The men cooked dinner. The women mixed the drinks.
The train stops here. However, it is always late.

The strong connecting word *however* becomes part of the second sentence.

Note how the following run-on sentence can be made into two sentences by inserting a question mark.

Did you go to the party I didn't.

can be changed into

Did you go to the party? I didn't.

Exercise: Point 3

Make each of the following run-on sentences into two separate sentences. Add correct punctuation and a capital letter.

1. She asked for a raise she got it.

    She asked for a raise. She got it.

2. That is a new hall the acoustics are fantastic.

3. He is a good father, he pays attention to his children.

4. The birds are chirping, they sound so happy.

5. The parade is beginning let's get a good spot.

6. Your paper is late, therefore it will lose a grade.

7. He failed the test, consequently he will have to take it again.

8. Why did you go partying you were tired.

_____

9. That suit fits you should buy it.

_____

10. Bowling is fun for the whole family, it is good exercise.

_____

Review Exercise: Points 1–3

Rewrite these run-ons in each of the three ways you know how to correct them.

1. The sun went down, the mosquitoes came out.

  The sun went down, and the mosquitoes came out.
  The sun went down; the mosquitoes came out.
  The sun went down. The mosquitoes came out.

2. Ben ran a good race, he came in second.

_____

_____

_____

3. We applauded the actress she came out for a second bow.

_____

_____

_____

4. I like Chaucer, I like Shakespeare even better.

_____

_____

_____

5. I am happy to be here, I'm glad you are with me.

_____

_____

_____

6. Turn right here park where you can.

_____

_____

_____

7. I quit smoking, I feel much better.

_____

_____

_____

8. I love visiting you, you treat me so well.

_____

_____

_____

9. I have hay fever I take allergy pills.

_____

_____

_____

10. I'm in my second childhood I feel young again.

_____

_____

_____

| **POINT 4** **Change one of the independent clauses into a dependent clause.**

- _Remember:_ When a dependent clause comes at the beginning of a sentence, it is followed by a comma. (See Chapter 4, Point 4.)

    When students write papers, teachers correct them.

The addition of the word _when_ makes _students write papers_ a dependent clause. This sentence is now complete and correct.

    Before the men cooked dinner, the women mixed drinks.
    Though the train stops here, it is always late.

● Look back at Chapter 4, Point 3, if you need to review how to make independent clauses dependent.

Exercise: Point 4

Each of the following run-on sentences contains two independent clauses. Correct the sentence by making one of them into a dependent clause.

1. We went to the museum, Bob went to the ball game.

   While we went to the museum, Bob went to the ball game.

2. You are my friend I trust you.

   _____

3. I don't like crowds, I enjoy going to the beach.

   _____

4. The temperature dropped it started to rain.

   _____

5. I answered the phone, the caller hung up.

   _____

6. The kids are building sand castles, the adults have a conversation.

   _____

7. Let's find our seats, the show begins.

   _____

8. I locked the door, they still broke in.

   _____

9. You were fired the place has not been the same.

   _____

10. You were gone the plumber came.

   _____

Review Exercise: Points 3 and 4

All the following sentences are run-ons. Correct each of them in two ways: (1) separate the independent clauses into two sentences with a period and a capital letter;

(2) make one of the clauses into a dependent clause and add any necessary punctuation.

1. We moved here we have been very happy.

    We moved here. We have been very happy.

    Since we moved here, we have been very happy.

2. Trash is collected on Mondays it is taken to the dump.

3. There is no easy remedy we must research the matter further.

4. I started taking fiddle lessons I improved my style.

5. That type of defense will never work the other team is too good.

6. We go swimming every night during the summer the pond is nearby.

7. We drove cross-country we had no idea how beautiful America is.

8. You don't look well, lie down for a while.

9. The professor raised his voice he was sure angry.

10. He looks grubby, he has not shaved for weeks.

_____

_____

THE FOUR WAYS TO CORRECT A RUN-ON SENTENCE

1. Connect two independent clauses with a comma _plus_ one of these connecting words: _and, but, for, or, nor, yet, so._
2. Separate two independent clauses with a semicolon.
3. Make the two independent clauses into two sentences by using a period, a question mark, or an exclamation point.
4. Change one of the independent clauses into a dependent clause.

Chapter Review

I. Mark _C_ for a complete sentence or _RO_ for a run-on. Draw a line between the independent clauses in run-ons. Cross out incorrect commas.

_____ 1. Shirts sometimes come with cardboard in them it protects them from wrinkling.

_____ 2. You need matches to start a fire.

_____ 3. Fred wears madras shirts, they have gone out of style.

_____ 4. Before you paint, you have to strip the surface.

_____ 5. She was hired because she was the best one for the job.

_____ 6. There is a late show tonight, what time does it start?

_____ 7. Al called last night he is getting married.

_____ 8. Rest is important vitamins will help.

_____ 9. It is your turn, roll the dice.

_____ 10. Max takes flying lessons, he is getting a license.

II. Mark _C_ for a complete sentence and _RO_ for a run-on. Correct the run-ons by using one of the four points.

_____ 1. Guns are dangerous, they can cause a lot of trouble.

_____

_____ 2. After the guests left, we cleaned up.

_____

_____ 3. Lilacs are fragrant, we should grow some.

_____

_____ 4. Construction workers wear hard hats they need protection.

_____

_____ 5. Come outside you want to see the stars.

_____

_____ 6. Poker is a great game, it takes skill as well as luck.

_____

_____ 7. I read a great novel you can borrow it.

_____

_____ 8. Shakespeare wrote comedies, tragedies, and histories.

_____

_____ 9. I chose a button-down shirt, I like that style.

_____

_____ 10. I wrote a letter to the editor, it was printed.

_____

III. Each of the following run-on sentences can be corrected by adding proper punctuation and sometimes a capital letter. Circle the correction that makes the run-on into a complete and correct sentence.

1. We want to buy a new car (, ;) but it is too expensive.

2. She is a teacher (, ;) therefore (,) she has her summers off.

3. I wrote my member of Congress (, . H) he replied with a form letter.

4. He started slowly (, . T) then (,) he speeded up and won the race.

5. Al went to the ball game (, ;) he ate peanuts and drank beer.

6. Italy is a lovely country (, . A) and so is Spain.

7. We had a picnic (, ;) and Marie played the guitar.

8. Although we got lost (, . W) we arrived on time.

9. Young people are often energetic (, ;) furthermore (,) they have great ambition.

10. Since we bought the fan (, ;) it has been much cooler in here.

IV. Each of the following run-ons can be corrected by the addition of a connecting word. Fill in the blank with an appropriate word.

1. Bring me my slippers, _____ see if you can find my pipe.

2. I've never been there, _____ I don't want to go.

3. I would like to get a bird's-eye view of things, _____ I can't fly.

4. You must do your homework, _____ you'll get a poor grade.

5. I don't usually read that magazine, _____ I did see the article.

6. The movie was hilarious, _____ I saw it twice.

7. I like playing tennis, _____ I'm not very good at it.

8. I take lessons, _____ I practice every day.

9. She wears army boots, _____ she rides a motorcycle.

10. I have hay fever, _____ it only bothers me in August.

V. Make each of the following run-on sentences into a complete and correct sentence. Use each of the four ways at least once.

1. Farming is hard work, it is satisfying.

   _____

2. We listened to oldies on the radio, it was an evening of memories.

   _____

3. Some people say horse races are fixed they are fun to watch.

_____

4. Avoid poison ivy, it can irritate your skin.

_____

5. A fireplace is romantic it can keep you warm.

_____

6. My teacher was close to me she was almost my best friend.

_____

7. I arrived late, I missed the interview.

_____

8. I can balance my checkbook, I cannot complete my income-tax forms.

_____

9. My sign is Libra however my wife is an Aquarian.

_____

10. Writing is an important skill it takes time to develop.

_____

VI. Tell one way to correct a run-on sentence.

Connect two _____ clauses with a comma *plus* one of

these connecting words: _____ , _____ ,

_____ , _____ , _____ ,

_____ , _____ .

VII. Correct these run-ons in each of the four ways you have learned.

1. Andy loves golf, he plays a round every day.

_____

_____

_____

_____

2. I built a desk I keep it in my bedroom.

_____

_____

_____

_____

3. We traveled to Europe we saw the Eiffel Tower.

_____

_____

_____

_____

4. English is my favorite subject I get good grades.

_____

_____

_____

_____

5. I mixed the ingredients I put the batter in the oven.

_____

_____

_____

_____

6. I love summer, I don't like the humidity.

_____

_____

_____

_____

7. The mail arrives late here, the postman walks a long route.

_____

_____

_____

_____

8. I enjoyed the dinner I feel a bit bloated now.

_____

_____

_____

_____

9. I see moisture in the basement, there must be a leak somewhere.

_____

_____

_____

_____

10. The wine is imported from France it is very good.

_____

_____

_____

_____

VIII. As independent clauses, all the following thoughts are complete by themselves, but you can make more interesting sentences by combining pairs of them. Use a connecting word where appropriate. Write the new sentences on the lines provided. Be sure to use correct punctuation.

Mario is a whiz at photography
he was a great composer
cheeseburgers are absolutely scrumptious
Tom is lazy
he is going to school to get his degree
he knows how important exercise is
Sally is an excellent painter
John wants to be a registered nurse
hamburgers are delicious
Beethoven was deaf

1. _____

2. _____

3. _____

4. _____

5. _____

IX. Here is another set to work with:

a summer breeze is lovely
sometimes it seems he can communicate with us
she bought a Volkswagen
it requires a lot of stamina
he is my best friend
that dog is very smart
it cools the body and the mind
backpacking is a great way to spend the day
he has moved to Detroit
she traded in her Ford

1. _____

2. _____

3. _____

4. _____

5. _____

X. Rewrite each of the following paragraphs. Change the run-ons into complete and correct sentences.

The energy crisis affects us all, the price of home-heating fuel keeps rising, it gets too expensive to stay warm. One way to solve the problem is to buy a wood-burning stove, in some cases you can heat a whole house with the stove. Wood is also costly, if you have access to a supply it can save you money. Also, a stove is a beautiful addition to a house or apartment, it comes in many different styles each kind suits a different purpose.

_____

_____

_____

_____

_____

_____

_____

_____

Cats makes great pets, you have to be affectionate with them. They are rather independent animals they do not always come when you call them. Many people prefer dogs, you can train them to come, or sit, or fetch a bone. With cats, on the other hand you have to be willing to let them live their own lives if you attempt to train them you may become discouraged. If you put two cats in the same room you are in for quite a treat. They chase each other, usually all in fun and when one catches the other the real show begins. Oftentimes they will cuddle and clean each other sometimes they will fight. The wise pet owner will know when to break up a fight and when to let it go since it is only play for the cats. They can be great company if you understand them.

Tennis is a sport that has gained great popularity over the last ten years, both men and women enjoy it. Tennis courts are being built all over, they can be found in cities, in the country, in the suburbs. People of all ages can play in fact some of the greatest players in the world are in their teens or early twenties. The most important and prestigious tournament is held every summer at Wimbledon, a suburb of London however America's most important tournament is the U.S. Open it is held at Flushing Meadows, New York. One does not have to be a star athlete to enjoy tennis, it is great fun even for those who just want some fresh air and exercise.

_____

_____

_____

_____

_____

_____

_____

_____

_____

_____

_____

_____

6

Misplaced Modifiers

Clear and logical word order is a very important aspect of effective sentence writing. Most of the time, you order the words in sentences without giving them much thought. For example, you would never write "Independence Day today is." You would just naturally write "Today is Independence Day." The words fall into the right order easily and make sense.

There are, however, certain times when your choice of word order is not so clear-cut. If you use the wrong order, your sentence may turn out to be confusing, if not downright silly.

> We were told at midnight the show would begin.
> The man dived into the pool with the moustache.

These sentences are confusing or silly because the modifiers are misplaced. In this chapter you'll learn how to avoid misplaced modifiers that result in confusing or silly sentences.

POINT 1 **A *modifier* is a word (or group of words) that describes or explains another word (or group of words) in a sentence.**

> He wore a **ragged** suit.

The word *ragged* modifies *suit*. That is, it describes the suit.

> The **short** woman wore **high-heeled** shoes.

This sentence contains two modifiers; *short* and *high-heeled*. *Short* tells us something about the woman, and *high-heeled* describes her shoes.

101

That man **on the corner** is playing the clarinet.

Here we see how a group of words, *on the corner*, describes the word *man*. The modifier distinguishes that man from any other man—he is *on the corner*.

All these modifiers describe a noun (a person, place, or thing). Modifiers can also describe verbs.

Hank ran **quickly** after the ball.

Quickly describes, or modifies, the verb *ran*. It tells us *how* Hank ran after the ball.

We left the party **early**.

Here the modifier, *early*, tells *when* we left.

She swam **alongside** the boat.

The modifier, *alongside the boat*, explains the verb, *swam*. It tells us *where* she swam.

Exercise: Point 1

Either a noun or a verb is underlined in each of the following sentences. Circle the word or words that modify the underlined word.

1. The (sunken) ship held many treasures.

2. The cat tiptoed silently through the room.

3. Ernie is repairing the picket fence.

4. She smiled with all her charm at the young man.

5. With some reluctance, Lucy moved away from her family.

6. Home-made ice cream is tastier than this stuff.

7. The house with grey shingles is weathered.

8. Anthony plays lovingly with his niece.

9. The bike with three red stripes is mine.

10. That handsome man is my boyfriend.

POINT 2 Place a modifier as close as possible to the word it modifies.

I showed my tooth to the dentist with a crack in it.

As this sentence is written, the dentist him- or herself has a crack. It is obvious that the phrase *with a crack in it* modifies the noun *tooth*. As it stands, the modifer is misplaced. The word order should be changed to

I showed my tooth with a crack in it to the dentist.

Now the modifier has been placed as close as possible to the word it modifies, and the sentence is clear.

> He told me he was going to the movie that night in the morning.

This sounds as if the night is in the morning. Actually the modifier, *in the morning,* explains when he *told* me. The sentence should read,

> In the morning he told me he was going to the movie that night.

Notice that in this sentence, the modifier cannot be placed right next to the word it modifies. The subject, *he,* is in the way. This often happens with words that modify verbs.

Exercise: Point 2

Place the modifier given in the parentheses in an appropriate spot in the sentence. Rewrite the entire sentence in the space provided, and underline the word that is modified.

1. (in a sharkskin coat) A man sold us a lottery ticket.

   A man in a sharkskin coat sold us a lottery ticket.

2. (along the boardwalk) We strolled until the sun set.

   _____

3. (excitedly) The crowd cheered when Yaz came to the plate.

   _____

4. (yellow) The banana comes in its own natural wrapper.

   _____

5. (climbing the steps) I saw my grandmother in her house.

   _____

6. (as usual) He spoke only about himself.

   _____

7. (approaching the finish line) We watched the horses.

   _____

8. (happily) Alex smiled when he heard the news.

   _____

9. (in a whisper) She warned me never to do that again.

   _____

10. (elastic) The man in the circus is a sideshow attraction.

Review Exercise: Points 1 and 2

Write *C* if the modifier is correctly placed in the sentence or *MM* if it is misplaced. Where the modifier is misplaced, correct the sentence as shown in the first example.

MM   1. Rick got an A on the test. Amazingly,

_____ 2. The monster waited in the ugly cave.

_____ 3. There was a rat waiting for us behind the door.

_____ 4. The quarterback made the decision to run, instantaneously.

_____ 5. Heading for a crash we watched the motorcyclist.

_____ 6. The city council voted to fund the project unanimously.

_____ 7. Max was chasing the dog wearing only his underwear.

_____ 8. The panhandler approached the millionaire without a cent to his name.

_____ 9. The furnace exploded, but no one was hurt with a crash.

_____ 10. My father bought a toupee who is bald.

POINT 3   When dealing with modifiers, ask yourself, *what goes with what?*

> The flowers appealed to the woman displayed in the vase.

The modifier, *displayed in the vase*, certainly does not refer to the woman. It is important to determine that the modifier *goes with* the noun *flowers*. The sentence should read:

> The flowers displayed in the vase appealed to the woman.

By determining that *displayed in the vase* goes with *flowers*, we can now place the modifier in its proper position—near the word it modifies.

> The man dived into the pool with the moustache.

Again, the moustache surely does not belong to the pool. The sentence should read,

> The man with the moustache dived into the pool.

Problems with misplaced modifiers often occur because you think faster than you can write. The key to this type of writing problem lies in proofreading—in checking what you have written. Reread what you write, asking yourself, "Is this what I mean to say?" Look at the modifiers and ask, "What goes with what?"

Exercise: Point 3

Determine what goes with the underlined word in each of the following sentences. Rewrite the modifer in the space provided.

1. <u>Poetry</u> appeals to many Americans of the fifteenth century.

   of the fifteenth century goes with <u>poetry</u>.

2. Suddenly riding her bicycle he saw the <u>child</u>.

   _____ goes with <u>child</u>.

3. Dressed in many colors we saw the <u>clown</u>.

   _____ goes with <u>clown</u>.

4. The <u>bureau</u> belonged to his great-aunt in the basement.

   _____ goes with <u>bureau</u>.

5. That <u>dog</u> belongs to the woman with the floppy ears.

   _____ goes with <u>dog</u>.

6. The siren <u>wailed</u> and we covered our ears loudly.

   _____ goes with <u>wailed</u>.

7. Promising better times for all we listened to the <u>politician</u>.

   _____ goes with <u>politician</u>.

8. The <u>check</u> was cashed the next day for fifty dollars.

   _____ goes with <u>check</u>.

9. The <u>girl</u> fed the lions with the creamy complexion.

   _____ goes with <u>girl</u>.

10. Barking at the fire hydrant we watched the <u>dog</u>.

    _____ goes with <u>dog</u>.

POINT 4   **Be sure that words such as *almost, even, hardly, just, merely, only, nearly,* and *scarcely* refer clearly to the words they modify.**

Consider the difference in meaning between these two sentences:

I almost ate all the vegetables.
I ate almost all the vegetables.

In the first sentence, *almost* is a misplaced modifier. If you think about it, you can see that to almost eat something is not to eat it at all. The second sentence, however, is much clearer. In this case, the speaker ate *almost* all the vegetables: that is, the speaker ate many of them, but not all.

Johnny, we **hardly** knew you.

The modifier, *hardly,* is placed right next to the verb *knew.* Like all modifiers, it explains the word it modifies. We can tell *how well* the speaker knew Johnny.
In which of these sentences is the modifier properly placed?

I read the newspaper **nearly** every day.
I **nearly** read the newspaper every day.

The first sentence is correct. The second is wrong, because you cannot *nearly read* a newspaper. Either you read it or you don't.

Exercise: Point 4

For each sentence, a modifier is given in parentheses. Place it near the word it modifies.

1. (almost) After an hour, she was ready to go.

2. (even) She does not know his name.

3. (hardly) You are the one I need for this job.

4. (just) She had finished painting when I touched the doorknob.

5. (just) There are three eggs left in the refrigerator.

6. (only) I received the passing grade on the exam.

7. (nearly) I put on a last burst of speed and won the race.

8. (scarcely) The host had provided enough food for all the guests.

9. (merely) The police officer informed us of our rights.

10. (nearly) This time we made it.

Review Exercise: Points 1–4

Each of the following sentences contains a misplaced modifier. Correct them by placing the modifier near the word it describes.

1. The birds are singing (in the trees) their songs of love.

2. I heard about the big music festival on the radio.

3. I fell over from almost laughing so hard.

4. She sighed when the good news came happily.

5. Everyone nearly loves a barbecue.

6. Pete turned away when he saw the girl of his dreams bashfully.

7. He sat watching his neighbors below on the roof.

8. We needed someone to work overtime badly.

9. I am talking and relaxing on the telephone.

10. You are the one for me only.

POINT 5 **Avoid placing a modifier between two words when its explanation can apply to either word.**

> His teacher told him **frequently** to study.

Does *frequently* refer to *told him* or to *to study?* We cannot tell if the teacher told him many times or if the teacher told him to study often. This sentence may be rewritten as either

> His teacher frequently told him to study.

or

> His teacher told him to study frequently.
> She said **before she left** she would visit him.

In this example, we cannot tell what part of the sentence the modifier refers to. Does *before she left* refer to when she was speaking or to when she would visit him? There is simply no way of knowing. This sentence may be rewritten as either

> Before she left, she said she would visit him.

or

> She said she would visit him before she left.

Once again, the rule to follow here is *make sure the modifier refers clearly to the words it modifies.*

Exercise: Point 5

Rewrite each of the following sentences in two different ways.

1. She told him every day to change his socks.

   Every day she told him to change his socks.

   She told him to change his socks every day.

2. Clara said after her operation she felt better.

   _____

   _____

3. He told me always to be practical.

   _____

   _____

4. We were told at midnight the show would begin.

   _____

   _____

5. Ruth promised on her way out to close the door.

   _____

   _____

HOW TO AVOID MISPLACED MODIFIERS

1. Keep the modifiers near the words they modify.
2. Ask yourself, "What goes with what?"
3. Be sure that words such as *almost, even, hardly, merely, only, nearly,* and *scarcely* refer clearly to the words they modify.
4. Don't place a modifier between two words when its explanation may apply to either word.

Chapter Review

I. Write *C* if the modifier is correctly placed. Write *MM* if it is misplaced. Then, in the MM sentences, circle the modifier and draw an arrow to show where it should go.

   _____ 1. The man was stopped for speeding in the blue sweater.

   _____ 2. I almost saw the whole movie, but I fell asleep around

   midnight.

_____ 3. Hanging on one hinge, Joe left the door.

_____ 4. The initials were those of the lovers carved on the tree.

_____ 5. There are only two parking spaces left in the lot.

_____ 6. Every four hours the doctor told him to take a pill.

_____ 7. Sitting on the porch, I smoked my last cigarette.

_____ 8. The woman walked into the elevator with high heels.

_____ 9. The jet crashed into a cliff carrying 155 passengers.

_____ 10. I can hardly remember my own name.

II. Do these examples the same way you did the last set. Write _C_ or _MM_ and show where the misplaced modifiers should be correctly placed.

_____ 1. I watched the mechanic fix the car with admiration.

_____ 2. He made it in time barely.

_____ 3. Reaching into the cupboard, I found the bag of cookies.

_____ 4. We borrowed a mower from a neighbor that was broken.

_____ 5. Climbing up a telephone pole we saw a squirrel.

_____ 6. Mel, as usual, was lagging behind.

_____ 7. The cat was rescued after the building had been set on fire by a firefighter.

_____ 8. We've almost found all the pieces to the puzzle.

_____ 9. Vandals from the corner stole the sign.

_____ 10. I need food badly.

III. Again, mark _C_ for correct and _MM_ for misplaced modifier. Then correct the MM sentences with an arrow.

_____ 1. Cathy was driven to the party by her mother.

_____ 2. I've hardly seen any of those films.

_____ 3. The signal, which was flashing intermittently, turned red.

_____ 4. By my favorite author, I read a new book.

_____ 5. Charlie visited his family in Baltimore.

_____ 6. The boy waved to the Queen with a crew cut.

_____ 7. Nearly everyone we invited showed up.

_____ 8. She said in an interview she was happy.

_____ 9. We flew in a plane through a terrible storm with a faulty
engine.

_____ 10. Lucy was skiing when she broke her ankle down the slope.

IV. Place the modifier given in the parentheses in an appropriate spot in the
sentence. Use an arrow.

1. (after the game) The coach treated the team to beers.

2. (wearing a ten-gallon hat) We saw a cowboy in the street.

3. (happily) She giggled when she saw him.

4. (in the supermarket) We buy vegetables five miles from here.

5. (running down the hall) The principal stopped the students.

6. (in the crib) She gave the baby a bottle.

7. (red) I bought a shirt to go with my yellow slacks.

8. (that had been painted) We bought a picture by an artist from New
Mexico.

9. (that she bought yesterday) She used a shampoo and then her usual
conditioner.

10. (when she reaches sixteen) I promised to kiss her.

V. Do this exercise the same way you did the last one.

1. (almost) The criminal laughed when he was arrested.

2. (with brass buttons) He bought a suit and treated himself to a fancy
dinner.

3. (around town) Sammy loves to ride his scooter.

4. (barely) The cat escaped before the blaze spread.

5. (in the attic) We put insulation down, and now we are cool.

6. (friendly) There is a teller in that bank.

7. (noisy) There is a dog in our neighborhood.

8. (occasionally) He surprised his wife with a rose.

9. (made of brass) She bought a tie clasp for her husband.

10. (just) We are about ready to leave.

VI. Each of the following sentences contains a misplaced modifier. In the space provided, rewrite the sentence in its correct form.

1. Susie fixed the pocket with a needle and thread which had a hole in it.

   _____

2. I said when I got home I would tell you about my trip.

   _____

3. The tire went flat with the puncture.

   _____

4. The hunter escaped from the bear's claws barely.

   _____

5. In swimsuits the judges watched the models parade on stage.

   _____

6. Robin brought her dog to the veterinarian with an injured tail.

   _____

7. He vowed to love, honor, and cherish her on his wedding day.

   _____

8. My mother-in-law snores when she sleeps loudly.

   _____

9. She bought a ring from the jeweler that was made of gold and enamel.

   _____

10. We first baked a cake for our friends in the new oven.

   _____

11. I ran into the barefooted street.

   _____

12. We sent invitations to all our friends in blue envelopes.

   _____

13. He left the clothing store and bought a newspaper with a new pair of socks.

   _____

14. That salesperson sold me a Pontiac with a bow tie.

_____

15. Jumping rope I watched my sister from the car.

_____

16. Sally said before she was twenty she would be a millionaire.

_____

17. I would like a banana and a glass of water in my sundae.

_____

18. The suit is at the cleaners with the brass buttons.

_____

19. The hospital has been torn down where I was born.

_____

20. I banged up a car in an accident that did not belong to me.

_____

VII. Rewrite each passage, correcting any sentences that contain misplaced modifers.

I forgot to nearly send Christmas cards this year. All my relatives would have been disappointed in other parts of the country. It really is not that much of a strain since I need to send about ten cards only. It is as easy as writing "Hi, How are you?" and mailing it on a note in an envelope. I usually work from a list that I keep in my desk of my friends' and relatives' names. I luckily remembered about the cards three days before the holiday; I just hope that too late I did not mail them.

_____

_____

_____

_____

_____

_____

_____

_____

Raising a family really is an easy task. Everyone thinks he knows the best way; anyone scarcely does it perfectly. Many people read Dr. Spock's book which presents clearly one accepted method. Everyone nearly has heard of that book at least.

No matter what method they follow, parents are advised constantly to be kind and affectionate toward their children. Some parents say after the baby is born their lives are changed completely for the better. They don't mind if the baby cries even. They rock the baby pacing the floor back to sleep. They accept the trouble calmly, knowing the baby will outgrow soon that stage. If they have prepared themselves for the new arrival as they could early and completely, they are never really upset almost by the little problems that come up.

These days, many people are trying health foods in all parts of the country. The "back to nature" movement has nearly affected everyone in one way or another. Producers of health foods use no perservatives in their products which they claim are bad for the system. Cereals such as granola a totally natural food are especially popular. People are also eating unstarched rice which is supposed to be good for the digestive system particularly. Ice cream even comes in new, natural flavors such as banana and coconut which is made with fresh bananas. Certainly health food companies are trying hard to attract customers interested in better nutrition.

7

Dangling Modifiers

In Chapter 6, we saw the problems that can come from a misplaced modifier. If we read, "Running at 70 miles per hour, I saw a cheetah," we may get a mental picture of an amazingly fast human. Still, with a bit of thought, we realize that it is the cheetah that is the speedy one. But what about this: "Running at 70 miles per hour, it was time to take a picture." Who or what was running? We don't know; there is absolutely nothing in the sentence to tell us. What we have here is a *dangling modifier*. It is a modifier with nothing to refer to. But, as you will see, the problem is easy to recognize and easy to correct.

POINT 1   A modifier is said to be *dangling* when there is no word in the sentence for it to modify.

Waiting for the bus, it started to rain.

The modifier, *waiting for the bus*, does not modify anything. It seems to modify *it*, but there is no logical connection between the words. *Who* was waiting for the bus? We cannnot tell from this sentence.

Listening to records, my stereo blew a fuse.

Was the *stereo* listening to the records? Of course not. The modifier, *listening to records*, is dangling because there is no word in the sentence for it to modify. We simply do not know who was taking part in the action of listening.

At the age of three, my mother told me bedtime stories.

In this sentence, it seems as if *my mother* was three years old when she was telling bedtime stories to her child. This, of course, is impossible. Who or what was three years old? Clearly, it is the speaker. Thus, the sentence should be rewritten as

When I was three, my mother told me bedtime stories.
Running in the race, sweat formed on my brow.

What word does *running in the race* modify? Unless the *sweat* was running in the race—which is highly unlikely—we again have a dangling modifier. There is no word in the sentence for *running in the race* to modify.

Exercise: Point 1

Draw one line under the dangling modifier in each of the following sentences.

1. Driving in heavy traffic, my head started to ache.

2. Seasoning meat, pepper is often used.

3. Crossing the border, my bags were searched.

4. Choosing a career, my counselor helped.

5. An iron was used, preparing my costume.

6. Mowing the lawn, lemonade is refreshing.

7. Examining philosophy, a text was helpful.

8. Thinking aloud, ideas came to me.

9. Suntan lotion helps, getting a tan.

10. Practicing the piano, a metronome is useful.

Can you see why the modifier in each of these sentences is dangling?

POINT 2   When a sentence begins with a group of words introduced by an -*ing* word, the person or thing performing the action (the subject) should be identified right after the -*ing* phrase.

Pondering my future, a decision was reached.

The modifier, *pondering my future*, is dangling, since there is no word for it to modify. Clearly, *a decision* is not pondering my future. We must determine who or what is performing the action (who or what is pondering my future). It would make perfect sense for the subject to be *I*. Therefore, this sentence should be revised to read:

Pondering my future, I reached a decision.

The subject, *I*, is placed directly after the -*ing* phrase.

Expecting trouble, our plans were changed.

Again we have a dangling modifier in *expecting trouble*. Who or what was expecting trouble? We need a subject, and since the sentence refers to *our* plans, the subject should be *we*. The sentence should read:

Expecting trouble, *we* changed our plans.

Walking down the aisle, tickets were collected.

should be changed to

Walking down the aisle, the *conductor* collected tickets.

or

Walking down the aisle, *he* collected tickets.

- Notice that after the modifier, the subject introduces an *independent clause*. Notice also that a comma is placed between the modifier and the independent clause.

- *Remember:* Always ask *who* or *what* performs the action indicated by the modifier.

Exercise: Point 2

Write *DM* if the modifier is dangling or *C* if it has a subject to refer to and the sentence is, therefore, correct. Underline the subject.

___*C*___ 1. Chasing his sister, <u>Billy</u> fell and bruised his knee.

_____ 2. Feeling happy, cheers were given.

_____ 3. Running scared, the cat climbed up the tree.

_____ 4. Being alone, I spent the evening reading.

_____ 5. Laughing hysterically, the joke was repeated.

_____ 6. Following the recipe, Patty cooked a great meal.

_____ 7. Slipping on the ice, her leg was broken.

_____ 8. Rollerskating, knee pads are useful.

_____ 9. Appreciating the performance, the audience applauded.

_____ 10. Throwing curveballs, a young pitcher must be careful not to hurt his arm.

Review Exercise: Points 1 and 2

Complete these sentences by adding an independent clause with an appropriate subject.

1. Preparing to land, _____*the pilot radioed the tower.*_____

2. Making a decision, _____

   3. Training for the marathon, _____

   4. Staring out the window, _____

   5. Adjusting her rear-view mirror, _____

   6. Checking my shoe size, _____

   7. Following close behind, _____

   8. Growing prematurely bald, _____

   9. Crying in the crib, _____

  10. Finally breaking through the clouds, _____

Another Review Exercise: Points 1 and 2

Complete these sentences in the same way you did those in the preceding exercise.

   1. When ready, _____ *the dinner will be served.* _____

   2. Although a stranger, _____

   3. At my high school graduation, _____

   4. While shopping for a home computer, _____

   5. From under the table, _____

   6. In her younger days, _____

   7. By the way you dress, _____

   8. On my stereo television, _____

   9. If damaged in shipment, _____

  10. When used properly, _____

Sometimes the sentence has a word for the dangling phrase to modify, but it is in the wrong place. Therefore:

| POINT 3 Put the modifier as close as possible to the word it explains.

This is the same rule we encountered in Chapter 6, when we were dealing with misplaced modifiers.

   Charging at the matador, the bull snorted and kicked.

Who or what was charging at the matador? The bull, of course. In this sentence, the modifier, *charging at the matador,* applies clearly to the word it modifies—*the bull.*

Attending college, four courses are taken by Ethel each semester.

Who or what is attending college? *Four courses* certainly are not. *Ethel* is attending college. In this sentence, it is not clear which noun the modifier applies to. The best way to correct this sentence is to rewrite the independent clause:

Attending college, Ethel takes four courses each semester.

Notice that in both corrected examples, the (former) dangling modifier modifies the subject of the main clause.

Exercise: Point 3

In all the following sentences, there are modifiers that do not apply clearly to the word they modify. Underline the subject and rewrite the sentence, making the modifier apply clearly to the word it modifies. If there is no subject, supply an appropriate one.

1. Reaching the finals, the game was won by the Tigers.

   Reaching the finals, the Tigers won the game.

2. Playing skillfully, a touchdown was made by the home team.

   _____

3. Shouting, an opinion was offered by Joe.

   _____

4. Painting the ceiling, her hair turned white.

   _____

5. Speaking for the community, the issue was raised by Mrs. Santos.

   _____

6. Losing his temper, shouts came from his father.

   _____

7. Running frantically, a loose shoelace tripped the ball carrier.

   _____

8. Being fond of romance, late-night movies appeal to Julie.

   _____

9. Endorsing the check and handing it to the teller, twenty dollars was paid to Alex.

   _____

10. Lighting the candle, hot wax got all over me.

POINT 4   Sometimes you can turn a dangling modifier into a dependent clause.

Refer back to Chapter 4, Point 3, if you need to refresh your memory about dependent clauses.

> Walking to school, a dog bit my ankle.

Here it seems as if the dog was walking to school, which is doubtful. The dangling modifier can be made into a dependent clause, and the sentence made into a correct one, by rewriting the sentence as follows:

> While I was walking to school, a dog bit my ankle.

The dependent clause *while I was walking to school* is placed next to *dog*. Obviously, it does not describe or modify the dog. Yet this is a correct sentence. Why? The answer is that a dependent clause is no longer a modifier, so it does not need to come at a precise place in the sentence. This sentence could just as well have been written:

> A dog bit my ankle while I was walking to school.
> Charging extra for delivery, the pizza is still reasonably priced.

may be changed to

> Although the restaurant charges extra for delivery, the pizza is still reasonably priced.

or

> The pizza is still reasonably priced, although the restaurant charges extra for delivery.
> When in high school, my grandmother gave me a fountain pen.

It is highly unlikely that the fountain pen was presented when the grandmother was in high school. This sentence should be changed to:

> When I was in high school, my grandmother gave me a fountain pen.

or

> When in high school, I was given a fountain pen by my grandmother.

Exercise: Point 4

Correct the following sentences by making the dangling modifier into a dependent clause. Rewrite the entire sentence in the space provided.

1. Fooling around, the lamps got broken.

   While we were fooling around, the lamps got broken.

2. Dashing through the snow, a stone upset the sleigh.

_____

3. Pedaling fiercely, my bicycle moved faster.

_____

4. Eating dinner, the dishes got dirty.

_____

5. Leaving the stadium, a section of the bleachers collapsed.

_____

6. Taking out the garbage, snow started to fall.

_____

7. Calling her on the phone for the first time, my throat was dry.

_____

8. Watching a horror movie, her palms started to sweat.

_____

9. Going into the sixth grade, my father's company transferred him to a different town.

_____

10. Spending a lot of time partying, her grades slipped.

_____

Review Exercise: Points 1–4

Revise the following sentences to eliminate the dangling modifiers.

1. Scoring in the final seconds, the game was won.
   Scoring in the final seconds, our team won the game.

2. Going to the supermarket, food for dinner was purchased.

_____

3. Traveling alone, the plane took Jan from Los Angeles to Boston.

_____

4. Running for mayor, handshakes were given to everyone by Ms. James.

_____

5. Flexing his muscles, his biceps bulged.

_____

6. Escaping from prison, the warden captured the convict.

_____

7. Smiling broadly, her hair blew in the wind.

_____

8. Recalling the past, a memory of her friend came to mind.

_____

9. Crying and kicking, the parents sent the child to his room.

_____

10. Smoking a cigar, the room started to stink.

_____

In addition to groups of words beginning with an *-ing* word, there are other types of modifiers which dangle if the writer is not careful. Each of these types is described in one of the following points.

_____

POINT 5   A group of words that has an *-ing* word *somewhere* in it must refer clearly to the subject of the sentence.

After **sneezing**, my handkerchief was used.

The modifier, *sneezing*, seems to apply to *handkerchief*. Handkerchiefs, however, do not sneeze all by themselves. As was the case with the other dangling modifiers, we need a subject. This sentence may be revised to read,

After sneezing, **I** used my handkerchief.

The addition of the subject, *I*, makes the sentence complete and correct. *I* was the one who did the sneezing.

Before eating, her hands are washed.

should be changed to

Before eating, she washes her hands.

● *Remember:* The *-ing* word tells us that there is some action taking place; it is important to identify *who* or *what* takes part in this action.

Exercise: Point 5

Complete these sentences.

1. Since moving to Nebraska, *I have learned to appreciate open land.*

2. Before selecting a business partner, _____

3. While waiting for the Sears man, _____

4. After getting a credit card, _____

5. By having the oil filter changed, _____

6. On hearing about your divorce, _____

7. While installing a skylight in my house, _____

8. While riding my bicycle, _____

9. Since moving to the country, _____

10. By choosing to live in the city, _____

POINT 6   **Modifiers beginning with α *to* form of α verb must refer clearly to the word they modify. That is, like other modifiers, they should be placed as close as possible to the word they modify.**

To see Jupiter, a telescope is necessary.

The modifier, *to see Jupiter,* cannot logically apply to *telescope.* A telescope does not see Jupiter. The sentence may be rewritten as follows:

To see Jupiter, one must use a telescope.

Now we have a subject—*one.* Who or what is seeing Jupiter? One—that is, some-one—is.

To play tennis, a racquet is necessary.

The racquet itself certainly doesn't play tennis. Only people can play. Thus, we need a subject for the modifier, *to play tennis,* to apply to. The sentence might read,

To play tennis, **you** need a racquet.

To answer the question, Chapter Six should have been read.

should be changed to

To answer the question, students should have read Chapter Six.

Exercise: Point 6

Complete these sentences.

1. To appreciate the music, _____ *you should turn up the volume.* _____

2. To clean the roof gutters, _____

3. To be a good friend, _____

4. To stay healthy, _____

5. To understand poetry, _____

6. To find the secret of life, _____

7. To avoid trouble, _____

8. To play professional baseball, _____

9. To prepare lasagna, _____

10. To finish a cabinet, _____

Review Exercise: Points 1–6

Rewrite the following sentences, eliminating any dangling modifiers.

1. Skating on the frozen pond, his ankles buckled.
   While he was skating on the frozen pond, his ankles buckled.

2. To run for public office, certain requirements must be met.

   _____

3. After putting up a scarecrow, the birds tore it apart.

   _____

4. While marching in the parade, the drum Carl was playing broke.

   _____

5. Jumping rope, Andrea's ankle was sprained.

   _____

6. To make a decision, convictions must be firm.

   _____

7. To go camping, a tent and a flashlight are necessary.

   _____

8. When reading the book, the character reminded me of you.

_____

9. Singing in the rain, an umbrella was carried by Gene Kelly.

_____

10. To pass this course, one paper each week is required.

_____

HOW TO AVOID DANGLING MODIFIERS

1. Ask yourself if there is a word in the sentence for the modifier to refer to.
2. Put the modifier as close as possible to the word it explains.
3. Solve the problem by rewriting the dangling modifier as a dependent clause.

Chapter Review

I. Circle the modifier and draw an arrow from it to the word it modifies.

1. Making a pizza, the chef flipped the dough into the air.

2. To learn to play the violin, a fellow must have patience and neighbors who realy like him.

3. To work up a sweat, Arnie jogs four miles.

4. Since starting college, Tracy has learned the meaning of hard work.

5. While filling the gas tank, the attendant told us about the new show in town.

6. Barking furiously, the puppy chased the cat.

7. Pretending to be asleep, she listened to the transistor radio.

8. Before finding a parking space, they had driven around the block three times.

9. Not paying attention, the students dozed off.

10. To relax, you can put your feet up and read a good book.

II. Fill in the blank with an appropriate subject.

1. Barking and wagging his tail, _____ showed his affection for his master.

2. Swerving to the left, _____ hit a lamppost.

3. To be a movie star, _____ need good looks and talent.

4. When lost in a strange city, _____ always use my CB to get directions.

5. In New England, _____ is generally very cold, and there is always a lot of snow.

6. Playing his role, _____ persuaded the audience that he really was Hamlet.

7. After dialing the wrong number, _____ asked the operator for assistance.

8. When scrambled with cheese and onions, _____ are absolutely delicious.

9. At the age of sixty, _____ retired from her job.

10. Using his professional knowledge, _____ repaired our leaky faucet.

III. Complete these sentences.

1. By sending her children to camp, _____

2. To make a Spanish omelet, _____

3. After realizing he had made the wrong turn, _____

4. When Kitty voices her opinion, _____

5. When feeling blue, _____

6. Thinking of you, _____

7. On being appointed president of the club, _____

8. While working in that restaurant, _____

9. To cancel your appointment, _____

10. During her career as a newscaster, _____

11. Ordering everyone around, _____

12. Scrubbing the kitchen floor, _____

13. To lend me a hand in this job, _____

14. After vacationing in Canada, _____

15. At the age of two, _____

16. Expecting to see her boyfriend, _____

17. To change engine oil, _____

18. When looking up a word in the dictionary, _____

19. Seeing his arch rival, _____

20. To show me that you love me, _____

IV. Write *C* if the sentence is correct as it stands. Write *D* if it contains a dangling modifier and underline the word that the modifier is supposed to modify. If the sentence contains no such word, put a circle around the *D*.

_____ 1. Risking his life, the passengers were saved by the captain.

_____ 2. Speeding on his motorcycle, the police officer gave him a ticket.

_____ 3. To make a good impression, you should wear a tie.

_____ 4. After crossing the finish line, the officials awarded a medal to the winner.

_____ 5. To learn to play a musical instrument, lessons are helpful.

_____ 6. Before going down into the cave, our backpacks were secured.

_____ 7. After lighting his cigarette, the match went out.

_____ 8. Seeing my wife, I raced to her arms.

_____ 9. Before losing your temper, you should find out exactly what happened.

_____ 10. When cooked properly, I love to eat chicken.

V. All the following sentences contain dangling modifiers. Rewrite each sentence, eliminating the dangling modifier.

1. Forgetting his meal ticket, lunch was not given to the student.

_____

2. Before pruning the trees, the blades had to be sharpened.

_____

3. To get the student rate, certain requirements must be met.

_____

4. When playing the guitar, finger picks are often used.

_____

5. Driving at night, his vision was impaired.

_____

6. While making the frappe, the blender broke.

_____

7. At the age of six, my finger was fractured.

_____

8. Sailing on the lake, her hat blew away.

_____

9. To lose weight, a diet must be followed.

_____

10. To play golf, a set of clubs is necessary.

_____

11. Before hitting the jackpot, a good-luck dance was performed.

_____

12. While laid up in a cast, the nurse told me to take it easy.

_____

13. Since firing Ben, business has improved.

_____

14. By considering the options, a decision was made.

_____

15. Being a pirate, a patch covered his right eye.

_____

16. Foaming at the mouth, the dogcatcher chased the rabid dog.

_____

17. Exploding in brilliant colors, the crowd watched the fireworks.

_____

18. To put the car in reverse, the stick shift must be used.

_____

19. When tired and hungry, a ham and cheese sandwich really hits the spot.

_____

20. In setting a table, forks, knives, and spoons must be placed correctly.

_____

VI. Rewrite the following passages, correcting any sentences which contain dangling modifiers.

On arriving in America, the sights and sounds amazed Pierre. Having traveled alone, so many people hurrying around and shouting came as a jolt to him. Coming from a small village in the south of France, so much commotion had never before been witnessed by the young traveler. And being only eight years old and a bit nervous, his luggage seemed to be his only companion. On this trip, his cousins in Philadelphia would be his hosts. After looking for them at the gate, and not being able to find them, an attendant took him to the information booth. Over the loudspeaker, Pierre's cousins were paged. To locate them, an announcement had to be made twice by the attendant. Then, running through the terminal, from the other end of the building, Pierre recognized his relatives. Feeling relieved, Pierre ran to them and escaped the crazy crowds of America.

_____

_____

_____

_____

_____

_____

_____

_____

_____

_____

_____

_____

To throw a successful party, several factors must be taken into consideration. When making up a list of people to invite, they should be compatible. After deciding on the guests, the amount of food and drink must be decided. If preparing a fruit punch, a large bowl and a ladle are necessary. To save money, a fruit punch is often better than serving everyone individual cocktails. Preparing the food in advance is also a good idea. When planning the meal, the number of guests must, of course, be considered. By cooking ahead of time, a lot of bother may be avoided. To make a suggestion, lasagna is always a favorite. When a host serves punch and lasagna, you can be almost certain that the party will be a success.

_____

_____

_____

_____

_____

_____

_____

_____

_____

_____

_____

_____

As a way of fighting the high cost of travel and of conserving fuel, smaller automobiles are common. On the highway, mileage is improved in a small car. In the city, when driving in traffic, gasoline is saved. After an average of 10,000 miles of rolling on the roads, the driver should bring his small car in for a tuneup. After receiving the proper care, any car owner will find that his vehicle is ready for continued efficient use. When you think about it, the day of the big car is gone.

_____

_____

_____

_____

8

Pronouns and Faulty Pronoun Reference

Suppose I run into you in the hallway and say, "Hey, I saw Bill and Jim yesterday, and he has a great new job!" Your response will probably be, "*Who* has a great new job? Bill or Jim?" If I answer, "Bill, of course," you will be quite justified in saying that there is no "of course" about it. From my original sentence, you could not possibly tell whether "he" referred to Bill or to Jim. This is an example of *faulty pronoun reference*.

A *pronoun* is a word that can be substituted for a noun. Pronouns are valuable because they save a lot of clumsy repetition. Instead of saying, "That's Virginia's dorm. Virginia lives on the second floor, and Virginia keeps a cat in Virginia's room," we can say, "That's Virginia's dorm. She lives on the second floor, and she keeps a cat in her room."

But like other parts of a sentence, pronouns must be used correctly. Otherwise the meaning of the sentence will not be clear. The basic rule is simple: Make sure the pronoun refers clearly to the noun whose place it takes in a sentence.

POINT 1   A pronoun may be used as the subject of a sentence.

- *Remember:* A subject tells who or what is taking part in the action described by the verb.

    Ronnie works on a farm.

Ronnie is the subject of the sentence.

    He works on a farm.

The pronoun, *he,* takes the place of *Ronnie,* and becomes the subject.

> **Shirley and Ruth** went to the movies.
> **They** went to the movies.

The pronoun, *they,* takes the place of *Shirley and Ruth,* and becomes the subject.

Pronouns as subjects were discussed in Chapter 3, Point 2. Look back to that section if you need to refresh your memory.

Exercise: Point 1

Rewrite each of the following sentences, using a single pronoun as the subject.

1. Andy's parents are going on a vacation.

   They are going on a vacation.

2. You and I will haul this stuff to the dump.

   _____

3. Brenda is learning how to water-ski.

   _____

4. The car antenna has been snapped in half.

   _____

5. The union members are planning a strike.

   _____

6. My uncle served in Vietnam.

   _____

7. Mary's parents are celebrating an anniversary.

   _____

8. Sally, Art, and I spent the day at the museum.

   _____

9. His sister is going for her Ph.D.

   _____

10. Weightlifting gives Fritz great pleasure.

    _____

POINT 2   A pronoun may be used as the *object* of a verb in a sentence.

An *object* is a word (or a group of words) that is affected by the action of a verb.

To determine the subject of a sentence, we ask who or what performed the action. To determine the object of a sentence, we ask who or what was affected by the action.

Steve rode the horse.

Who or what performed the action? Steve rode the horse; therefore *Steve* is the subject. Who or what was affected by the action? The horse was affected by Steve's action; therefore *the horse* is the object.

Cathy cooked breakfast.

Can you identify the subject and the object in this sentence?

Objects are also used following such words as *in, on, by, at, to, for, around, between, near, among, through, upon.*

Gene went to the game.

Gene is the subject; *game* is the object.

The rabbit ran through our yard.

Rabbit is the subject; *yard* is the object.

You already know what pronouns can be used as subjects. For objects, you must use a different set of pronouns.

Subjects	Objects
I	me
you	you
he	him
she	her
it	it
we	us
you	you
they	them

- To take the place of a noun that is affected by the action of a verb, always use an object pronoun. Use object pronouns following such words as *in, on, by,* and so on.

Jack repaired the broken **window.**

Jack is the subject; *window* is the object.

Jack repaired **it**.

Jack is the subject; *it* is the object.

He repaired the **window.**

He is the subject; *window* is the object.

> **He** repaired **it**.

He is the subject; *it* is the object.

> **Marcia** spoke to **Mr. Otis**.

Marcia is the subject; *Mr. Otis* is the object.

> Marcia spoke to **him**.
> **She** spoke to Mr. Otis.
> **She** spoke to **him**.

Exercise: Point 2

Rewrite the following sentences, changing all the nouns to pronouns.

1. Lori hit George with a stick.

   She hit him with it.

2. I wrote a poem about my girlfriend.

   _____

3. The twins starred in the school play.

   _____

4. Ms. Alexander bought that sofa.

   _____

5. Robbie paid for that suit.

   _____

6. The police officer told Jim and Carl to move their van right away.

   _____

7. Lou and Barbara called Danielle and me.

   _____

8. Danielle and I called Lou and Barbara.

   _____

9. Do you smoke that corncob pipe?

   _____

10. Honesty is important to Jane and Max.

    _____

Review Exercise: Points 1 and 2

Fill in the blank with a pronoun that can take the place of the noun given in the parentheses.

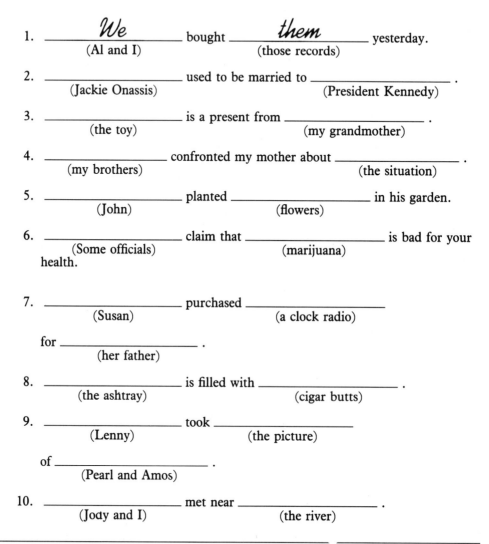

1. _____*We*_____ bought _____*them*_____ yesterday.
   (Al and I)　　　　　　　　(those records)

2. _____ used to be married to _____ .
   (Jackie Onassis)　　　　　　　　　(President Kennedy)

3. _____ is a present from _____ .
   (the toy)　　　　　　　　　(my grandmother)

4. _____ confronted my mother about _____ .
   (my brothers)　　　　　　　　　(the situation)

5. _____ planted _____ in his garden.
   (John)　　　　　　　　(flowers)

6. _____ claim that _____ is bad for your
   (Some officials)　　　　　(marijuana)
   health.

7. _____ purchased _____
   (Susan)　　　　　　　　(a clock radio)

   for _____ .
   (her father)

8. _____ is filled with _____ .
   (the ashtray)　　　　　　　　(cigar butts)

9. _____ took _____
   (Lenny)　　　　　　　(the picture)

   of _____ .
   (Pearl and Amos)

10. _____ met near _____ .
    (Jody and I)　　　　　　　(the river)

POINT 3　**Often a sentence contains both a noun and a pronoun that refers to the noun. To decide whether to use a subject pronoun or an object pronoun, look at the pronoun's relation to *its own verb*.**

　　　Carla brought the ice cream and the boys thanked her.

The pronoun *her* refers to Carla. *Carla* is the subject of the verb *brought*, but *her* is the object of the verb *thanked*. Therefore an object pronoun is needed.

Usually, you can *hear* the correct choice of pronoun. You would never write:

Carla brought the ice cream and the boys thanked *she*.

I saw Mel yesterday and he told me about his trip.

The pronoun *he* is the subject of *told*, so a subject pronoun is needed.

Exercise: Point 3

Fill in the blank with the appropriate pronoun, and underline the word to which it refers. Mark *S* or *O* above the noun and the pronoun to show whether each is a subject or an object. Some sentences have more than one blank.

1. The <u>boat</u> drifted for three weeks before the Coast Guard found ____*it.*____

2. I entered a dress in the design contest and _____ won

   second prize.

3. Martha and I are going to Mexico this summer; her cousins will join

   _____ there.

4. Tom and his friend just left for Cape Code, where _____

   hope to find summer jobs.

5. If _____ can find the money, Dolores hopes to go back

   to school next year.

6. Larry has gotten interested in skateboarding; it seems as if everyone is

   trying _____ .

7. Willie's adviser told _____ that he has to pass this

   course if _____ wants to be a physical therapist.

8. Ted had a flat tire last night. _____ had to change _____

   in the pouring rain, while other cars kept passing _____ .

9. I want to go to the movie, but I have a big test in consumer economics

   tomorrow. Oh, well, I'll be back in time to study for _____

10. I need to get a notebook and some pens at the bookstore. Having spent all my

    money on that trip yesterday, I'll have to charge _____ .

POINT 4   When a sentence contains two or more nouns, place the pronoun as close as possible to the noun it refers to, and make sure the reference is clear.

When the fans met the players, they were excited.

Who was excited? Was it the fans or the players? We cannot tell, because *they* could refer to either *fans* or *players*. We could rewrite the sentence this way:

The fans were excited when they met the players.

Now we know that the fans were the ones who were excited. Or

The players were excited when they met the fans.

In this case, *they* refers to *players*.
On the other hand, what about this sentence?

When Dave met the players, they were excited.

Now it is clear that the players were excited. *Players* is the only noun in this sentence to which *they* can refer.
Sentences with *told*, *said to*, and similar words need to be fixed differently.

Cindy told Marie that she was jealous.

Whom does the pronoun *she* refer to? Was it Cindy or Marie who was jealous? We cannot tell. In this sentence, there is nowhere else to put the pronoun *she*. We might rewrite it like this:

Cindy told Marie, "I am jealous."

Now it is clear that Cindy is the one who is jealous. The pronoun *I* refers to Cindy. Or, on the other hand,

Cindy told Marie, "You are jealous."

You refers to Marie, so now it is Marie who is jealous.
The words inside the " " marks in these sentences are *quotations*. The " " marks, or *quotation marks*, tell us that these are the exact words the person spoke. We will have more to say about quotations in Chapter 11.

Exercise: Point 4

All the following sentences contain faulty pronoun references. Rewrite each sentence, making the pronoun references clear. There may be more than one correct way to rewrite the sentence. Choose one.

1. Stan told Barbara that she would be elected class president.

   Stan told Barbara, "you will be elected class president."

2. He added pepper and salt and then some more of it.

3. When the White Sox played the Red Sox, they won.

_____

4. Before Ms. Sanchez adopted Maria, she lived in an orphanage.

_____

5. When Bill finally approached his father, he felt great.

_____

6. When the car hit the telephone pole, it was damaged.

_____

7. When my mother scolded my little sister, she was quite upset.

_____

8. Paul told his nephew that he would be a great man some day.

_____

9. The doctor told her patient that she would have to take some time off.

_____

10. When the boys asked the girls to dance, they were embarrassed.

_____

Review Exercise: Points 1–4

Underline the pronoun in each of the following sentences and draw an arrow from it to the noun it refers to. Mark _S_ in the blank if the pronoun is used as a subject or _O_ if it is used as an object. (Some sentences have more than one pronoun.)

___*O*___ 1. The counselor called one of the boys and sent him to find Jim.

_____ 2. Lee called and said she will be here by seven.

_____ 3. The traffic gets very bad around nine in the morning; Anita avoids it by leaving early.

_____ 4. The senator was glad when his bill was passed; he had put a lot of work into it.

_____ 5. Eddie said to Ivan, "You're a real friend to stand by me this way."

_____ 6. The vase broke when the wind knocked it over.

——— 7. Gail acted shy when Craig asked her to dance.

——— 8. Dave and Sandy, can you lend a hand with this box of books?

——— 9. Carol told her parents that she was leaving home.

——— 10. The carton had to be taped when the bottom of it fell out.

POINT 5 Be sure that pronouns refer to a single noun and not to a whole idea.

Such words as *it, this, that,* and *which* should not be used to refer to a whole idea.

The weather was going to be beautiful, which made me very happy.

Which, in this example, refers to an entire idea rather than to a single noun. This is a faulty pronoun reference. The sentence may be rewritten:

I was very happy that the weather was going to be beautiful.
Barney said he is sure that Charles can't do the work. **This** is untrue.

What is untrue? Is it untrue that Barney is sure, or is it untrue that Charles can't do the work? The faulty pronoun reference makes it impossible to tell. The sentence may be rewritten as follows:

It is untrue that Barney said he is sure Charles can't do the work.

or

Barney was mistaken when he said he is sure that Charles can't do the work.

Exercise: Point 5

Write *C* if the pronoun reference is correct or *F* if the pronoun reference is faulty. Underline the pronoun (*it, this, that,* or *which*), and circle the word or whole idea it refers to.

__*F*__ 1. (The class show was a great success,) which greatly pleased all who

worked on it.

——— 2. He hadn't heard about the change in plans, which caused him to be

late.

——— 3. It made her angry that the mattress did not arrive on the day it was

supposed to.

——— 4. People continue to drive after drinking. This is ridiculous.

_____ 5. Every American has the chance to be whatever he or she chooses. This is one of the basic concepts of democracy.

_____ 6. Buses never seem to keep to the schedules anymore. It is really getting out of hand.

_____ 7. I miss my family, and that is why I go home for the holidays every year.

_____ 8. She takes a ballet lesson every Thursday, which helps to strengthen her leg muscles.

_____ 9. When I was younger, my mother always bugged me about keeping my room clean. But this changed as I grew older and more mature.

_____ 10. He always carries a slide rule with him, which makes his work a lot easier.

POINT 6   Be sure that a pronoun has a word, and not an unexpressed idea, to refer to.

To get a job in a department store, you have to dress the way **they** tell you to.

Who are *they?* Are *they* a department store? We have here a faulty pronoun reference, because *they* does not refer to any particular word in the sentence. Instead, it refers to an idea that has not been expressed. The sentence may be rewritten:

To get a job in a department store, you have to dress the way the managers tell you to.

Kate is always happy to see me, but **it** rarely shows.

To what word does *it* refer? Remember, pronouns refer to nouns. Is *happy* a noun? Since there is no noun for *it* to refer to, the pronoun reference is faulty. The sentence may be rewritten as follows:

Kate is always happy to see me, but her happiness rarely shows.

Her happiness has taken the place of *it.*

I don't mind going to the dentist's office, because **he** is so friendly.

Is *he* a dentist's office?

Because the dentist is so friendly, I don't mind going to his office.

Exercise: Point 6

All the following sentences contain faulty pronoun references. Identify the word to which the pronoun *should* refer by answering the question following each sentence.

1. Joseph is nervous about the upcoming event, but *it* doesn't show.

   What is *it*? _____ *his nervousness* _____

2. Whenever I swim in that lake, *they* always nip at my feet.

   Who are *they*? _____

3. Paula bought some red dye for her hair so she could become *one*.

   What is *one*? _____

4. He joined the fraternity because *they* enjoy the same things he does.

   Who are *they*? _____

5. Although he made *one*, he was intimidated by all the home-run hitters in the lineup.

   What is *one*? _____

6. Some teachers feel that their students are lazy, and that *it* is the result of too many hours spent watching television.

   What is *it*? _____

7. To avoid getting penalized for a late return, you have to send *them* your income tax forms by April 15.

   What are *they*? _____

8. The concert was sold out, so we will have to see *them* some other time.

   Who are *they*? _____

9. Her sandwich was stale, but *it* was because she had not wrapped it properly.

   What is *it*? _____

10. When we flew to Europe, I was surprised at how quickly *it* went.

    What is *it*? _____

Review Exercise: Points 1–6

To make use of the work you have done in the last two exercises, choose five sentences from the Point 5 exercise and five sentences from the Point 6 exercise, and rewrite them correctly in the following space. Number the sentences you choose by point number and sentence number.

1. _(5,1) Everyone who worked in the class show was pleased that it was a great success._

2. _____

_____

3. _____

_____

4. _____

_____

5. _____

_____

6. _____

_____

7. _____

_____

8. _____

_____

9. _____

_____

10. _____

_____

HOW TO AVOID TROUBLE WITH PRONOUNS

1. To decide whether you should use a subject or an object pronoun, think of the pronoun's relation to *its own verb*.
2. Be clear about which noun in the sentence each pronoun refers to.
3. Use a pronoun to refer to a single noun, not a group of words.

Chapter Review

I. Circle the correct pronoun given in the parentheses.

1. (I, me) plan to improve my grades next semester.

2. (She, her) sent (I, me) a package in the mail.

3. Have you seen (he, him) lately?

4. Wendy is somewhere around; have you seen (she, her)?

5. The commanding officer gave (him, he) a real bawling out.

6. They told (us, we) to look for (they, them) after the show.

7. (They, them) invited (we, us) over for cocktails.

8. I will never speak to (they, them) again.

9. Adrian chose (he, him) and (I, me) for teammates.

10. The bullies on the beach were bothering (we, us).

11. (We, us) don't know what is good for (we, us).

12. Federico saw (she, her) standing on the corner.

13. (They, them) will have to figure that out for themselves.

14. Maxine tried to visit (he, him) in the hospital, but the nurses would not let (she, her) in.

15. (He, him) and (I, me) are on the same bowling team.

16. Either (she, her) or (I, me) will have to save the seats while (he, him) gets the popcorn.

17. (We, us) wanted our luggage returned to (we, us).

18. Laurie has an amusing hobby; (her, she) collects toy hippopotamuses.

19. (He, him) is the best driver I know.

20. Both (we, us) and (they, them) had the chance to appear on the television game show.

II. Fill in the blank with an appropriate pronoun.

1. After spending two hours in the sun, _____ discovered that her back was badly burned.

2. We noticed that the turtle's shell was pink and purple, and we realized that _____ had been painted.

3. Since the family moved to a new apartment, _____ have been happier than ever.

4. The children were frightened when the pony chased _____ .

5. When Tony dated _____ , Sylvia was only sixteen years old.

6. Marco admitted that _____ was the one who made the phony phone call.

7. It was our turn to get the hot dogs, so _____ piled into Alan's car.

8. Theresa said to Judy, " _____ are the only one who will understand my problem."

9. Cheryl discovered that her new job with its overwhelming demands was simply too much for _____ .

10. Barry found his Swiss army knife in the drawer with a pile of T-shirts on top of _____ .

III. Write *C* if the pronoun reference is clear or *F* if it is faulty. Be prepared to defend your answers.

_____   1. Tom had had enough of school, which is why he decided to join the marines.

_____   2. He used a hacksaw instead of a wood saw to cut through the wire fence. This is an example of clear thinking.

_____   3. Donna is able to design and sew her own clothes. It is one way to save money.

_____   4. Jake told his brother that he ought to get out and enjoy the fresh air.

_____ 5. Ted threw the plate through the window and broke it.

_____ 6. After I talked with the therapist, she told me to come back once a week for consultation.

_____ 7. A rolling stone gathers no moss, which is why one must always be on the go.

_____ 8. There is never enough time to see all my friends when I come to town. It is a real shame.

_____ 9. Heidi told her mother that she should learn to type.

_____ 10. Sue has always enjoyed helping people, and she plans to study medicine when she completes her undergraduate studies.

_____ 11. I have a bucket, but it has a hole in it.

_____ 12. He joined a commune because they share everything there.

_____ 13. Life is peaceful on a farm, which is one good reason to escape the rat race of the city.

_____ 14. After I heard Segovia play the guitar, I decided that that was what I wanted to be.

_____ 15. Wheat is one grain from which they make bread.

_____ 16. There is relatively little traffic in the sky, which is one reason air travel is safer than driving.

_____ 17. I scored twenty points because I was very good at it.

_____ 18. When he worked with clay, he could mold it beautifully.

_____ 19. Gus told Jerome that he was an expert marksman.

_____ 20. Mike told Alice that she was the most intelligent person he had ever met.

IV. Rewrite the following sentences, eliminating any faulty pronoun references.

1. I changed my mind about buying a motorcycle, which pleased my wife.

_____

2. When he put the saw on the shelf, it fell down.

_____

3. Betty told Jenny that she was the best cook in the world.

   _____

4. I bought a new pair of sneakers, but my old ones are still pretty good, so
   I always wear them.

   _____

5. We could not find a parking space, which was why we were late.

   _____

6. Gene loves nature. That is why he moved there.

   _____

7. She told her sister that she had found true love.

   _____

8. I brought the broken tool to the hardware store because I don't know
   how to do it.

   _____

9. In New England they have plenty of snow.

   _____

10. As soon as I pumped up the tires, I went for a ride on it.

    _____

11. She appeared in a Shakespearean play, which was her debut.

    _____

12. When I used that coupon, it drove my wife crazy.

    _____

13. Vincent told Stephen that he was awarded a medal of honor.

    _____

14. Rudy said that he had heard I was moving to California. This is untrue.

    _____

15. He pays a great deal of attention to his children, which is what makes
    him a good father.

    _____

16. Oscar is happiest when he is working, but it never shows.

_____

17. I knew the president of the company, which is how I got the job.

_____

18. Sally told her mother that her plans were outrageous.

_____

19. When I went to the supermarket, I was happy to see that they had gone

down in price.

_____

20. Two plus two equals four, which is an elementary fact in mathematics.

_____

V. Rewrite these passages, eliminating any faulty pronoun references.

When I first learned to drive a car, it was a harrowing experience. I took ten weeks
of lessons at a driving school, which were very helpful. But it was not until I was
preparing for my road test that I found out how inexperienced I really was. That was
really the problem.

In my last trial run, I backed the car out of my driveway and hit a lamppost, but it
was not badly damaged. That was only the beginning. I finally got the car moving
smoothly, and was nervous about running into something else, but I didn't let it
show. I was cruising along at 25 miles per hour with the radio playing, which always
helped to calm me down. A police officer who was patrolling the neighborhood must
have thought I was going too slowly and pulled me over. We talked for a few minutes, and it turned out to be rather helpful: He suggested I use the headlights while
driving at night.

_____

_____

_____

_____

_____

_____

_____

_____

_____

_____

_____

_____

_____

_____

When I was informed of the rally, it was an exciting event. As soon as I heard about the demonstration, I got them ready. They had shiny leather tops, brand-new laces, and thick rubber soles, which put me into the right frame of mind for walking. I really believed in the cause, which was why I looked forward to the march with great anticipation. Sometimes I get weary during a long walk, but I never let it show. Besides, this was a truly important demonstration! When I slid my feet into my shoes, this time they did not ache at all.

_____

_____

_____

_____

_____

_____

_____

_____

_____

_____

_____

The nine-to-five workday, which millions of Americans experience five times a week, may be slowly dying out, which would make many people very happy. Employers are telling their employees that they could use some extra time to themselves. A four-day workweek may be with us shortly, and they are pleased to have the chance to spend more time with their families. Fathers and mothers will be able to take up new hobbies and pursue new interests, and it will serve to improve the health of many people. This applies to both physical and mental health. Working fewer hours would make millions of people very happy, but it would have to go along with a promise of no drop in income. There are still some problems in setting up the shortened working schedule, but they are confident that as the need for it becomes more apparent, it will come about.

_____

_____

_____

_____

_____

_____

_____

_____

_____

_____

_____

_____

9

Faulty Parallelism

Many sentences contain what we might call *parallel thoughts*. For example, you might say, "Lee had a great time scuba-diving and water-skiing on her vacation." *Scuba-diving* and *water-skiing* are parallel thoughts; that is, they are both things that Lee had a great time doing. By expressing both of them with *-ing* words, the sentence emphasizes this parallelism. A clumsier way of saying the same thing might be, "Lee had a great time scuba-diving and also she water-skied during her vacation." Here the two parallel thoughts are expressed in nonparallel forms of words, and the sense of their parallel relationship is weakened.

POINT 1 When elements are parallel in thought, use parallel forms to express them.

>   cooking, eating, cleaning

All the elements in this series are *-ing* words; they are arranged in a parallel structure.

>   to cook, to eat, to clean

All the elements are *to* forms of verbs; their structure is parallel.

>   have cooked, have eaten, have cleaned

Again, a parallel structure.

>   pretty, tall, friendly

All are words that are used to describe a person. These modifiers are arranged in a parallel structure.

151

If one form of a verb is mixed with another form of the same verb in a sentence, the parallel structure is lost:

cooking, to eat, have cleaned

Now the elements are of different forms; there is no parallel structure in this series.

● *Remember:* When you make any kind of list, put all the items in the same form.

Exercise: Point 1

Fill in the blank with the correct form of the verb given in the parentheses. The first verb in the series will tell you which form to use. Be sure to maintain parallel structure.

1. dancing, ___*singing*___ , ___*laughing*___
   (sing)   (laugh)

2. to blend, _____ , _____
   (mix)   (stir)

3. pushed, _____ , _____
   (pull)   (shove)

4. have written, _____ , _____
   (stamp)   (send)

5. fed, _____ , _____
   (swallow)   (digest)

6. building, _____ , _____
   (paint)   (whitewash)

7. rose, _____ , _____
   (sink)   (reappear)

8. to love, _____ , _____
   (honor)   (obey)

9. drove, _____ , _____
   (park)   (pay)

10. living, _____ , _____
   (laugh)   (love)

POINT 2 **Balance a noun with a noun, a verb with a verb, a modifier with a modifier, and so on.**

Whenever possible, words of the same kind should be used to do the same kinds of jobs in a sentence.

She is **charming** and **beautiful**.

In this sentence, *charming*, an *-ing* word, is balanced with *beautiful*. They are in parallel structure, however, because they are both modifiers; that is, they both describe a person.

> She **is charming** and **has beauty.**

Both phrases describe her, but *charming* is a modifier, whereas *beauty* is a noun. Therefore, the sentence has now lost its parallel structure.

> We like **tacos** and **to eat enchiladas.**

Tacos is a noun; *to eat enchiladas* is a combination of a verb form and a noun. Is this sentence in parallel structure?

> We like tacos and enchiladas.

Does this sentence have parallel structure? What words are parallel? What kind of words are they?

> We like to eat tacos and enchiladas.

Although this sentence may appear to have faulty parallelism, it actually does have a parallel structure. In this case, *tacos* and *enchiladas* are objects of the verb *to eat*. What do we like to eat? We like to eat tacos and we also like to eat enchiladas.

Exercise: Point 2

Add one element to each series. Make sure that the new element is parallel to those provided.

1. hungry, thirsty, _____*tired*_____
2. proud, brave, _____
3. brunette, brown-eyed, _____
4. weaving, crocheting, _____
5. bought, traded, _____
6. to replace, to repair, _____
7. playing baseball, playing football, _____
8. exciting, fantastic, _____
9. planting, reaping, _____
10. dreamed, desired, _____

POINT 3   **Use parallel constructions for words joined by such connectors as *and, but, nor, or.***

I enjoy **reading, writing,** and **conducting** experiments in a laboratory.

Note that the three elements are all *-ing* words. This sentence contains proper parallelism.

Our baby is **cute** and **behaves well.**

In this example, the parallelism is faulty. *Cute* is a modifier; *behaves well* is a form of a verb. This sentence may be rewritten as follows:

Our baby is **cute** and **well behaved.**

Now we have two modifiers describing the baby; the parallelism is proper.

Whenever I try to talk to him he is crabby, busy, or doesn't know what to say.

Crabby and *busy* are both modifiers, but *doesn't know what to say* is a form of a verb. It would be hard to find a modifier that would take the place of the verb form here. Instead, the sentence might be rewritten thus:

Whenever I try to talk to him he is crabby or busy or else he doesn't know what to say.

Now *crabby* and *busy* are parallel modifiers joined by *or*, whereas *he is* and *he does know* are parallel subjects and verbs joined by *or else*.

Exercise: Point 3

Complete the following sentences by filling in the blanks. Be sure to maintain parallel structure. Underline the original part of the sentence to which your addition is parallel.

1. Eduardo has always enjoyed <u>fishing</u> and _____*hunting*_____ .

2. You can see the moon and _____ in the sky tonight.

3. As an accountant, Phyllis adds and _____ figures all day long.

4. I will probably be washing the dishes or _____ when you arrive.

5. He is old but _____ .

6. Filling the gas tank and _____ are two of the responsibilities of a gas station attendant.

7. A teacher expects his students to do their homework, to attend classes

   regularly, and _____ .

8. Before she left, she combed her hair, polished her fingernails,

   and _____ .

9. When customers are not satisfied, they return the merchandise

   or _____ .

10. The day is sunny, hot, and _____ .

Review Exercise: Points 1–3

All the following sentences contain errors in parallel structure. Revise and rewrite the sentences in the space provided.

1. Put the cheese between two slices of bread and frying it.

   Put the cheese between two slices of bread and fry it.

2. He was a good lecturer, a kind man, and he worked hard.

   _____

3. A lifeguard supervises the beach, is flirting with girls, and rescues swimmers who are having difficulty.

   _____

4. Lynn is preparing her résumé, reading the want ads, and she will go for interviews.

   _____

5. A good friend is thoughtful, truthful, and he supports you.

   _____

6. I enjoy seeing shows, to read a good book, and going to the movies.

   _____

7. To be a doctor, one must have ambition, persistence, and be willing to work long hours.

   _____

8. The cat purred, meowed, and cleaning itself.

   _____

9. He was forced to pawn his watch, sell his radio, and trying to find a new job.

   _____

10. To be or not being; that is the question.

___

POINT 4   Use parallel structure with such constructions as either. . .or, neither. . .nor, not. . .but, not only. . .but also, both. . .and.

> Either **going for a ride** or **to lie in the sun** is my idea of a good time.

This sentence may be rewritten,

> Either **going for a ride** or **lying in the sun** is my idea of a good time.

Now the two elements are in a parallel structure.

> Not only was he a great man, but also an excellent writer.

What is wrong with the parallelism here? *Was he a great man* contains both a subject—*he*— and a verb—*was; an excellent writer* contains neither. This is an especially common error. The sentence may be rewritten as

> He was not only a great man but also an excellent writer.

Now the subject and verb have been moved out of the parallel sections, and there is proper parallelism between *a great man* and *an excellent writer*. Or

> Not only was he a great man but he was also an excellent writer.

Now each clause has a subject and a verb; again there is proper parallelism.

Exercise: Point 4

Write *P* if the sentence has proper parallelism or *X* if the parallelism is faulty.

_____ 1. Either you come here or I will go there.

_____ 2. He is neither fair nor aiming to please.

_____ 3. Janet is not only a good tennis player but also a fine golfer.

_____ 4. The dog is both noisy and he chases all the other animals on the block.

_____ 5. I can't decide whether to laugh or to cry.

_____ 6. Pete not only failed the test but also was caught trying to cheat.

_____ 7. Neither Josh nor I care to remain here.

_____ 8. He is both a gentleman and a scholar.

_____ 9. To be a good parent, one must be dedicated, caring, and want the
best for his children.

_____ 10. Either I am crazy or I heard that phone ring.

> | **POINT 5**   **Make sure that *parallel groups of words* in a sentence have parallel structure.**

> I promise **to be a good husband** and **that I will help clean the apartment.**

The two groups of words do not have a parallel structure in this sentence. One begins with the *to* form of a verb, and the other does not. This sentence may be rewritten as follows:

> I promise **that I will be a good husband** and **that I will help clean the apartment.**

Now the two elements are parallel. Note how the form of the first has been changed to go along with the second.

> **By changing the oil myself,** and **because I know how to do tune-ups,** I save money on the care of my car.

Again the two separate elements of this sentence do not coincide. There is no parallel structure. The sentence may be rewritten as follows:

> **By changing the oil myself** and **by doing my own tune-ups,** I save money on the care of my car.

> She got a new job **with a higher salary, increased benefits,** and **she also works fewer hours than before.**

may be changed to

> She got a new job with **a higher salary, increased benefits,** and **shorter working hours.**

Exercise: Point 5

Cross out the part of the sentence that is not parallel and write the correction in the space above it.

1. Our house is located near the bus station, the laundromat, and ~~is within~~
   the
   ~~walking distance of a~~ supermarket.

2. By taking lessons and because she practices daily, Andrea has become a fine violinist.

3. My dream is to have a good job, a family, and buying a house in the country.

4. Washing my car, removing the rust, and to get a good finish takes time.

5. He said that he would stop by our house, to deliver the package, and that he would eat dinner with us.

6. I bought a car with whitewall tires, leather seats, and it has an AM-FM radio.

7. She asked me where I went to school and my degree.

8. Waiting for the bus and to become a bit nervous, Hal started biting his nails.

9. I promise to dress properly and that I will arrive on time.

10. Doris wants to be a violinist, a music teacher, or she will learn to conduct.

Review Exercise: Points 1–5

All the following sentences lack parallel construction. Rewrite the sentences, eliminating the errors.

1. He accepted the money, promised to spend it wisely, and was going for a ride in his car.

   He accepted the money, promised to spend it wisely, and went for a ride in his car.

2. Not only was she attractive, but also she had a good sense of humor.

3. They went to Cape Cod on their vacation for camping and to have fun.

4. The book is boring and is too long.

5. Her coat has six brass button, flared sleeves, and there is a detachable hood.

6. Eating breakfast, eating lunch, and to eat dinner are my three favorite activities of the day.

7. Debra was either angry or she was just irritable.

_____

_____

8. The fullback is strong, big, and runs with speed.

_____

_____

9. We went to the concert with Fred, with Jane, and Zelda came along also.

_____

_____

10. They were interested in buying the air conditioner, but not willing to spend so much money.

_____

_____

HOW TO AVOID FAULTY PARALLELISM

1. Remember that elements that are parallel in thought should be expressed in parallel forms.
2. Use parallel structure for elements joined by such words as _and, but, or nor, either. . .or, neither. . .nor, not. . .but, not only. . .but also._
3. Make sure parallel groups of words in a sentence have parallel structure.

Chapter Review

I. Circle the word or phrase that maintains the parallel structure in each sentence.

1. I enjoy working hard, getting paid well, and (to get a sense of satisfaction, achieving a sense of satisfaction).

2. He admitted to robbing the store and (escaping in the green Ford, that he escaped in the green Ford).

3. She achieved her fame by working hard and (having good luck, she was lucky).

4. Terry hates to get up in the morning, to brush his teeth, and (combing his hair, to comb his hair).

5. I admire his talent, his ambition, and (his ability to keep cool, he was able to keep cool).

6. The drummer kept the beat, the guitarist played the melody, and (the singing was done by the piano player, the piano player sang).

7. She went either with my sister, with my brother, or (by herself, alone).

8. The bull was snorting and (charging at us, started to charge at us).

9. In grammar school I learned to read, to write, and (arithmetic, to do arithmetic).

10. My aunt was charming, helpful, and (kind, always doing kind things).

II. Cross out the element in each series that is not parallel to the other two.

1. standing in line
   to cash a check
   speaking to my friend

2. on my own
   in the forest
   looking out for bears

3. short
   ugly
   with pimples

4. looking outside
   was in the room
   wanted to open the window

5. in the city
   on a subway
   riding

6. to get undressed
   taking a shower
   watching television

7. by raking the leaves
   mowing the lawn
   by trimming the shrubs

8. sturdy
   made of wood
   has compartments for pencils

9. green eyes
   a long, curling tail
   on the sofa

10. to meet the neighbors talking
    outside telling stories

III. Complete the following sentences by filling in the blanks. Be careful to maintain parallel structure. Underline the original part of the sentence to which your addition is parallel.

1. It is my ambition to be successful and _____ .

2. Rod can speak both English and _____ .

3. She said that she would be on either the 7:00 bus or _____ .

4. The brown puppy was wagging its tail and _____ .

5. The cabinet he built is made of pine and _____ .

6. We strolled under the boardwalk _____ .

7. He wants to move to Mexico and _____ .

8. Judy kept a rabbit's foot, a four-leaf clover, and a _____

    in her drawer.

9. When we visited San Francisco, we rode the cable cars, went to

    Fisherman's Wharf, and _____ .

10. When left alone, he gets sad, lonely, and _____ .

IV. Each of the following sentences has an error in parallelism. Write a corrected version of each sentence in the space provided.

1. He admitted the crime and that he deserved to get caught.

    _____

2. We were disappointed with our grades but understanding them.

    _____

3. Batting, throwing, and to field are important skills in baseball.

    _____

4. The dog dug up the bone and finding it to his liking.

    _____

5. Ramon knows that he should work on his writing and to improve his spelling.

    _____

6. His lunch included soup, a roast beef sandwich, a peach, and there was also dessert.

    _____

7. I respected his intellect, his strength, and he was also very funny.

    _____

8. It would make my day complete to see you, going to a movie, and to have dinner with you.

    _____

9. That cigarette has a harsh taste and is probably stale.

    _____

10. Marianne spends her day attending classes, she studies, and to listen to music.

    _____

11. The day was sunny, bright, and with low humidity.

_____

12. The dean told the teacher that classes were suspended and to allow the students to go home.

_____

13. She could read on a bus, in an elevator, or when she waited in line at the bank.

_____

_____

14. The camper learned how to tie a knot, how to start a fire, and horseback riding.

_____

15. That car with four-wheel drive can get out of mud, of snow, and deep potholes.

_____

16. There were news items about the rising price of coffee, the increased crime rate, and how we are running short of energy.

_____

_____

17. The grass turned brown and was needing water.

_____

18. Going for a walk in the evening and to meet a friend on the street is a simple and great pleasure.

_____

19. The movie starred Richard Burton, Elizabeth Taylor, and George Segal and Sandy Dennis also had starring roles.

_____

_____

20. Stupid questions anger me and I am losing my temper.

_____

V. Compose a sentence, using the elements provided. If the elements are not parallel, make them so.

1. watching the ball game

   eating hot dogs

   _____

2. that we had won the lottery

   that we had become instant millionaires

   _____

3. to catch a butterfly

   running

   jumping

   _____

4. cooked our dinner

   then cleaned the dishes

   _____

5. to save money

   to buy presents

   _____

6. to go to the dance

   choosing a partner

   dancing

   _____

7. to listen to the radio

   putting my feet up

   relaxing

   _____

8. that he could stand no more

   that he would lose his temper

   _____

9. thin

   flimsy

   _____

10. keeping good notes

    to use a tape recorder

    _____

11. with my buddies

    to the stadium

    _____

12. applying for a job

    scheduled an interview

    _____

13. steep

    dangerous

    slippery

    _____

14. on Mother's Day

    on Father's Day

    Thanksgiving

    _____

15. laughing

    happy

    _____

16. around the corner

    in aisle three

    _____

17. if I got the job

    when I would start working

    _____

18. to build a fire

    roasting marshmallows

    _____

19. that I was her best friend

    that she wanted to read me her poetry

    _____

20. to have friends

    to be free

    _____

VI. Rewrite each passage, eliminating any cases of faulty parallelism.

A library is a good place to spend an afternoon and relaxing. You can read the newspaper from any major city, spend time looking for a good novel, or listening to a record. Librarians can tell you where to find a particular book and a quiet place to read it. Many libraries have display halls where you can observe artwork or just strolling around.

People find many different things to do in the library. There is usually someone studying or to write a research paper; there are those who read periodicals and those just chatting with a friend. All things considered, the library is an excellent place for meeting people, to read, or to relax.

_____

_____

_____

_____

_____

_____

_____

_____

When we heard that we had won the lottery, we wanted to jump for joy, scream our lungs out, and patting each other on the back. We immediately made plans for a car that we could rent, dining, and dancing. We went wild, spending the evening eating the best food we had ever tasted, drinking only the finest wines, and we rode to the top of the Hancock Tower to get a dramatic view of Boston. Finally at around 3:00 A.M. we decided that we were pooped, that we had to go home, and we wanted to climb into bed.

Paul Newman is one of America's most popular actors. Not only is he a big drawing card, he also has a lot of talent. He has played in many pictures including *The Hustler* and *The Sting,* and starring most of the time. Many women feel he is handsome and has sex appeal; he appears to be tough and have a strong will to many men.

In *Butch Cassidy and the Sundance Kid* he appeared with Robert Redford, another extremely popular American actor. In that movie, they robbed banks, diving off a steep cliff, and to live with a beautiful woman who was played by Katherine Ross.

Paul Newman lives with his wife, Joanne Woodward, in Connecticut. They live in a beautiful town, sharing a lovely house, and that the rumor is they have a very happy marriage.

_____

_____

_____

_____

_____

_____

_____

_____

_____

_____

_____

_____

10

Shifts in Number, Person, and Tense

Suppose you are watching a ball game on television when something goes wrong with the set and the image begins jumping all over the screen. Probably you'll be quite annoyed. It's pretty hard to keep track of the action if you can't tell where the player is going to be from one eyeblink to the next. If you can't fix the picture, you'll probably give up and turn off the set.

Something similar can occur in writing. If I say, "First you turn this knob, then one presses this lever, and finally we open the lid," you may get the idea, but you're likely to be a bit dizzy. There's too much jumping around in the sentence— from *you*, to *one*, to *we*. You can follow the instructions a lot more easily if I say, "First you turn this knob, then you press this lever, and finally you open the lid." Now all the subjects are *you*. There is a kind of parallelism in this sentence that was missing from the first sentence. Like the parallelism we studied in Chapter 9, it makes the sentence clearer and easier to understand.

This chapter is concerned with some of the jumps, or *shifts*, that often occur in sentences. Like the jumping image on the television screen, they get in the way of understanding. However, like faulty parallelism, they are easy to avoid once you know what to watch out for.

POINT 1 *Number* **refers to the number of units referred to. In English grammar, there are only two numbers: singular and plural.**

Singular refers to *one:*

> the student
> a cow
> the population
> I, me, my, mine
> you, your, yours
> he, she, him, her, his, hers, it, its

Plural refers to *more than one:*

the women
men
vegetables
we, us, our, ours
you, your, yours
they, them, their, theirs

Exercise: Point 1

Write *S* if the example is singular or *P* if it is plural.

_*S*_ 1. a romantic novel

_____ 2. an everyday problem

_____ 3. the members of Parliament

_____ 4. a drive-in movie

_____ 5. my relatives

_____ 6. dancing

_____ 7. cigar boxes

_____ 8. the news

_____ 9. somersaults

_____ 10. potato chips

| POINT 2   Be sure to keep number consistent throughout a sentence.

A man should be dedicated to **their** job.

Their is plural; if it is used to refer to *a man,* which is singular, the sentence will contain a faulty shift in number. The correct version would be

A man should be dedicated to **his** job.

A woman should be dedicated to **her** job.

Woman is singular, and so is *her.*

Men should be dedicated to **their** jobs.

Men and *their* are both plural.

Women should be dedicated to **their** jobs.

If a personal subject is not specifically female, the masculine forms *he, him,* and *his* are customarily used. This is not meant to slight women; it is simply a matter of accepted usage and style.

> A **senator** is responsible to the voters in **his** state.

In this sentence, *senator* is used in its general sense. That is, we are not speaking about any senator in particular. On the other hand, if we are speaking about Senator Karen Mills, we might write:

> The **Senator** is responsible to the voters in **her** state.

If you are using a word in its general sense and want to avoid suggesting a masculine slant, you can sometimes solve the problem by making the sentence plural:

> **Senators** are responsible to the voters in **their** states.

To refer to a singular, nonliving thing, use *it* or *its.*

> The **book** is in **its** place on the shelf.

> The **books** are in **their** places on the shelf.

Books is plural; it takes the plural pronoun *their.*

- Keep in mind the principles of correct pronoun reference. For a review of pronoun reference, turn to Chapter 8.

Exercise: Point 2

Circle the correct word given in the parentheses. Underline the word (or words) to which the circled word refers.

1. A <u>reporter</u> should always write (his, their) stories objectively.

2. If a driver is careful, (he, they) will avoid accidents.

3. A model should always look (their, his) best when (he, they) is being photographed.

4. Breakfast cereals are tasty, and (it, they) supply vitamins and minerals.

5. The headmaster works in (his, their) office.

6. A disc jockey plays records; also, (she, they) reads commercials.

7. A teacher should be familiar with (his, their) material; moreover, (they, he) should be able to present it in a clear manner.

8. Our boss is vacationing in (her, their) trailer.

9. My grandmother is making (her, their) special soup.

10. The fans are waiting in line for (his, their) turn.

Review Exercise: Points 1 and 2

Rewrite the following sentences, correcting any faulty shifts in number.

1. A successful comedian tries to get a sense of their audience.

   A successful comedian tries to get a sense of his audience.

2. A person should try to understand their limitations.

   _____

3. I was looking for my hat, but I could not find them.

   _____

4. You have two chances, so use it wisely.

   _____

5. A teacher grades papers, and sometimes they also write comments.

   _____

6. A lawyer advises their clients, but their fees are often excessive.

   _____

7. Athletes often get his back massaged.

   _____

8. The radio is broken, but they can be repaired.

   _____

9. Ms. Kanter is cooking their special pot roast.

   _____

10. A party can be a lot of fun, but they must be well planned.

    _____

POINT 3 **There are only three *persons* in English grammar. Each person may be either singular or plural.**

First person—used to indicate the person who is speaking or a group which includes that person. First-person words are

Singular	Plural
I, me, my, mine	we, us, our, ours

I am a sailor.
We are trying to change our lives.

Second person—used to indicate the person spoken to. Second-person words are

Both Singular and Plural

you, your, yours

Marty, **you** had better stop bothering me.
You are all invited to the party.

The forms of the second person are the same in both singular and plural.
Third person—used to indicate the person or persons spoken about. Third-person words are

Singular	**Plural**
he, him, his	they, them, their, theirs
she, her, hers	
it, its	

Words such as *one, anyone, everyone, everybody,* and *nobody* are also third-person. As we saw in Chapter 3, such words are singular. *Note: All nouns* are third-person.

She is an excellent cook.
I want to speak with **him**.
One must be careful these days.
Mr. Martinez works in the department store.
A **bird** sat on my windowsill.

Exercise: Point 3

Write *1* if the word is in the first person, *2* if it is in the second person, or *3* if it is in the third person.

___*3*___ 1. the flowers

_____ 2. I

_____ 3. your parrot

_____ 4. she

_____ 5. it

_____ 6. you

_____ 7. George Washington

_____ 8. we

_____ 9. the shopping center

_____ 10. anyone

POINT 4   Be sure to keep person consistent throughout a sentence.

When you write a sentence, choose *one person* to write in, and *stick with it*. It is confusing to shift person in the middle of a sentence, a paragraph, or an essay.
Note: Be especially careful of shifts from the third person to the second.

A **clerk** should always count change aloud or **you** are liable to make a mistake.

Clerk is third person; *you* is second person. This shift in person in the middle of the sentence makes its meaning unclear. This sentence may be rewritten as follows:

A **clerk** should always count change aloud or **he** is liable to make a mistake.

Now both a **clerk** and **he** are in the third person. If you are not sure why *he* is used, check Point 2.

In writing a paper, **one** should always keep **your** basic point in mind.

Again we see a shift from the third person—*one*—to the second person—*your*. This sentence should be revised:

In writing a paper, **one** should always keep **his** basic point in mind.

However, *one* should be used very sparingly. If you use it often, your writing is likely to sound stiff. It is sometimes better to rewrite the sentence, eliminating *one:*

In writing a paper, you should always keep your basic point in mind.

Exercise: Point 4

Circle the correct word given in the parentheses. Make sure there is no shift in person in the sentence.

1. A person can run for public office if (he, you) meets certain requirements.

2. If he were really my friend, (he, you) wouldn't have made that remark.

3. If one is running for office, (he, you) should always tell the truth.

4. One could ask her a question and (you, he) would never get an answer.

5. Anyone can quit smoking if (he, you) really puts (his, your) mind to it.

6. She sat in the sun for three hours, and (you, one) can't do that without getting a severe burn.

7. You can do it if (one, you) put your mind to it.

8. The bowler scored seven strikes in a row; (one, you) has to be skillful to do that.

9. After we left, (we, you) felt that (we, you) wanted to visit again.

10. A lawyer should advise (his, your) clients carefully.

Review Exercise: Points 1–4

All the following sentences contain shifts in number or person. Rewrite the sentences, correcting the errors, in the space provided.

1. A good businessman is always helpful to your clients.

   A good businessman is always helpful to his clients.

2. The student who studies hard is sure to find satisfaction for themselves.

   _____

3. A roller coaster is exciting to ride, but some think they are dangerous.

   _____

4. She likes to watch television, but you should spend some of your time reading.

   _____

5. A person should brush their teeth after every meal.

   _____

6. A son may sometimes try to take after their father.

   _____

7. Sherry always keeps their checkbook balanced.

   _____

8. A butcher must be careful not to back into his meat slicer, or you may get a little behind in your work.

   _____

9. A fool will soon part with your money.

   _____

10. A wise person looks ahead to the future; they do not get themselves forever tied up in the past.

   _____

POINT 5:   Be sure to keep *tense* consistent throughout a sentence.

A sentence, a paragraph, or an essay should be written in one tense. Do not shift tenses (from past to present, or present to past) in the middle of a sentence. If you need to review verb tenses, look back at Chapter 2.

He **calls** my name and **told** me to stand.

Calls is in the present tense; *told* is in the past tense. The shift in tense in the middle of the sentence results in an incorrect and misleading expression. The sentence may be rewritten as follows:

He **calls** my name and **tells** me to stand.

(both verbs are in the present tense) or

He **called** my name and **told** me to stand.

(both verbs are in the past tense).

In my haste I **tripped** over the skateboard and **fall.**

Again, we see a shift in tense. This sentence may be rewritten as

In my haste I **tripped** over the skateboard and **fell.**

or

In my haste I **trip** over the skateboard and **fall.**

Exercise: Point 5

Underline the first verb in each sentence. Then circle the correct form of the verb given in the parentheses. Make sure there is no shift in tense in the sentence.

1. She <u>gave</u> him good advice, but he (ignore, (ignored)) her.

2. I lost my library card, so I (get, got) a new one.

3. I could not find my way, so I (ask, asked) for help.

4. It was one of the weirdest experiences I ever (have, had).

5. The police officer stopped him because he (is, was) jaywalking.

6. I miss you and (want, wanted) you.

7. When I tell her that I (love, loved) her, she is happy.

8. She asked, "Are you coming?" and I (says, said), "No."

9. We stayed for the entire show and then (go, went) out for ice cream.

10. The road was rocky, but because he (is, was) driving carefully, we (arrive, arrived) safely.

Review Exercise: Points 1–5

All the following sentences contain shifts in number, person, or tense. Rewrite the sentences, correcting any errors, in the space provided.

1. We brought an air conditioner, so we stay cool all last summer.

   We bought an air conditioner, so we stayed cool all last summer.

2. He was a man who always put your best foot forward.

   _____

3. A teacher must prepare their lesson plans every night.

   _____

4. She berates her brother and hit him, too.

   _____

5. A great chef will never tell you their secret recipes.

   _____

6. Everyone who was there had your fanciest clothes on.

   _____

7. I saw her at a distance, and then I run to her.

   _____

8. A politician must know how to address their constituency.

   _____

9. If one intends to get an A in the course, you will have to work hard.

   _____

10. Man orbits the earth before he walked on the moon.

    _____

CONFUSING SHIFTS TO AVOID

> Make sure your sentences do not contain shifts in
> 1. Number—singular or plural.
> 2. Person—first, second, or third.
> 3. Tense—past, present, or future.

Chapter Review

I. Circle the correct word given in the parentheses. Make sure there is no shift in number, person, or tense.

1. A fashion designer has (his, their) work cut out for (him, them).

2. When you know the answer raise (your, his) hand.

3. She was hired yesterday and (celebrates, celebrated) last evening.

4. Whenever he sneezes, he (causes, caused) quite a ruckus.

5. Children should respect (his, her, their) parents.

6. The golfer measured the putt and tapped (his, your) ball in for a par.

7. A typewriter should be cleaned regularly or else (it, you) will not print clearly.

8. We went skiing, had drinks before a fireplace, and (get, got) to know each other better.

9. When a baby cries, it often means that (he, they) wants (his, their) mother.

10. Some people never get (their, your) car tuned.

11. Man's best friend is (his, your) dog.

12. Don't lose (your, his) cool!

13. We go for a ride, have a picnic, and then come home and (have, had) another party.

14. I came, I saw, I (conquer, conquered).

15. A typewriter is useful to (his, its) owner.

16. The Beatles wrote most of (its, their) songs.

17. Food is very expensive today; also, heating costs (are, were) higher.

18. She ran out of the room and (says, said), "I am leaving."

19. As Americans, we are supposed to have the opportunity to improve (their, our) future.

20. The singer signaled for (her, their) musicians to pick up the tempo.

II. Fill in the blank with an appropriate word. Make sure there is no shift in number, person, or tense.

1. A person may get his hair cut, or _____ may get it styled.

2. A doctor should be sympathetic with _____ patients.

3. We ate and _____ until we were full.

4. A dog is man's best friend; _____ always comes when _____calls.

5. I missed the bus, so I _____ for another.

6. Children should respect _____ parents.

7. If you cross the street in the middle of the block, _____ have to be very careful.

8. A public official should heed the opinions of _____ constituents.

9. The building inspector expressed _____ opinion that the old house should be torn down.

10. The dog chased the man and _____ his leg.

11. One should exercise _____ right to vote.

12. A student should try to hand in _____ papers on time.

13. The principal called the teachers in for a meeting and addressed _____ on methods of discipline.

14. The car swerved and _____ a telephone pole.

15. A person should try to make _____ dreams come true.

16. People should try to make _____ dreams come true.

17. You are my best friend, for _____ always listen when I have problems.

18. The bus driver wanted the exact change, but we _____ not have it.

19. She wanted _____ boss to give _____ a raise.

20. Go tell Aunt Rodie that the old gray goose _____

dead.

III. Circle any words in the following sentences that represent faulty shifts in number, person, or tense. Then, in the space provided, write what type of shift takes place.

1. If an employer is considerate, they are likely to get along well with their employees.

Shift in _____

2. We swam, sailed, and picnicked, and then decide it was time to go home.

Shift in _____

3. A professor may be exciting or boring; it depends on how you present your material.

Shift in _____

4. A father should teach your children right from wrong.

Shift in _____

5. I do all the work around here, and I never got a compliment.

Shift in _____

6. Bicyclists must be sure that his tires have the proper air pressure.

Shift in _____

7. One should be honest with your friends.

Shift in _____

8. He built that house with your own bare hands.

Shift in _____

9. Shakespeare's poetry is beautiful; they are an example of the form known as the sonnet.

Shift in _____

10. I was playing the guitar and use an amplifier.

Shift in _____

IV. All the following sentences contain faulty shifts in number, person, or tense. In the space provided, rewrite the sentences to eliminate the errors.

1. First you read the novel; then he wrote the paper.

_____

2. A sportscaster should be objective, but they always seem to root for the home team.

   _____

3. If a student studies regularly, they will not have to cram the night before a test.

   _____

4. She enjoys reading, but she disliked writing.

   _____

5. One must participate in class discussion, or your grade will suffer.

   _____

6. Anyone can learn home repair if you concentrate.

   _____

7. Hansel and Gretel finally found his way home.

   _____

8. She counts to ten before she lost her temper.

   _____

9. Pilots always try to make his passengers feel at ease.

   _____

10. A person can educate themselves if they put their minds to it.

    _____

11. King Arthur ate with all of their knights at the Round Table.

    _____

12. Every morning she washes her face, brushes her teeth, and combed her hair.

    _____

13. If you want to see an enjoyable movie, they should see _E.T._

    _____

14. A fisherman should always carry extra hooks with them.

    _____

15. He whines whenever he did not get his way.

_____

16. Many taxpayers need an accountant to figure out your returns.

_____

17. I don't enjoy shopping for clothes because you have to spend so much time in dressing rooms.

_____

18. If one intends to quit your job, he should give two weeks' notice.

_____

19. A pediatrician must like children, because they deal with them every day.

_____

20. I went to the movies and see *Fantasia*.

_____

V. Rewrite these passages, eliminating any faulty shifts in number, person, or tense.

If one intends to be a writer, you must first learn the great task of self-discipline. Most novelists, or poets, or dramatists do not work in an office; he often works at home. If he is unable to rid himself of distractions, they will probably find that they do very little work. There are always plenty of reasons or excuses not to write, but if the writer is able to set his mind to their work, he will not bother them. Some writers make schedules for themselves; others chose to work when they were inspired. Whatever the case, the point remained the same: If one wants to write, you write; if one does not, you don't.

Today, news programs and magazines were quite the rage. Everywhere you look, I can see news of this strike or that tax increase thrown at you. A newspaper should be objective, but they always seem to inject their own opinion into the stories. Because of the subjective nature of the news, more and more magazines find its way onto the newsstands. Moreover, these magazines often produced more in-depth accounts of the news. I suppose every form of the news media has their place.

I work in a bank, and when you have that type of job, you have to be willing to wake up at a very early hour. Each morning, I drive to work, park my car, and walked a block to work. I get a lunch break every day at noon, and they love to eat at the delicatessen around the corner. I worked at the bank for over a year, and decided that I had had enough. After looking around for a new job, I found one where you had to be at work by 6:00 A.M. This job was in a restaurant where you had to stand up all day, and after six months, I decided to go back to the bank. The manager was very nice to me and says, "You can have your old job back if one promises to stay at least two years." I take the job, and I enjoyed an extra hour of sleep every morning.

_____

_____

_____

_____

_____

_____

_____

_____

_____

_____

_____

_____

Part III

PUNCTUATION

11

Period, Question Mark, Exclamation Point, Quotation Marks

When we talk, we do not merely recite a string of words. We pause or let our voices rise or fall in pitch or put extra stress on some words. If I say, "She wants to marry him," I drop the pitch of my voice at the end. The listener knows from this that I have simply told a fact. But if, instead, I raise my voice and put extra stress on the word "marry," the listener knows I am expressing surprise. The sentence has become an exclamation: "She wants to *marry* him!" A change in the tone of my voice has made the same set of words into a completely different kind of sentence.

In writing, of course, we cannot use changes in sound to help express our meaning. Instead, we use *punctuation marks*— periods, commas, question marks, and so on. A few simple rules will help you use them correctly and effectively.

POINT 1   Use α *period* at the end of α sentence that makes α statement.

> We went to the movies last night.

This sentence makes a clear statement; that is, it *states* a piece of information. It is followed by a *period*.

> She said that she was an Aquarian.

Again we have a sentence that makes a statement. Note the period at the end.

> James wanted to know if he could come with us.

Although this sentence *sounds* as if it is asking a question, it is not. It is making a statement about someone else's question. This kind of statement is sometimes called

187

an indirect question. However, since it is still a statement, we still use the period at the end.

Exercise: Point 1

Write *S* if the sentence makes a statement or *X* if it does not. If the sentence *does* make a statement, put a period in its proper position.

___*S*___ 1. They promised to arrive on time.

_____ 2. The humidity bothers me

_____ 3. Will you speak to her for me

_____ 4. The repairman asked whether we had fooled around with the plug

_____ 5. Why

_____ 6. Vote for me

_____ 7. I bought a new needle for my record player

_____ 8. Let's build a bonfire tonight

_____ 9. They danced the tango

_____ 10. Why do you treat me this way

POINT 2 Use a period after an abbreviation.

Mr.	oz.	gal
lbs.	Dr.	Oct.
etc.	Ms.	Mon.
Mrs.	tsp.	ft.

Some abbreviations consist of the first letters of several words. In this case, put a period after the abbreviation of each word:

C.P.A.	Ph.D.
M.D.	M.A.

Certain agencies or organizations have abbreviations which do not require a period:

CETA	AFL-CIO
FCC	AMA
ASPCA	NATO

If an abbreviation comes at the end of a sentence that makes a statement, only one period is necessary.

He studies biology, chemistry, physics, etc.
Add the butter, reserving one tsp.

Too many abbreviations can confuse the reader. What is your reaction to this example?

On Sat., Dec. 4, I test drove a new Buick. At speeds over 40 mph, it got only 12 miles to the gal. The engine has a lot of h.p. By 9:00 P.M., I had decided to buy the car. It cost $6,050 F.O.B. Detroit. Since I am a C.P.A. (with a B.A. in accounting) I had no trouble estimating my monthly payments.

Review Exercise: Points 1 and 2

Add periods where they are necessary in the following sentences.

1. Dr. Mitchell cancelled my appointment.

2. *Ms* magazine is very popular reading these days

3. A PhD is an advanced degree

4. Combine two oz butter with four oz sugar

5. Now I get it

6. Mrs Ames raised an objection

7. I have been instructed to report on Sept 30

8. Sen Rosser is a great man

9. There are never enough hours in the day

10. The room measured 20 sq ft

POINT 3   Use a *question mark* after a direct question.

Were you invited to the party?

The direct question is followed by a question mark.

He is your brother, isn't he?

Again the direct question, *isn't he,* is followed by a question mark. However, you *should not* use a question mark if the question in the sentence is asked *indirectly.*

He asked whether the new job offered a higher salary.

This is an indirect question, like the example under Point 1. In this type of sentence, use a period instead of a question mark.

Does the new job offer a higher salary?

Now the sentence has been changed so that the question is asked *directly*. Note that the end punctuation has been changed to a question mark.

Exercise: Point 3

Write *C* if the sentence is punctuated correctly or *X* if it is punctuated incorrectly.

_*C*_ 1. Will the rain never stop?

_____ 2. He asked her if she would marry him?

_____ 3. Have you ever pondered the fate of the earth.

_____ 4. She is your closest friend, isn't she?

_____ 5. Can you tell me why you did that.

_____ 6. We wondered whether the movie would be shown on television?

_____ 7. To be or not to be, that is the question?

_____ 8. Are you going to study chemistry tonight.

_____ 9. She wondered if he would call?

_____ 10. You live in Illinois now, don't you.

POINT 4   Use an *exclamation point* after an expression or statement that shows strong feeling, including a forceful command.

The exclamation point should not be overused. It gives real emphasis to individual expressions when used carefully.

> Fire!
> Get out of here!

This expression shows strong feeling and deserves an exclamation point.

> Unemployment must end!
> We've made it!

When the exclamation point is overused, it tends to take the emphasis away from the expressions that really need it.

> Disneyland is great! There are thrilling rides and beautiful exhibits! Mickey Mouse and Donald Duck stroll around the grounds! There is a fireworks display every evening!

As you can see, too many exclamation points make the passage sound almost ridiculous.

Exercise: Point 4

The following paragraph contains far too many exclamation points. Circle the ones you think should be kept, and cross out the others. You should have no more than two or three exclamation points when you finish.

> The alarm clock was shrieking! I woke up with a start! When I looked at the clock, it said 8:30! Oh, no! I had meant to set it for 7:30! Now I'd never get to the bus stop on time! I jumped out of bed, yanked on my clothes, and grabbed a couple of dough-nuts from last night's party! They would have to do for breakfast; I couldn't even take time to make coffee! With the doughnuts in one hand and my purse in the other, I dashed out the door and ran down the street! The bus was coming! I would never make it! Then, at the last minute, the traffic light turned red! The bus had to wait! I put on a last burst of speed and made it to the bus stop just as the bus rolled up! As I scrambled aboard, panting, the driver grinned! "I saw you coming," he said! "I would have waited for you!" I ought to have thanked him, but the way he grinned made me want to hit him instead! I collapsed into the nearest seat, puffing like an overweight elephant! It didn't matter—I had caught the bus!

Review Exercise: Points 1–4

Insert the proper punctuation at the end of each sentence.

1. Working by candlelight can be inspiring.

2. Has the mail arrived yet

3. She asked him if he would like to go out for dinner

4. We do not take credit cards here

5. I would like a corned beef sandwich

6. Are you still taking violin lessons

7. Good grief, he's having a heart attack

8. Is there any reason to continue

9. You had better comb your hair and straighten your tie

10. I hope I don't have any cavities

POINT 5   Use *quotation marks* to enclose the exact words of a speaker or writer.

> She said, "I am finally ready to go."

The exact words of the speaker have been placed inside the quotation marks.

The politician said, "There will be no new taxes. I will see to it that the crime rate declines. I will be a representative of the people."

Note that the entire speech, even though it consists of more than one sentence, is enclosed by *one set* of quotation marks.

A new paragraph should be begun whenever there is a change of speaker:

"Doctor, I think I'm a dog," the patient said.
"Lie down on the couch and we'll talk about it," replied the doctor.
The patient looked sad, and said, "Oh no, I'm not allowed on the couch."

Note that in this example, a new paragraph was begun each time the speaker changed. Quotation marks were used any time the exact words of the speaker were written.

However, you should *not* use quotation marks if the quotation is indirect, that is, if the exact words of the speaker are not used:

She said that supper is almost ready.

This indirect quotation does not require quotation marks.

She said, "Supper is almost ready."

We have added quotation marks and removed the word *that*.

Make sure that the quotations themselves begin with a capital letter:

The professor announced, "There will be an exam next Wednesday."

Use *There* instead of *there*.

However, if the quotation is split, as in the following sentence, you should not begin the second part with a capital letter:

"We'll see the movie," he said, "and then we'll go out for dessert."

Two sets of quotation marks are needed here to separate the speaker's words from *he said*.

Two sets of quotation marks are also needed to separate the speaker's words from *she said*, but this example is not a split quotation; it consists of *two* quotations by the same speaker.

"I'm cold," she said. "Please hand me my sweater."

Exercise: Point 5

Place quotation marks where they are needed in each of the following sentences.

1. The teller said, "I'm sorry, but your check has bounced."

2. I'll never lie again, he said I promise.

3. This assignment is due Tuesday, the teacher announced.

4. I warned him to drive slowly on the icy roads.

5. Do you know the answer? the teacher asked.

6. The doctor said, Take two aspirins and go to sleep.

7. Carol asked me if she could have a ride home.

8. You can't get there from here, said the tour guide.

9. I am telling the truth, he said. Then he added, I know you won't believe me.

10. Why don't you and Jane come for dinner, she asked.

POINT 6 (a) Periods and commas are always placed *inside* quotation marks; (b) question marks and exclamation points are placed *outside* quotation marks except when the quotation itself is a direct question or an exclamation; (c) semicolons and colons are placed outside the closing quotation marks.

> He said, "I enjoy working on automobile engines."
> "I enjoy working on automobile engines," he said.

Note the comma in the second sentence. When the end of a quoted statement comes before the end of the whole sentence, its period is replaced by a comma.

> I said, "Tell me that you love me."
> "Tell me that you love me," I said.

> Did you say, "We are going away together"?

The entire sentence is a question, but the quoted material itself is a statement.

> She asked, "Are you coming?"

The quotation itself is a direct question; therefore the question mark is placed *inside* the quotation marks.

> "Are you coming?" she asked.

Again the quotation itself is a direct question.

> He yelled, "Get out!"

The quotation itself is an exclamation; the exclamation point is placed *inside* the quotation marks.

Did you notice that in three of the last four sentences, one punctuation mark has been dropped? For instance, "We are going away together" is a statement, but there is no period or comma at the end of it. Why not? When the end of a quotation comes at the end of the whole sentence, only the *stronger punctuation mark* is used. Question marks and exclamation points are strong; periods and commas are weak. A question mark is usually stronger than an exclamation point. When both the whole sentence and the quotation are statements, only one period is used, inside the quotation marks.

Also, have you noticed that in every example we have seen so far, a *comma* follows the word just before a direct quotation? Look back over the previous examples and note how the comma is used in this way.

Notice in the following example how the semicolon is used in relation to quotation marks. In Chapter 5, Point 2, you learned how a semicolon can connect two independent clauses; more information on the semicolon and the colon will be provided in Chapter 12.

> "The only seats left," shouted the usher, "are in the first row"; by then, however, we had settled into comfortable seats in the middle of the theater.

Here are some more examples of sentences with quotations. They are all correctly written. See if you can tell why certain punctuation is used in each case. if you have difficulty, reread Points 5 and 6.

> Gail asked, "Whose record is this?"
> "Will you come if I ask you nicely?" he inquired.
> Did you say,"Cows have three legs," or am I crazy?
> Roger screamed, "So this is my destiny!"
> "Time!" the coach shouted.
> I said, "These phone bills are getting out of hand."
> "I have always been a loner," the old man whispered.
> Fire anyone who says, "I'm too tired"!
> Was it you who asked, "Is anybody home?"

Exercise: Point 6

Write *C* if the sentence is punctuated correctly or *X* if it is not. Rewrite the incorrect sentences, correcting the punctuation.

__*X*__ 1. Joyce said, "I think I have a cold".

_____ *Joyce said, "I think I have a cold."*

_____ 2. "Do you love me," he asked?

_____

_____ 3. "Mend your ways!" I screamed!

_____

_____ 4. Billy asked, "Why is it always me."

_____

_____ 5. I can't believe you actually said, "Fishing is for the birds."; you have a weird sense of humor.

_____

_____ 6. "Does this car need oil"? the attendant inquired.

_____

_____ 7. "Out, damn Spot," she screamed, throwing her dog out the door!

_____

_____ 8. "I am trying not to lose my temper," said Mr. Dobbs.

_____

_____ 9. Did you shout, "Bargains galore!"?

_____

_____ 10. Cries of "Help"! echoed through the building.

_____

> **POINT 7   Use quotation marks to enclose the title of a short work such as a story, essay, short poem, or song.**

> We heard "Lucy in the Sky with Diamonds" on the radio.
> "The Lottery" was written by Shirley Jackson.
> Have you ever read "The Charge of the Light Brigade"?

Note that what appears in the quotation marks is the *exact* title. If there is no punctuation in the title itself, there should be no punctuation within the quotation marks.

For longer words such as novels, plays, movies, newspapers, full-length books, and magazines, use underlining instead of quotation marks. In printed material, the names of such works usually appear in italics.

> Have you seen *Jaws?*
> I read about the blackout in the *New York Times*.
> During the semester we will read Tolstoy's *War and Peace*.

Exercise: Point 7

Use quotation marks or underlining where necessary in each of the following sentences.

1. Last night we saw <u>Gone with the Wind</u> for the fifth time.

2. Don't Think Twice was written and sung by Bob Dylan.

3. Grammar Review is the first part of Troubleshooting.

4. I read an article entitled A Day with the President.

5. Harrison Ford starred in the film Indiana Jones and the Temple of Doom.

6. Great Expectations is one of Dickens' most enjoyable novels.

7. The Star-Spangled Banner is America's national anthem.

8. No Way to Treat A Lady is a frightening movie.

9. Coleridge wrote a poem entitled Kubla Khan.

10. Tradition is the opening song in the musical Fiddler on the Roof.

Review Exercise: Points 5–7

The following sentences contain errors in the use of quotation marks or other elements covered in Points 5–7. Rewrite each sentence, making the necessary corrections.

1. Annie asked are you going to sing that song again?

   Annie asked, "Are you going to sing that song again?"

2. I plan to read Moby Dick this summer.

   _____

3. "Are you my friend or aren't you," she asked?

   _____

4. The time is right he said for us to move on.

   _____

5. Have you heard the Rolling Stones perform "Brown Sugar?"

   _____

6. She said that "she would be studying all night."

   _____

7. John said Come visit us next weekend.

   _____

8. "Before I go", she said, "Let me ask you one question?"

   _____

9. Do you read The New Yorker she asked.

   _____

10. Get that car out of my driveway, the man hollered.

    _____

HOW TO PUNCTUATE SENTENCES

> 1. Use a *period* at the end of a statement or an indirect question and at the end of an abbreviation.
> 2. Use a *question mark* after a direct question.
> 3. Use an *exclamation point* after an expression of strong feeling.
> 4. Use *quotation marks* to enclose a direct quotation.

Chapter Review

I. Write *C* if the sentence is punctuated correctly or *X* if it contains any error in punctuation.

_____ 1. "Do you want to have a good time" he asked?

_____ 2. I read Toni Morrison's novel Tar Baby this summer.

_____ 3. Ms Katz has seventeen cats.

_____ 4. She wanted to know whether the sauce was too spicy?

_____ 5. Will you join us?

_____ 6. "I don't care," she said, "and I will not change my mind."

_____ 7. "Are you a man she inquired or a mouse?"

_____ 8. "You must be kidding!" she cried.

_____ 9. Did you ask her if she was in the right seat.

_____ 10. "What"?

II. Punctuate the following sentences.

1. I am spending more time in the library these days

2. Have you ever eaten smelts

3. Don't try any funny business with me

4. I wonder why they say blondes have more fun

5. The show is on Channel 5

6. He has a lighter with his initials on it

7. Did you say that you were driving to California this summer

8. The bellboy asked whether we needed any help with our bags

9. Dr. McCarthy is the new chairman

10. Debbie is working toward her Phd

11. What kind of fool am I

12. Get lost, Buster

13. Where were you on the night of June 3

14. Should I wait for her

15. Let's go, Mets

16. She asked whether she could expect a raise

17. Have you heard about Hugo and Kim

18. A rolling stone gathers no moss

19. Sgt Anderson is an excellent detective

20. Should we call you Miss Burns or Mrs Burns

III. Add or change punctuation where necessary in each of the following sentences.

1. I'm thinking. Give me some time! Peter snapped.

2. Rita asked, Will there be an essay question on the test?

3. We're late, she cried, hurry up

4. Have you seen The Big Chill?

5. In the musical Oliver, Fagin sings a song called Reviewing the Situation.

6. The metric system is too confusing, he complained.

7. Don't you get the joke? she asked.

8. Block that kick, the crowd chanted rhythmically.

9. His mother pleaded, Finish your vegetables. There are people starving in India.

10. Why don't you come up and see me sometime? she sang.

11. Get lost! we screamed at the hoodlums.

12. Anything Goes is one of Cole Porter's most popular songs.

13. The doctor asked, Are you feeling better?

14. This won't hurt a bit, the nurse said as she stuck the needle into my arm.

15. What is your hurry, asked the old timer?

16. Stevie Wonder wrote You Are the Sunshine of My Life.

17. I heard her say, This is the worst party I've ever been to.

18. Hold it right there! the police officer shouted.

19. I hate peas, wailed the child!

20. Run a mile a day, she adivsed, and you're sure to feel better.

IV. Complete these sentences. Be sure to use *all* necessary punctuation marks.

1. Earl asked⎯⎯⎯⎯⎯⎯⎯⎯⎯⎯⎯⎯⎯⎯⎯⎯⎯⎯⎯⎯⎯⎯⎯

2. The little boy cried⎯⎯⎯⎯⎯⎯⎯⎯⎯⎯⎯⎯⎯⎯⎯⎯⎯⎯

3. Inez asked her brother⎯⎯⎯⎯⎯⎯⎯⎯⎯⎯⎯⎯⎯⎯⎯⎯

4. She wondered if⎯⎯⎯⎯⎯⎯⎯⎯⎯⎯⎯⎯⎯⎯⎯⎯⎯⎯⎯⎯

5. As I always say⎯⎯⎯⎯⎯⎯⎯⎯⎯⎯⎯⎯⎯⎯⎯⎯⎯⎯⎯⎯

6. Ms. Yee said⎯⎯⎯⎯⎯⎯⎯⎯⎯⎯⎯⎯⎯⎯⎯⎯⎯⎯⎯⎯⎯⎯

7. He responded by saying⎯⎯⎯⎯⎯⎯⎯⎯⎯⎯⎯⎯⎯⎯⎯

8. Do you know that song⎯⎯⎯⎯⎯⎯⎯⎯⎯⎯⎯⎯⎯⎯⎯⎯

9. My favorite movie is⎯⎯⎯⎯⎯⎯⎯⎯⎯⎯⎯⎯⎯⎯⎯⎯⎯

10. The doctor warned us⎯⎯⎯⎯⎯⎯⎯⎯⎯⎯⎯⎯⎯⎯⎯⎯

V. All of the following sentences contain errors in punctuation. Rewrite each correctly in the space provided.

1. "I love scary movies my sister informed us."

   ⎯⎯⎯⎯⎯⎯⎯⎯⎯⎯⎯⎯⎯⎯⎯⎯⎯⎯⎯⎯⎯⎯⎯⎯⎯⎯⎯⎯⎯

2. Dr. Gomez is an M D

   ⎯⎯⎯⎯⎯⎯⎯⎯⎯⎯⎯⎯⎯⎯⎯⎯⎯⎯⎯⎯⎯⎯⎯⎯⎯⎯⎯⎯⎯

3. "Where do you think you're going," my mother asked.

   ⎯⎯⎯⎯⎯⎯⎯⎯⎯⎯⎯⎯⎯⎯⎯⎯⎯⎯⎯⎯⎯⎯⎯⎯⎯⎯⎯⎯⎯

4. I wonder, he said, if the economy will ever improve.

   ⎯⎯⎯⎯⎯⎯⎯⎯⎯⎯⎯⎯⎯⎯⎯⎯⎯⎯⎯⎯⎯⎯⎯⎯⎯⎯⎯⎯⎯

5. My sister said that "she was going to run off to the Orient."

   ⎯⎯⎯⎯⎯⎯⎯⎯⎯⎯⎯⎯⎯⎯⎯⎯⎯⎯⎯⎯⎯⎯⎯⎯⎯⎯⎯⎯⎯

6. Why must you always complain, I asked her?

   _____

7. *A Child's Christmas in Wales* is a short story by Dylan Thomas.

   _____

8. Full speed ahead shouted the captain.

   _____

9. What's the deal, he whispered.

   _____

10. The lyrics are Candy is dandy, but liquor is quicker.

    _____

11. "I'm working as a file clerk this summer he said."

    _____

12. Was it you who asked "that stupid question?"

    _____

13. "There's no green cheese up here," said the astronaut

    _____

14. As Time Goes By was a very popular love song.

    _____

15. "Get out of my life, she cried, I've had enough!"

    _____

16. While I'm away he said please water my plants.

    _____

17. Why are you so good to me, she sighed?

    _____

18. You fool screamed the man whose car I had just hit.

    _____

19. Al Jolson made a movie called "The Jazz Singer."

    _____

20. "You will be a great writer", his teacher told him.

_____

VI. Rewrite these passages, correcting any errors in the usage of periods, question marks, exclamation points, and quotation marks.

"This is the third paper of the semester that you have turned in late said Professor Martin and you are simply going to have to change your work habits." I know said Bruce, and I promise to change my ways. Mr. Martin said, Don't tell me your dog chewed up the paper. What happened. "I don't have a dog, replied Bruce, but I do have a little brother. "And he tore it up? Mr. Martin asked." "No, said Bruce," but he wrote it for me, and since his spelling was so bad, it took me two whole days to correct it."

_____

_____

_____

_____

_____

_____

_____

_____

_____

_____

_____

_____

_____

Three men were stationed in the farthest reaches of Alaska, and their supply of whiskey was running low. Two of the men felt that they could take advantage of the third, so they told him to go out into the blizzard and buy some more whiskey in the nearest town. The third man said I will go only if you promise to save the last drop of this remaining whiskey for me. Don't worry the others said we promise. I will definitely not go if you drink that last drop the third man said. We promise, we promise, the others assured him. With that, the third man left. A day went by Two days went by A week and then two weeks went by. The two men figured that the third must have died in the blizzard and decided "to drink the last bit of whiskey." They took the bottle down from the shelf, said Cheers, and were about to indulge when the third man flung the door open. I told you he announced I wasn't going to go if you drank that last drop!

_____

_____

_____

_____

_____

_____

_____

_____

_____

_____

_____

_____

12

Semicolon and Colon

Now we come to two punctuation marks that are used only within sentences, never at the end. They are the *semicolon* (;) and the *colon* (:). As you can see, they look very much alike, and poeple often get them confused. However, they are used in quite different ways. You have already learned one way to use semicolons, in Chapter 5. Just for a refresher, we will review that way and then go on to some new ones.

POINT 1   Use a *semicolon* to separate two independent clauses.

If you need to review independent clauses, look back at Chapter 4, Point 3, and Chapter 5, Point 2.

> The movie started late; we had enough time to buy popcorn.

In this sentence we have two independent clauses; that is, each clause can stand alone as a complete sentence, since it has a subject and a verb. The two clauses are separated by a semicolon.

> The record was scratched; I returned it the next day.

Again we have two independent clauses separated by a semicolon.

> My sister calls me once a week; we have a good relationship.

Exercise: Point 1

Each of the following sentences contains two independent clauses. Separate the two clauses with a semicolon.

1. My family vacationed in Canada; we visited Toronto and Montreal.

2. The baseball game was exciting it went into extra innings.

3. We always see the latest horror films we like being scared.

4. Mary lost her I.D. card she couldn't get the student rate.

5. The lawn was overgrown Dave volunteered to mow it.

6. Firefighters have to be brave they risk their lives almost every day.

7. We got the mortgage we bought the house.

8. I will use a road map I will not lose my way.

9. The concert was given outdoors it was free of charge.

10. He talks to his house plants they just don't want to grow.

Note: Sometimes you may wonder whether to put a semicolon at the end of one line or the beginning of the next. *Never* put a semicolon at the beginning of a line. You should write

> He was late for dinner every night for a week;
> I was really getting fed up.

not

> He was late for dinner every night for a week
> ; I was really getting fed up.

Follow this rule with all punctuation marks except opening quotation marks.

POINT 2   Do not use a semicolon when two independent clauses are joined by such connecting words as *and, but, for, nor, or, so, yet.*

> I wanted to play for the team; but I was cut.

The semicolon is used incorrectly in this sentence. Two independent clauses are connected by the word *but*. The sentence may be rewritten as follows:

> I wanted to play for the team; I was cut.

(now we have two independent clauses joined by only a semicolon) or

> I wanted to play for the team, but I was cut.

(a comma has been substituted for the semicolon). This gives us a sentence like those discussed in Chapter 5, Point 1.

> She got an A on her final; so she threw a party.

Again we have an incorrect use of the semicolon. Can you see why? This sentence may be rewritten:

She got an A on her final; she threw a party.

However, if the clauses are joined by stronger connecting words, such as *also, however, therefore, then, otherwise, nevertheless,* and *moreover,* you should use a semicolon.

Bottle-cutting can be great fun; however, one must have great patience.

Two independent clauses are joined by a semicolon and the connecting word *however*. This sentence is complete and correct as it stands. Finally, note the placement of the comma after *however*.

Exercise: Point 2

Write *C* if the semicolon is used correctly or *X* if it is used incorrectly. Be prepared to explain your answers.

___*X*___ 1. That is a difficult question; but I can tell you the answer.

_____ 2. I sat on the beach for five hours; I got an awful sunburn.

_____ 3. We bought a huge bagful of groceries; then we cooked a stupendous dinner.

_____ 4. We gave it our best; yet we still finished second.

_____ 5. He was not happy about the decision; nor did he accept it quietly.

_____ 6. I think; therefore I am.

_____ 7. It is a shame; moreover, it is a disgrace.

_____ 8. A disc jockey must know a lot about popular music; and he must be able to sell products.

_____ 9. You have treated me unfairly; nevertheless, I remain your friend.

_____ 10. The garbage disposal was clogged; so we had to scrape out the orange rinds.

Review Exercise: Points 1 and 2

Rewrite the following sentences, using a semicolon in each one. Remember to put commas where they are needed.

1. The weather was miserable it rained all day.

The weather was miserable; it rained all day.

2. The cabinet is handcrafted it is made of oak.

_____

3. Mr. Ryan got a new job however he is not very happy in it.

_____

4. We went skiing last weekend the snow was perfectly packed.

_____

5. I witnessed the accident therefore I will testify in court.

_____

6. Alice missed a week of class nevertheless she passed the exam.

_____

7. I enjoy reading novels of the occult however I find the movies boring.

_____

8. Reporters have strict deadlines they work under great pressure.

_____

9. Raking leaves is spiritually rewarding it is also exhausting.

_____

10. I have planted a garden I expect tomatoes by the end of the summer.

_____

POINT 3   Use semicolons to separate items in a series when the items (a) have internal punctuation or (b) are long.

Ordinarily commas are used to separate items in a series, but in the two instances just stated, a semicolon is less confusing.

> We visited Cooperstown, New York, Niagara Falls, and Syracuse, New York.

Cooperstown, New York, is one town, but from the way the sentence is punctuated we might just as well be talking about Cooperstown *and* New York City. The sentence doesn't distinguish between punctuation *within* a series item and punctuation at the *end* of an item. A better version would be

> We visited Cooperstown, New York; Niagara Falls; and Syracuse, New York.

Now it is clear just what towns we are talking about.

The importance of semicolons is even more obvious when the items are longer:

> We visited Cooperstown, New York, where we went to the Baseball Hall of Fame, Niagara Falls, where we took a boat ride under the falls, and Syracuse, New York, where we spent the afternoon at the university.

The semicolons make clear what happened where.

> We visited Cooperstown, New York, where we went to the Baseball Hall of Fame; Niagara Falls, where we took a boat ride under the falls; and Syracuse, New York, where we spent the afternoon at the university.

Exercise: Point 3

Put semicolons where necessary in each of the following sentences.

1. I read in the newspaper about the governor's efforts to lower automobile insurance rates the latest troubles in the Middle East and a new program for providing hot meals for the elderly on holidays.

2. In my refrigerator are the remains of a bacon, lettuce, and tomato sandwich, which I made two weeks ago, some cheddar cheese, which could probably be used for penicillin, a fried egg, and two bottles of beer, which I should probably drink to forget about the sad state of my refrigerator.

3. Nancy has lived at three different addresses: 505 South Street, Miami, Florida, 71 Granite Avenue, Atlanta, Georgia, and 12–47 Maxwell Boulevard, Charlotte, North Carolina.

4. Our neighborhood council has resolved that street lights will be turned on every evening at 7:30 that parents should keep a close watch on their children to see that vandalism declines and that a recycling drop-off point will be established at the corner of Northend and Pleasant Streets.

5. The terms of the contract stated that the work must be finished by August 15 that payment would be made in two installments, one by September 30, the other by December 30 and that all work must be presented in a manner judged acceptable by the employer.

POINT 4   Use a *colon* to introduce a list following a noun that *names* the list.

I have three favorite actors: Paul Newman, Jimmy Stewart, and Woody Allen.

Note the placement of the colon. It introduces a list and follows a noun, *actors*, that names the list.

In the last two months, Nathan has read four books: *The Scarlet Letter; Rabbit, Run; The Sicilian;* and *The Interpretation of Dreams.*

Books is the noun that names the list to follow; therefore a colon is used to introduce the list. Why have semicolons been used to separate the items in the series? Do not be tempted to write this sentence as follows:

Nathan read: *The Scarlet Letter; Rabbit, Run; The Sicilian;* and *The Interpretation of Dreams.*

This sentence is punctuated incorrectly because there is *no noun* that names the list.

Exercise: Point 4

Write *C* if the colon is used correctly or *X* if it is used incorrectly. Circle the noun, if there is one, that names the list.

C ____   1. I bought two (records:) "J.T." by James Taylor and "Judith" by Judy Collins.

____   2. The teacher said: that there would be an exam and that we had better study.

____   3. My talents: guitar playing, cooking, carpentry.

____   4. We packed: swimsuits, suntan lotion, plastic cups, and a thermos filled with lemonade.

____   5. I was worried about: my financial state, my health, and my future.

____   6. Uses of the semicolon: to separate items in a series and to join two independent clauses.

____   7. Vices: gambling, smoking, and drinking.

____   8. We were: ready, willing, and able.

____   9. Cups are made of: glass, clay, or plastic.

____   10. Types of cups: glass, clay, and plastic.

POINT 5 Use a colon to set off a list or statement that is introduced by the words *the following* or *as follows*.

The crooks stole the following: a television set, a radio, a camera, and a silver serving platter.

The list of items is preceded by a colon because it is introduced by the phrase *the following*.

The teacher instructed us as follows: "Read the chapter carefully, take notes, reread the chapter, and finally, reread your notes."

The statement is introduced by the words *as follows* and a colon.

Review Exercise: Points 4 and 5

Write *C* if the colon is used correctly or *X* if it is used incorrectly. If the sentence is faulty, rewrite it in the space provided.

  1. Every morning I eat: cereal, eggs, and toast.

   Every morning I eat cereal, eggs, and toast.

_____ 2. She has promised: to love, to honor, and to cherish.

_____ 3. We took the following: a tent, two sleeping bags, and a lantern.

_____ 4. I am learning: to drive, to swim, and to type.

_____ 5. Important English skills: grammar, spelling, and punctuation.

_____ 6. Equipment necessary for tennis: sneakers, tennis balls, and a racquet.

_____ 7. Directions: north, east, south, west.

_____ 8. Line up: two by two, and in order of your height.

_____ 9. Steps in cooking spaghetti: boil the water, add the spaghetti, cook for ten minutes, and drain.

_____ 10. She directed us as follows: "Go three blocks south, turn to the right, and look for a mailbox with a picture of a collie on it."

HOW TO USE A SEMICOLON

1. To separate two independent clauses, unless the clauses are joined by a weak connecting word.
2. To separate items in a list, when the items are long or have internal punctuation.

HOW TO USE A COLON

1. To introduce a list following a noun that names the list.
2. To set off a list or statement that is introduced by *the following* or *as follows*.

Chapter Review

I. Write *C* if the sentence is punctuated correctly or *X* if it is punctuated incorrectly.

_____ 1. The firefighter rescued the baby; however, the building was destroyed.

_____ 2. We will invite: Jack and Jill from the hill.

_____ 3. I like you: I want you to like me.

_____ 4. We forgot the following: a toothbrush, a shaving kit, and a good book to read.

_____ 5. Sports: baseball, football, basketball, golf.

_____ 6. Hamlet had to make a choice: to be or not to be.

_____ 7. I'd love to meet her; but I am busy tonight.

_____ 8. He is usually unlucky at games: however, he won tonight.

_____ 9. Sophia has four brothers: Tommy, Sal, Joe, and Robert.

_____ 10. You are in trouble; and you know it.

II. Circle the correct punctuation mark given in the parentheses.

1. The car has a flat tire(; :)there is a spare in the trunk.

2. I didn't finish the assignment(; :)I was too busy.

3. That dress comes in three colors(; :)red, blue, and yellow.

4. We've never traveled so much(; :)it's fun.

5. He told me the following(; :)that he was fed up with the city and that he was moving to the country.

6. I'm exhausted(; :)moreover, I still have more to study.

7. Carl has only two desires(; :)to be rich and to be famous.

8. Linda had two boyfriends before she met me(; :)Jack and Frankie.

9. Russian dressing is good(; :)nevertheless, I prefer Italian.

10. We were late for the concert(; :)the usher made us wait until the first number had been completed.

11. President Kennedy once said, "Ask not what your country can do for you(; :)ask what you can do for your country."

12. They drove through three states(; :)Oregon, Idaho, and Washington.

13. You cook with love(; :)therefore, your dinners are wonderful.

14. We went horseback riding in the afternoon(; :)then we settled down to an evening of food and good talk.

15. Human needs(; :)food, clothing, and shelter.

16. I don't enjoy flying(; :)nevertheless, we flew to Europe last summer.

17. Norm used to smoke cigarettes(; :)now he smokes a pipe.

18. Intramural sports are great(; :)they give you a chance to exercise without high-pressure competition.

19. Ingredients for a salad(; :)lettuce, tomatoes, carrots, and peppers.

20. You have been given three wishes(; :)make them carefully.

III. In each of the following examples, draw one line under the first independent clause and two lines under the second independent clause. Then put a semicolon or other punctuation where it is necessary.

1. We bought tickets well in advance therefore we got good seats.

2. I would love to go however I am too tired.

3. Choose one essay question answer it in 500 words or less.

4. I keep losing my ball-point pens I should get one with a clip.

5. Our team won the championship we were awarded a trophy.

6. You must learn to control your temper it can get you into trouble.

7. Robert Redford starred in the movie he gave a great performance.

8. A calendar watch can be a great convenience however it has to be reset once a month.

9. A sense of humor is important try to develop one.

10. I get hay fever attacks every August however, they do not bother me much with my new allergy pills.

IV. In each of the following examples, underline the noun that names the list, and supply a colon where necessary.

1. I have two reasons to be depressed my girlfriend left me, and I'm developing dandruff.

2. Shakespeare wrote plays in different styles comedy, tragedy, and history.

3. We had a great dinner veal, spaghetti, green beans, and wine.

4. Aspects of a novel plot, character, setting, theme, and tone.

5. Our teacher stressed two points that we should attend class regularly and that we should hand assignments in on time.

6. Hank has two pairs of sneakers one for tennis and one for basketball.

7. You will receive the following a demonstration lesson and a free career brochure.

8. We learned two new dance steps the tango and the hustle.

9. We saw two movies last weekend *Ghostbusters* and *The Karate Kid*.

10. Choose one main dish chicken chow mein or chop suey.

V. Write five sentences of your own, using semicolons.

1. _____

2. _____

3. _____

4. _____

5. _____

VI. All the following sentences contain errors in the use of semicolons or colons. In the space provided, rewrite the sentences to correct the errors.

1. Janet works in the library: she is a page.

_____

2. You don't understand: I apologize for my thoughtlessness.

_____

3. That store sells: jeans, jeans, and more jeans.

_____

4. I have been to that part of town once; but I will never go back.

_____

5. He was arrested on the following charges; assault and battery and armed robbery.

_____

6. Beatrice exercises daily; and it shows in her fine physique.

_____

7. Call me anytime: I'm here when you need me.

_____

8. Birds fly; fish swim; and snakes crawl.

_____

9. He sang as follows; off-key and very loud.

_____

10. The cast rehearsed for weeks: still they were nervous on opening night.

_____

11. There's no business like show business: I should know.

_____

12. She appeared calm: on the inside, though, she was scared.

_____

13. It was Melvin's fault: he is such a klutz.

_____

14. Tomorrow is her birthday: she'll be twenty-five.

_____

15. We watch: the news and the _Tonight Show_ every night.

_____

16. He is responsible for; tending the garden, painting the house, and washing the car.

_____

17. The jury announced its verdict as follows guilty of first-degree murder.

_____

18. First the leaves turn colors: then they fall.

_____

19. I want bigger muscles: therefore; I lift weights.

_____

20. Ralph doesn't take care of his teeth: consequently, he gets at least six cavities a year.

_____

VII. Rewrite the following passages, correcting any errors in the use of semicolons or colons.

The team was in trouble: it had dropped from first place to last in three weeks. The manager called a meeting of the players at which the following issues were discussed; the importance of developing a winning attitude, whereby the players would place the goals of the team over their individual achievements, the imposition of a strict curfew so that the players would be well rested for the games, the problem of teammates competing among themselves for higher salaries and greater coverage in the newspapers, and last but not least, the general lack of hustle and determination on the part of the team's stars.

My friends and I recently spent a day driving around New England trying to hit as many hamburger joints as we could in 16 hours. Our travels took us to the following places; Burlington, Massachusetts, where we prepared our stomachs with thick shakes and French fries, Concord, New Hampshire, where we indulged in double cheeseburgers, Canaan, New Hampshire, where we settled for soft drinks, Woodstock, Vermont, where we each downed a filet of fish, and finally to Worcester, Massachusetts, where we celebrated with chicken sandwiches; we ate dessert at the quick lunch bar at Boston University, Boston, Massachusetts.

13

Comma

Commas are the most used and most frequently misused punctuation marks. Basically the comma is used to signal a pause. It can help make the meaning of a sentence more clear, but if it is used carelessly, it can cloud the meaning of a sentence entirely. The most important rule of thumb regarding commas is to use a comma only when you are sure you need it.

POINT 1 Use *commas* to separate three or more items in a series.

> I enjoy baseball, basketball, and tennis.

In this sentence, the items in the series are separated by commas. Note that the comma follows the item. Since the last item is the last word of the sentence, there is no need to put a comma after it; it is followed by a period.

> She knows how to sing, dance, and play the piano.

Again the items in the series are separated by commas.

> We bought groceries and liquor.

Note that there are no commas in this sentence. There are only two items in the series; therefore, no comma is required.

Exercise: Point 1

Put commas where necessary in each of the following sentences.

1. She was lonely, depressed, and nostalgic.

2. Kathy planted tulips daffodils and roses.

217

3. It is hot and muggy today.

4. He stormed out of the house went for a walk and came back the next morning.

5. I've been to South America Central America and Canada.

6. Bend me shake me break me; do anything you want.

7. The letter was signed sealed and delivered.

8. We strolled along the beach and gathered shells.

9. This library has books books and more books.

10. For lunch we had soup salad and a sandwich.

POINT 2   Use a *comma* between two independent clauses if they are connected by such words as *and, but, for, or, nor, yet, so.*

This is something that has been covered before, but it will be useful to review it now.

> I wanted to go, but I didn't have enough money.

This sentence contains two independent clauses; they are separated by a comma.

> I was hired for the job, and I start work Monday.

Again we have two independent clauses, which are connected by a comma and *and.* Note that the comma *precedes* the connecting word.

> You should pay your bills when they are due, or you will have to pay an interest charge.

Two independent clauses are connected by a comma and *or.* Note the placement of the comma.

When connecting independent clauses in this way, be sure to use the comma *plus* the connecting word. The use of the comma without the connecting word creates a serious error in sentence structure—the run-on sentence. Go back to chapter 5 if you need to review run-ons.

> Trish ran for office and was elected.

In this sentence there is no comma because we do not have two independent clauses. There is only one subject, *Trish* the two verbs refer to the same subject.

> He tried his best but failed.

Is this sentence correct as it stands?

Exercise: Point 2

Put commas where necessary in the following sentences.

1. He thinks he should be a star, but he really isn't very talented.

2. I can type very fast but I make a lot of mistakes.

3. That's the way it goes and you will have to accept it.

4. My wife tries to rush me yet I always take my time.

5. She had a cold so she stayed in bed all day.

6. I'm taking flying lessons but I can't seem to get the hang of making turns.

7. Randy will graduate this year and he hopes to get a job in the clothing industry.

8. Friendship is simple yet complex.

9. Be truthful with me or I will leave you.

10. He is very bright but can't seem to get his head together.

Review Exercise: Points 1 and 2

All the following sentences contain errors in comma usage. In the space provided, rewrite the sentences to correct the errors.

1. Joe, Sue and Anne were invited to the party.

    Joe, Sue, and Anne were invited to the party.

2. We hoped the humidity would end but it didn't.

    _____

3. There were cows, and horses roaming around the field.

    _____

4. I ate pizza and she ate a grinder.

    _____

5. We spoke seriously, yet insincerely.

    _____

6. She used parsley, garlic and tarragon in the sauce.

    _____

7. She is superstitious and her husband is a nervous wreck.

_____

8. We got to the show on time but we left at the intermission.

_____

9. Reading writing and arithmetic are the basics of education.

_____

10. We sang laughed and drank all night long.

_____

POINT 3   **Use a comma after a long introductory phrase or clause. Use a comma after a short introductory phrase if it is necessary to avoid unclear meaning.**

When the time comes, everything will be settled.

When the time comes is a dependent clause. As we saw in Chapter 4, Point 4, a dependent clause at the beginning of a sentence is usually followed by a comma.

All through the long drive, my mind kept going back to last night's conversation.

All through the long drive is not part of the main idea.

While eating, the group discussed plans for the afternoon.

Without a comma, it might look as though someone were eating the group.

As captain, Mike decided the lineup.

Again, without a comma there could be confusion. But

At eight o'clock he opened the doors.

Here there is no real danger of confusion, so a comma is not needed.

The words *yes* and *no* are generally followed by a comma when they begin a sentence. So are words such as the following:

however	of course	by the way
in fact	incidentally	well

No, there is no need for concern.
However, you will have to talk to your adviser.
Well, I haven't seen her in three weeks.

It is important for a writer to develop a good ear if he is to use commas efficiently. Learn to listen to your words. If a sentence seems to have a natural pause, it *may* need a comma.

Exercise: Point 3

Put commas where necessary in each of the following sentences.

1. After the party ended, we cleaned the apartment.

2. Yes we have no bananas.

3. As I said before the lecture is canceled.

4. Not wanting to go I said I wasn't feeling well.

5. Since you wanted popsicles I bought some.

6. By the way you have been promoted.

7. Whenever I hear that album I feel better.

8. As I feared the end is near.

9. Thinking about the past I always get melancholy.

10. Unfortunately your plan will never work.

Another Exercise: Point 3

Write five sentences of your own, using introductory phrases.

1. _____

2. _____

3. _____

4. _____

5. _____

POINT 4   **Use commas on both sides of a word (or group of words) that interrupts the flow of the sentence.**

> The fact is, Bob, that I feel quite unhappy about it.

Bob interrupts the flow of the sentence and therefore is set off from the rest of the sentence with commas.

> Croissants, for example, are delicious with coffee.

For example interrupts the flow of the sentence and therefore is set off with commas.

Other expressions that are generally set off with commas include

however	in fact	at any rate
of course	to tell the truth	I think
therefore	by the way	finally

We are, of course, pleased with your grades.

Note the placement of the commas.

Your last letter, by the way, was very puzzling.
Ricky, not knowing what the question was, was dumbfounded.

In the preceding sentence, the interrupting phrase adds information to or comments on the situation. It is set off with commas.

I am sorry, sir, for what I have done.

The interrupting word, *sir*, ells us to whom the statement is being made.

Exercise: Point 4

Put commas where necessary in each of the following sentences.

1. I told you once, Margie, and I will not tell you again.

2. Shakespeare for example wrote beautiful sonnets.

3. I think therefore that we should adjourn immediately.

4. My grandmother strangely enough bought a motorcycle.

5. Watch out Hubert!

6. I believe on the other hand that there is too much violence on television.

7. Her illness of course is the reason for her absence.

8. Jogging as it turns out has helped me lose weight.

9. Your theory I am certain is worthy of more consideration.

10. A car if it is not tuned regularly is likely to break down.

Review Exercise: Points 1–4

Put commas where necessary in each of the following sentences.

1. At the barbecue, we had hamburgers, hot dogs, and chicken.

2. We saw the game at the ballpark and we watched the highlights on television.

3. After we finished eating Harry and Gail went for a walk.

4. I am asking you Mr. Maxwell to give me a direct answer.

5. A bagel with cream cheese makes a great snack.

6. The manager however refused to listen to the demands of the employees.

7. During her road test Trudy had to parallel park back up and make a U-turn and park the car on a hill.

8. He made copies of the article and circulated them among the students.

9. Without taking much time Pat answered all the questions on the test.

10. A parent if he wants his child to do well in school should encourage him to work his hardest.

Another Review Exercise: Points 1–4

All the following sentences contain errors in the use of commas. Rewrite the sentences, correcting the errors, in the space provided.

1. The poet spoke to the audience, and answered questions.

   The poet spoke to the audience and answered questions.

2. Before making up her mind Linda asked her counselor for advice.

   _____

3. We cast our votes as usual, just before the polls closed.

   _____

4. By the way Mom happy Mother's Day.

   _____

5. Reading, *Sports Illustrated,* is my favorite way to relax.

   _____

6. In addition, to mastering the use of commas you have, improved your vocabulary.

   _____

7. I am have always been and always will be your best friend.

   _____

8. Those wind chimes are lovely but, they are too expensive.

   _____

9. Never before in my life, have I met such a man.

_____

10. That puppy, with the floppy ears, is mine.

_____

| POINT 5   Use commas to set off nonessential material.

Nonessential material, simply defined, is material that may be interesting but is not absolutely necessary for the main idea of the sentence. That is, any material that can be left out of the sentence without changing the main idea is nonessential.

> Mr. Turner, who was defeated in the election four years ago, is running for office again.

The material set off by commas is nonessential; that is, the main idea of the sentence would not be changed if that material were omitted.

> A hiccough remedy that usually works is hard to come by.

There is no nonessential material in this sentence. Do not be tempted to write this sentence as follows:

> A hiccough remedy, that usually works, is hard to find.

This is incorrect because the group of words _that usually works_ is essential to the meaning of the sentence. If this group of words were omitted, the sentence would read, "A hiccough remedy is hard to find." An important part of its meaning would be lost.

> _Jaws,_ which is about killer sharks, was written by Peter Benchley.

If we omit the nonessential material between the commas, the sentence would read: _Jaws_ was written by Peter Benchley. The main idea of the original sentence still stands; the group of words _which is about killer sharks_ is nonessential.

> Peter Benchley's _Jaws_ is about killer sharks.

In this sentence there is no nonessential material.

Exercise: Point 5

Put commas where necessary in each of the following sentences.

1. His car, which had been repaired at Moe's Garage, broke down again.

2. My sister an Aquarian was born in January.

3. Mr. Thomas the coach of our football team called practice off for today.

4. Her suggestion that we feed the cats was reinforced by a chorus of meows.

5. This cottage which was built in 1901 is our favorite vacation spot.

6. The tea kettle that I bought at the bazaar is an antique.

7. Tomorrow June 20 is our wedding anniversary.

8. Joey smiling like a fool looked ridiculous.

9. The kerosene lamp which we always use in an emergency came in very handy.

10. The job that you applied for has been filled.

Another Exercise: Point 5

Write five sentences of your own in which you use commas to set off nonessential material.

1. _____

2. _____

3. _____

4. _____

5. _____

Review Exercise: Points 1–5

All the following sentences contain errors in the use of commas. Rewrite each sentence, correcting the error, in the space provided.

1. A fool, and his money, are soon parted.

   A fool and his money are soon parted.

2. It is I think the best way to solve the problem.

   _____

3. Chicken soup which some people believe can cure diseases, is delicious.

   _____

4. He can play the flute, the clarinet the oboe and the trumpet.

   _____

5. After a while even the most exciting entertainment can become boring.

   _____

6. That in fact is exactly the reason I am here.

_____

7. As sure as I'm breathing you're a double for my brother.

_____

8. Backgammon a game which involves gambling, is very popular.

_____

9. Nuclear plants, which some people feel are destructive to the environment are being built in many states.

_____

10. We browsed, in the bookstore, for an hour.

_____

POINT 6   Use a comma after every item in an address or date.

> 610 South Street, Dayton, Ohio
> Apt. 5, Wellington Arms, 1515 Broadway, St. Paul, Minn.
> Sunday, January 1, 1978
> On March 8, 1977, we were married in Atlanta, Georgia.

A one-item address or date is an exception to this rule:

> May 5 is my brother's birthday.
> The house at 412 Fisher Street is the one that people say is haunted.

Exercise: Point 6

Put commas where necessary in each of the following sentences.

1. Paul was born on September 3 1953.

2. Renee works at State Hospital 600 Washington Street Evanstown Kansas.

3. The paper is due on Monday May 15.

4. The play opens on September 1, 1985 at the Stoner Theater 50 Broad Street

   Fresno California.

5. We celebrated our anniversary July 19 in Charleston South Carolina.

Write one sentence in which you tell when and where you were born.

_____

Review Exercise: Points 1–6

All the following sentences contain errors in the use of commas. Rewrite the sentences, correcting the errors, in the space provided.

1. There were no runs two hits and two men left on base.

   There were no runs, two hits, and two men left on base.

2. That guy, in the blue suede shoes, is really wild.

   _____

3. After deliberating for two hours the jury reached a verdict.

   _____

4. Toby Al and Dave have moved to Palo Alto California.

   _____

5. Biology the study of living things is my favorite subject.

   _____

6. I have, after much thought reached a decision.

   _____

7. We walked, and talked all night long.

   _____

8. I'm afraid it will rain although I hope it doesn't.

   _____

9. I have up until now, handed in my assignments on time.

   _____

10. Are you sure pal that you want to come along?

   _____

HOW TO USE COMMAS

1. Use them to separate three or more items in a series.
2. Use them between two independent clauses joined by a weak connecting word.
3. Use them after introductory material when it is long or the meaning might otherwise be unclear.
4. Use them to set off nonessential material or words that interrupt the flow of the sentence.

Chapter Review

I. Write *C* if the sentence is punctuated correctly or *X* if it contains an error in comma usage. Be prepared to explain your answers.

_____ 1. We have never since we moved here had to lock our doors.

_____ 2. As Socrates said, "Know thyself."

_____ 3. I brush my teeth, twice a day.

_____ 4. The bread, that you were baking, is burned.

_____ 5. Yes, sir, I know what you mean.

_____ 6. This couch, which we bought at a flea market is very comfortable.

_____ 7. On December 5 I will be twenty-six years old.

_____ 8. You must, however have a library card.

_____ 9. Do you know what I mean, or are you confused?

_____ 10. When the time is right you will know it.

II. Put commas where necessary in each of the following sentences.

1. This section therefore will be closed.

2. Hey wait!

3. While waiting for the bus we told each other jokes.

4. Why Mr. Carl must you be so rude?

5. The television set which was stolen last week was found in the basement of a warehouse.

6. The store is located at 520 Elm Street Lewistown Michigan.

7. We must if we are ever to change our ways begin today.

8. I'd love to go but she won't let me.

9. Sometimes when I am feeling blue a good record can lift my spirits.

10. You know of course that our television is broken.

11. In a sense you are right.

12. We plan if the weather is good to go swimming tomorrow.

13. He had always wanted to participate in the Olympics but he had never trained properly for the trials.

14. The recipe directs you to mix the batter with one egg add the premeasured packet of chocolate chips and bake the mixture for forty-five minutes in an oven set at 350°.

15. Time as it always does has a way of changing things.

16. While showering I sing to myself.

17. That novel which by the way I have never read is supposed to be excellent.

18. A sandwich if made with whole wheat bread is delicious and healthful.

19. There has never been as far as I can remember such a destructive storm.

20. Well how do you like that!

III. Here are four rules governing the use of commas:
    (1) Use commas to separate items in a series.

    (2) Use a comma between two independent clauses if they are connected by one of the weak connecting words.

    (3) Use a comma after a long introductory phrase or clause and after a short introductory phrase if it is needed to make the meaning clear.

    (4) Use commas around words that interrupt the flow of a sentence and around nonessential material.

All the following sentences are punctuated *correctly*. Write the *number* of the rule that applies to the use of the comma in each sentence.

_____ 1. One of my friends, Mark, is planning to get married.

_____ 2. The scarecrow, which was made of straw, was dragged to the ground.

_____ 3. I watered the plants, fed the dog, and cleaned the kitchen.

_____ 4. They had a golden opportunity, but they could not capitalize on it.

_____ 5. As a student of the arts, I am required to go to the museum once a week.

_____ 6. The dean, however, was willing to listen to the demands of the student committee.

_____ 7. Since I hurt my back, I have never shoveled snow.

_____ 8. Dorothy, in her early years, was a dancer.

_____ 9. The pitcher, who was brought up from the minor league last week, threw a shutout.

_____ 10. We visited my parents, my wife's parents, and my sister.

_____ 11. I will not repeat myself, so you had better listen carefully.

_____ 12. This, of all things, you call a surprise!

_____ 13. I'm sorry, Dad, for banging up the car.

_____ 14. We played chess, checkers, and cribbage.

_____ 15. So, after all that, you want to apologize!

_____ 16. Shopping wisely, we bought sheets and pillowcases that matched.

_____ 17. And now, for my final number, I will play a sonata by Beethoven.

_____ 18. Have you ever, in your whole life, met such a man?

_____ 19. This, above all, is what is important.

_____ 20. I met her in the morning, and I married her in the evening.

IV. Write sentences of your own, using the rule indicated by the number in the parentheses. The numbers refer to the rules in the previous exercise. If, for example, you are directed to write a sentence using (1), you should apply the rule that states, "Use commas to separate items in a series."

(1)_____

_____

(1)_____

_____

(2)_____

_____

(2)_____

_____

(3)_____

_____

(3)_____

_____

(4)_____

_____

(4)_____

V. All the following sentences contain errors in the use of commas. Rewrite the sentences, correcting the errors, in the space provided.

1. Waving her wand the princess performed some magic.

   _____

2. Never never will you get away with that.

   _____

3. I had a bacon lettuce and tomato sandwich for lunch.

   _____

4. Who in your opinion is the world's greatest athlete?

   _____

5. Her latest poem, is superb.

   _____

6. As of next week the prisoner will be a free man.

   _____

7. His answer which was wrong made the class laugh.

   _____

8. That dog barking at the tree, is mine.

   _____

9. We were wed on April 17 1977.

   _____

10. When our guests arrived we greeted them at the door.

_____

11. Once upon a time there was a dog who could fly.

_____

12. We met as usual at the corner of Hollywood, and Vine.

_____

13. I waited, for nearly a month for your letter.

_____

14. It is my choice however to travel alone.

_____

15. For once try studying.

_____

16. You are mine and I am yours.

_____

17. Write to me at 65 Market Street Portland Maine.

_____

18. You are all prepared I'm sure for the test.

_____

19. Ice cream if it is made at home is very good.

_____

20. As long as I live I will love to dance.

_____

VI. Rewrite the following passages, correcting any errors in comma usage.

When we spent the day at my grandmother's cottage, on the beach, we had a great time. My wife and I, together with two friends, drove about sixty miles, from our home to the small two-room beach house which had been built over a hundred years ago. We stopped at a small market, to pick up some food, for sandwiches, and ate as soon as we arrived at the cottage. We spent the rest of the day, eating drinking sunning ourselves going for walks and swimming. By the time the sun went down we were thoroughly exhausted. Isn't is strange I ask you that doing nothing can make someone so tired?

Liberal arts contrary to what some people think provides a good basis for an education. It is important I believe for every student to be well grounded in such subjects as art history science, politics and English. These subjects give students a good idea, of what has been accomplished in the history of the world, and what is yet to be accomplished. By the time one completes a full program in liberal arts he or she will be ready to live with vigor, and vitality.

PART IV
MECHANICS

14

Capital Letters

One of the ways to make important words stand out is to *capitalize* them—that is, begin them with a capital letter. There are a lot of rules for capitalization. However, they will be easier to learn if you keep in mind that most of them have to do with *names:* names of people, names of books, names of places, and so on. For instance, you would write,

> John Morrison
> The Whole Earth Catalog.
> San Francisco, California

Moreover, as you can see, capitalization usually has to do with very *specific* names. We would write

> Wayne Community College   but   a two-year college
> Green Bay Packers   but   the football team

There are few other uses of capital letters. For instance, you probably know already that the word *I* is always capitalized and that the first word of every sentence is capitalized. But keep in mind the principle of specific names. With this to help, you should not have much trouble learning when and when not to capitalize.

POINT 1   Capitalize the first, last, and important words in a title.

> Lady Sings the Blues

In the title of this movie, the first word, the last word, and the important word *Sings* begin with capital letters. *The* is not quite as important as the other words and is therefore not capitalized.

<u>A Tale of Two Cities</u>
<u>Where the Wild Things Are</u>

Remember: In a sentence, the title of a work of some length should be underlined. (See Chapter 11, Point 7)

Exercise: Point 1

Circle any letters that should be capitalized in the following sentences.

1. have you ever seen the agony and the ecstasy?

2. i read an article entitled "the history of jazz."

3. one of Freud's most important books is called *the interpretation of dreams.*

4. We saw a production of Shakespeare's *the taming of the shrew.*

5. i have a book called *how to grow beautiful house plants.*

Another Exercise: Point 1

Write five sentences of your own in which you use titles. Be sure to use capital letters when necessary.

1. _____

2. _____

3. _____

4. _____

5. _____

POINT 2   Capitalize the names of specific persons, places, languages, nations, and nationalities.

Alice J. Brock	English
Mr. Farnsworth	Italian
Denver, Colorado	Chicano
Mississippi River	American
Oriental	Canadian
Spanish-American	Harlem
Latin America	France

He works at the hardware store on Mill Street.

Mill Street, the name of a specific place, is capitalized.

We went canoeing on the Concord River.

Again the name of a specific place is capitalized.

Ms. Warren can speak English and French.

A specific person's name is capitalized; names of languages are capitalized.

Names of races used to be capitalized, but today they frequently are not. You will be on fairly safe ground if you capitalize *Oriental* and *Indian,* but do not capitalize *white* and *black.* The words *Chicano* and *Caucasian* are usually capitalized, but some writers prefer not to capitalize them. Whichever you choose to do, be consistent about it within each piece of writing.

Exercise: Point 2

Circle any letters that should be capitalized in the following sentences.

1. the fowlers always spend their vacation in the caribbean.

2. mel gave up his united states citizenship when he moved to canada.

3. joe perry has moved to los angeles, california.

4. does lori know how to speak german?

5. venezuela, argentina, mexico, and most of latin america have been free

   countries since they rebelled against spain.

6. lou takes great pride in his italian-american heritage.

7. the school is going to offer a course in black history next semester.

Another Exercise: Point 2

Write five sentences of your own in which you use capital letters to name a specific person, place, language, or nationality.

1. _____

2. _____

3. _____

4. _____

5. _____

POINT 3   **Capitalize names of days of the week, months, and holidays; do not capitalize names of the seasons.**

> Thanksgiving falls on the last Thursday of November.

The names of a holiday, a day of the week, and a month are capitalized.

> It has been a hard winter.

The name of a season, *winter*, is not capitalized.

> Summer brings heat and humidity.

Summer is capitalized only because it is the first word of the sentence.

> Next Monday is Washington's Birthday.

The name of the holiday contains two words—both are capitalized.

Exercise: Point 3

Circle any letters that should be capitalized in the following sentences.

1. september 21 is the first day of autumn.

2. i am on the road on monday and thursday.

3. independence day falls on july 4.

4. we visit my family on the first sunday of every month.

5. september and october are the loveliest months of the year.

Another Exercise: Point 3

Write five sentences of your own in which you use capital letters in the names of days of the week, months, and holidays.

1. _____

2. _____

3. _____

4. _____

5. _____

Review Exercise: Points 1–3

All the following sentences contain errors in the use of capital letters. Rewrite the sentences, correcting the errors, in the space provided.

1. i read *the boys from brazil* last spring.

   I read The Boys from Brazil last spring.

2. barry smith works in new york, but he lives on long island.

   _____

3. on monday we will discuss ibsen's play entitled *a doll's house*.

   _____

4. i travel to the mountains every autumn.

   _____

5. marcia was born in canada, but she lives in kansas and considers herself an american.

   _____

6. the police found the stolen car in norfolk county.

   _____

7. have you read the article "a way to understand the universe"?

   _____

8. be careful on april fool's day.

   _____

9. she is reading a book about american indians.

   _____

10. last Summer we visited texas, oklahoma, and nevada.

    _____

POINT 4   Capitalize the first word of a direct quotation.

My teacher said, "This is a brilliant answer!"

The first word of the direct quotation, *This*, is capitalized.

"Are you planning to move?" she asked.

Again the first word of the direct quotation is capitalized.

She wanted to know whether dinner was ready.

There is no direct quotation in this sentence.

If you need to review the use of quotation marks in these sentences, look back at Chapter 11, Point 5.

Exercise: Point 4

Circle any letters that should be capitalized in the following sentences.

1. john asked lucy, "will you come to the dance with me?"
2. the pharmacist said, "here is your prescription."
3. "when will we get out tests back?" i asked.
4. "you are all invited to the victory party," the candidate announced.
5. "please pick up some tomatoes," she said.

Another Exercise: Point 4

Write five sentences of your own in which you use capital letters to begin direct quotations.

1. _____
2. _____
3. _____
4. _____
5. _____

POINT 5 **Capitalize words of family relationship when they are used as names.**

Are you coming, Mother?

Mother, a word of family relationship, is capitalized because it is used as a name.

My husband's Uncle Mike came to visit us.

Uncle is used as part of a name.

Come on, Dad, let's go to the ball game.

However, if a *possessive* word is used before the word, the word should not be capitalized. Such possessives include *my, our, your, his, her, its, their, Bill's, the doctor's,* and similar words.

My mother is coming.
Our uncle came to visit us.
We went to the ball game with Steve's dad.

Exercise: Point 5

Circle any letters that should be capitalized in the following sentences.

1. Happy Birthday, sister.

2. I'm not eating these lima beans, mom.

3. my aunt is a champion at poker.

4. Have you heard from uncle ebenezer?

5. My brother is also my best friend.

6. I heard that ed's father used to play professional baseball.

7. My grandmother married a man half her age.

8. Is it true that father knows best?

9. I visited grandpa mac in his office.

10. abby's cousin lisa is very pretty.

POINT 6   **Capitalize words such as *college, doctor,* and *building* when they are part of the names of specific people or things.**

I am a student at Jones College.

Jones College is the name of a specific thing; therefore it is capitalized.

She has an appointment with Dr. Miller.

Dr. Miller is a specific person.

Professor Chapman teaches that course.

Professor Chapman is a specific person.

We went to the top of the Empire State Building.

The *Empire State Building* is the name of a specific thing.

When such words are not part of specific names, they should not be capitalized.

I am a student in college.
She has an appointment with the doctor.

Our professor teaches that course.
We went to the top of the building.

Exercise: Point 6

Circle any letters that should be capitalized in the following sentences.

1. We took a boat ride on the colorado river.

2. The ice cream shop is located on franklin drive.

3. She teaches literature at thomas university.

4. He has been our senator for twelve years.

5. Mr. michaels is our professor.

6. He expects us to call him professor michaels.

7. She was the architect for the wilson county courthouse.

8. Have you ever visited phoenix park in dublin?

9. They went swimming in the pond.

10. They went swimming in walden pond.

Review Exercise: Points 1–6

All the following sentences contain errors in the use of capital letters. Rewrite the sentences, correcting the errors, in the space provided.

1. dr. meyer's office is on state street.

   Dr. Meyer's office is on State Street.

2. on the first night of Chanukah, we visited grandma and grandpa.

3. we went to Times Square on new year's eve.

4. our teacher is from the iberian peninsula.

5. "when will you hand in that paper?" the Professor asked.

6. i answered, "i will hand it in next tuesday."

_____

7. have you seen *terms of endearment?*

_____

8. i liked *an officer and a gentleman* even better.

_____

9. does your Brother still work at the Plant?

_____

10. In the Fall we will go camping at bear mountain.

_____

Another Review Exercise: Points 1–6

Write your own sentences, using the word given in the parentheses. Use the word *exactly* as it appears.

1. (River) _____

2. (grandmother) _____

3. (Sister) _____

4. (Winter) _____

5. (building) _____

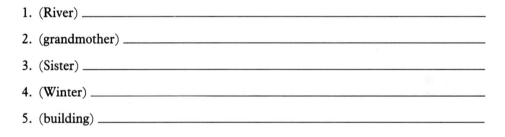

POINT 7   Capitalize events in history, movements, and periods.

The Civil War was an important event in American history.

The *Civil War,* an event in history, is capitalized.

The Impressionists did much to change people's thinking about art.

Impressionists refers to a group of artists who were part of the movement called Impressionism.

Much of our terrain was formed during the Ice Age.

Ice Age refers to a period in history.

The years after World War I are known as the Roaring Twenties.

Exercise: Point 7

Circle any letters that should be capitalized in the following sentences.

1. (t)he (d)eclaration of (i)ndependence was signed in 1776.

2. life was exciting in the frontier age.

3. the vietnam war was thought by many to be a tragedy.

4. Leonardo da Vinci was an important figure during the renaissance.

5. the gettysburg address was delivered by abraham lincoln.

Another Exercise: Point 7

Write five sentences of your own in which you use the names of historical events, movements, or periods.

1. _____

2. _____

3. _____

4. _____

5. _____

POINT 8   Capitalize the names of specific school courses, but do not capitalize general words that refer to the courses.

> I take Spanish 10 and Chemistry 101.

The names of these specific courses are capitalized.

> I am studying history, foreign language, and mathematics.

No specific course is mentioned in this sentence.

> I take Spanish and chemistry.

Spanish is capitalized because it is the name of a language; *chemistry* is not capitalized because there is no mention of a *specific* course.

Exercise: Point 8

Circle any letters that should be capitalized in the following sentences.

1. She is studying (e)nglish with (p)rofessor (r)oss.

2. do you expect to take german 101 next semester?

3. Esther plans to major in anthropology.

4. i wanted to take english 2a, but my advisor suggested i take basic composition.

5. He got an A on his physics final.

Another Exercise: Point 8

Write sentences of your own in which you name five courses you have taken in your academic career.

1. _____

2. _____

3. _____

4. _____

5. _____

Review Exercise: Points 1–8

All the following sentences contain errors in the use of capital letters. Rewrite the sentences, correcting the errors, in the space provided.

1. who was responsible for the break-in at watergate?

   Who was responsible for the break-in at Watergate?

2. aunt tilly is preparing her annual christmas dinner.

   _____

3. next winter we will ski in the alps.

   _____

4. "why didn't you fill that prescription?" dr. cohen asked.

   _____

5. do you refer to taj mahal the singer or to taj mahal the building?

   _____

6. chrissy got a B in biology 2a last term.

   _____

7. so, mom, do you think i should buy a ford or a chevy?

_____

8. the united states entered world war II after the attack on pearl harbor.

_____

9. can we try that new french restaurant?

_____

10. peter sellers is the star of *the return of the pink panther.*

_____

WHEN TO USE CAPITAL LETTERS

1. Capitalize the names of specific persons, places, languages, nations, nationalities, and some races.
2. Capitalize the names of days of the week, months, and holidays (but *not* seasons).
3. Capitalize the first, last, and important words in a title.
4. Capitalize the first word of a direct quotation.
5. Capitalize the first word of a sentence.
6. Capitalize the word *I.*

Chapter Review

I. Write *C* if the sentence makes correct use of capital letters or *X* if it contains an error in the use of capital letters.

_____ 1. *The Catcher in the rye* was written by J.D. Salinger.

_____ 2. Mr. Morrison has been named dean of the College.

_____ 3. he is the lieutenant governor of Kansas.

_____ 4. The conductor said, "Tickets, please."

_____ 5. I will be an english major.

_____ 6. Next Friday is her Thirteenth Birthday.

_____ 7. Aunt Martha is sally's favorite relative.

_____ 8. Oh, mom!

_____ 9. New england is beautiful in the Autumn.

_____ 10. King Kong was seen atop the Empire State building.

II. Circle any letters that should be capitalized in the following sentences.

1. He is my uncle from las vegas.

2. the professor asked, "who knows the answer to this question?"

3. I always buy the newspaper on sunday.

4. jefferson city is the capital of missouri.

5. the boutique is located on willis avenue.

6. don't capitalize every letter you see!

7. i just finished reading *the double helix*.

8. Did you see the football game on new year's day?

9. When, dad, will you ever understand me?

10. Zelda lives a zesty life in zanzibar.

11. mr. Fisher, our biology teacher, is also coach of the basketball team.

12. I will play basketball for the detroit pistons.

13. You can find the book you want at the Atlanta public library.

14. For the second time, I flunked economics 101.

15. "I live near the charles river," he said.

16. Richard plans to join the peace corps.

17. in october the leaves begin to fall.

18. When we were in california we visited the la brea tar pits.

19. She teaches spanish at Billings high school.

20. He was born in mexico city, and he lives in san antonio, Texas.

III. Write sentences of your own, using the word given in the parentheses. Use the word *exactly* as it appears.

1. (Captain _____

2. (summer) _____

3. (Uncle) _____

4. (March) _____

5. (history) _____

6. (Revolution) _____

7. (Dad) _____

8. (mother) _____

9. (Autumn) _____

10. (Park) _____

IV. Circle the correct word given in the parentheses.

1. Last (summer, Summer) I worked in a gas station.

2. My (father, Father) served in World War II.

3. Erich Segal had a best seller with *Love (story, Story)*.

4. She asked me, "(why, Why) must you treat me this way?"

5. I think (Doctor, doctor) Martin is a veterinarian.

6. I have been studying (latin, Latin).

7. Did you write a letter to your (aunt, Aunt)?

8. Our (teacher, Teacher) is not here today.

9. I hope the (yankees, Yankees) win the pennant.

10. We went sailing on the Hudson (river, River).

11. Did you ever read *Women (in, In) Love?*

12. We're going to Vancouver over the Labor Day (weekend, Weekend).

13. "How," I said, "(do, Do) you expect to pass that exam?"

14. Many fairy tales begin, "Once upon a (time, Time)."

15. He learned to play the (bagpipes, Bagpipes) in Scotland.

16. (winter, Winter) is my favorite season.

17. Life was very different in the Middle (ages, Ages).

18. My (sister, Sister) has dropped out of (school, School).

19. It's (greek, Greek) to me!

20. He asked me (whether, Whether) I planned to get a haircut.

V. All the following sentences contain errors in the use of capital letters. Rewrite the sentences, correcting the errors, in the space provided.

1. "Lucy In the Sky With Diamonds" is a Beatles' song.

   _____

2. he was born in mexico, and he has lived there all his life.

   _____

3. i would like to drive a rolls royce.

   _____

4. I'm only asking you, dad, to give me another chance.

   _____

5. The Babysitter pleaded, "behave yourself."

   _____

6. My Grandfather will be ninety years old next month.

   _____

7. The Chicago cubs are in the national league.

   _____

8. Let's see the fireworks on independence day!

   _____

9. albert's aunt alberta has arrived.

   _____

10. We ate dinner in the restaurant at the top of the Building.

    _____

11. Is there a Doctor in the house?

    _____

12. when you are in new york, visit Macy's.

    _____

13. Come on, horatio, you're holding us up.

    _____

14. i asked Dr. Simmons if I could change my appointment.

    _____

15. Mario is the Manager of a big department store.

_____

16. Mail the form to john doe, anytown, u.s.a.

_____

17. i read the bestseller called _sophie's choice._

_____

18. Everyone wants to know When the stock market will improve.

_____

19. My Brother exclaimed, "so this is your apartment!"

_____

20. Martin Luther King headed the civil rights movement.

_____

VI. Rewrite the following passages, correcting any errors in capitalization.

many people think of Baseball as the great american game. And why not? fans get to sit in beautiful parks such as yankee stadium, eat Hot Dogs, watch an exciting event, and Yell Their Lungs Out. All the Fun and Excitement typifies the spirit of america. A great writer, roger angell, has examined the intricacies of the sport, and of the event, in his collection of essays entitled _five seasons: a baseball companion._ it makes great reading for the serious and even the not-so-serious fan.

_____

_____

_____

_____

_____

_____

_____

_____

_____

_____

if you need someone to fix something in your apartment or house, don't call me! i have read *The Book Of Home Repair,* and still cannot manage to hang a picture or fix a leaky faucet. whenever something goes wrong in my home, i always call my Uncle, who is a whiz at such things. last Fall—i believe it was around thanksgiving—our garbage disposal overflowed. as usual, i called my Uncle, who said, "this is getting a bit out of hand. you can't expect me to drive all the way from cleveland to fix your garbage disposal!" seeing as we lived in chicago, he was right. i called a Plumber instead, who charged me fifty dollars for the job; the Lake on the kitchen floor vanished, but i vowed i would either learn something about home repair or move to cleveland.

15

Spelling

Spelling—ugh! How do you *ever* know whether something is spelled right or not? And who cares, anyway, as long as the word can be understood?

Fortunately or unfortunately, such people as teachers and bosses do seem to care about correct spelling. And it's not just fussiness; often a word *is* harder to understand if it's not spelled in the way people are used to seeing it. So it's worthwhile making the effort to learn the rules for correct spelling.

Of course, there are a lot of cases that aren't covered by the rules. English-language spelling is full of irregularities. Many of them can be learned only by using them often enough so that they become familiar. In the meantime, perhaps the best spelling rule is this: *When in doubt, check the dictionary.*

Still, there are *some* rules that hold for most words. The most basic rules are given in this chapter, and if you master them you will be able to avoid many common errors. Also included in the chapter is a list of frequently misspelled words, which you may find it helpful to memorize.

A final point: In using many of the following rules, you will need to be aware of the difference between vowels and consonants. Five letters of the alphabet are known as *vowels: a, e, i, o,* and *u.* All other letters are consonants.

POINT 1 Use *i* before *e*
Except after *c*
Or when sounded as *a*
As in neighbor or weigh.

i before e	ei after c	ei when sounded as a
believe	receive	eight
chief	ceiling	vein
niece	deceive	sleigh
thief	conceive	freight

This rule works in most cases, but there are a few exceptions you should memorize:

either	height
neither	leisure
weird	seize

Exercise: Point 1

Write *C* if the word is spelled correctly; if it is spelled incorrectly, write the proper spelling in the space provided.

1. preist _____ *priest* _____
2. reign _____
3. reciept _____
4. wieght _____
5. retreive _____
6. die _____
7. peice _____
8. fiegn _____
9. sliegh _____
10. height _____

POINT 2   In putting an additional ending on a word, drop a *final silent e* when the ending begins with a vowel; keep a final silent e when the ending begins with a consonant.

Endings Beginning with Vowels	Endings Beginning with Consonants
-ing	-ly
-ure	-ment
-ion	-ness
-ance	-ty
-able	-ful
-ed	-less
-ish	

1. Drop the *e* when the ending begins with a vowel:

love + ing = loving
please + ure = pleasure

recreate + ion = recreation
resemble + ance = resemblance
move + able = movable
scare + ed = scared
peeve + ish = peevish

2. Keep the *e* when the ending begins with consonant:

like + ly = likely
arrange + ment = arrangement
white + ness = whiteness
nine + ty = ninety
hope + ful = hopeful
care + less = careless

There are, however, some exceptions to this rule. As always, it is wise to check with a dictionary. The exceptions:

notice + able = noticeable
change + able = changeable
dye + ing = dyeing (This differs from die + ing = dying.)
awe + ful = awful
true + ly = truly

Exercise: Point 2

Form each of the following words.

1. entire + ly = _____ *entirely* _____

2. come + ing = _____

3. improve + ment = _____

4. guide + ance = _____

5. love + less = _____

6. smoke + ed = _____

7. safe + ty = _____

8. like + able = _____

9. use + ful = _____

10. complete + ion = _____

Review Exercise: Points 1 and 2

All the following sentences contain spelling errors. Rewrite the sentences, correcting the errors, in the space provided.

1. Fernando wieghs 165 pounds.

   Fernando weighs 165 pounds.

2. You will need a stepladder to paint that cieling.

   _____

3. Your pleasure is my pleaseure.

   _____

4. Gail bears a great likness to her mother.

   _____

5. We expressed our condoleences at the funeral.

   _____

6. The hobo scrambled aboard the frieght train.

   _____

7. She always speaks sincerly about the most delicate of issues.

   _____

8. This is one wierd party!

   _____

9. I was truely amazed at the feats the sword-swallower performed.

   _____

10. One pays a price for being fameous.

    _____

A letter that behaves a bit differently from most others is *y*. The following rules will cover most situations involving this letter.

POINT 3   Change *y* to *i* when it is preceded by a consonant and followed by any letter other than *i*.

try + ed = tried	*but* try + ing = trying
greasy + er = greasier	forty + ish = fortyish
merry + ly = merrily	
plenty + ful = plentiful	
penny + less = penniless	

Exception: In most cases, change *y* to *ie* when it is preceded by a consonant and followed by the ending -*s.*

    try + s = tries
    baby + s = babies
    hurry + s = hurries

Do not change *y* when it is preceded by a vowel.

    stay + s = stays
    play + ed = played
    enjoy + able = enjoyable

Exceptions: a few common words:

    day + ly = daily
    gay + ly = gaily

Exercise: Point 3

Form each of the following words by using the rules you have learned in this step.

1. gully + s = _____ *gullies* _____

2. worry + ed = _____

3. happy + ness = _____

4. repay + ing = _____

5. attorney + s = _____

6. stray + ed = _____

7. fry + ing = _____

8. necessary + ly = _____

9. apply + ed = _____

10. lonely + est = _____

POINT 4   Add -*s* to form the plural of most nouns; add -*es* when the plural has an extra syllable, unless the singular ends in a silent e.

Same Number of Syllables

Singular	*Plural*
step	steps
picture	pictures

Singular	*Plural*
radio	radios
key	keys
flower	flowers
boy	boys

Note that all these examples have been changed from singular to plural merely by adding -*s*.

Most words that have an extra syllable in the plural are words in which the singular form ends in an *s*-like sound.

Extra Syllable in Plural

Singular	*Plural*
bush	bushes
fox	foxes
mattress	mattresses
spice	spices

Note that all these examples have been changed from singular to plural by adding -*es*, except the last, which already has a silent *e* in the singular.

Some words, such as *tomato* and *potato*, do not follow the rule. The plural forms of these words are *tomatoes* and *potatoes*. As always, it is a good idea to check with a dictionary when you are in doubt.

Certain other nouns do not follow a regular pattern in changing from singular to plural. It is wise to memorize the following list of common irregular plural nouns, but you should also remember to consult the dictionary whenever you have a question about how to use a word.

Singular	*Plural*
wife	wives
life	lives
knife	knives
man	men
woman	women
crisis	crises

Exercise: Point 4

Form the plurals of the following words by adding -*s* or -*es*.

1. girl _____ *girls* _____

2. typewriter _____

3. church _____

4. trace _____

5. cigar _____

6. apartment _____

7. porch _____

8. bus _____

9. ache _____

10. tax _____

Review Exercise: Points 1–4

All the following sentences contain spelling errors. Rewrite the sentences, correcting the errors, in the space provided.

1. Norman was curseing his fate.

   Norman was cursing his fate.

2. I have already applyed to three graduate schools.

   _____

3. I'm looking for a peice of the action.

   _____

4. His whole apartment is lighted by gas lampes.

   _____

5. There are three different styles of couchs to choose from.

   _____

6. That is a great wieght off my shoulders.

   _____

7. We are looking ahead hopfully to the next election.

   _____

8. Richard is pursueing a new career.

   _____

9. Honey, you are my shineing star.

   _____

10. This sandwich is just aweful.

   _____

POINT 5   Double a *final single consonant* before an ending beginning with a vowel when *both* of the following occur: (1) a single vowel precedes the consonant, *and* (2) the accent is on the last syllable.

hop + ing = hopping
Final single consonant?	*p*
Single vowel precedes consonant?	*o*
Ending beginning with a vowel?	*i*
Accent on last syllable?	*only one syllable*

omit + ed = omitted
Final single consonant?	*t*
Single vowel precedes consonant?	*i*
Ending beginning with a vowel?	*e*
Accent on last syllable?	*yes*

labor + ing = laboring
Final single consonant?	*r*
Single vowel precedes consonant?	*o*
Ending beginning with a vowel?	*i*
Accent on last syllable?	*no*

Since the accent is not on the last syllable in *labor,* we do not double the *r* to form laboring.

keep + ing = keeping
Final single consonant?	*p*
Single vowel precedes consonant?	*no*
Ending beginning with a vowel?	*i*
Accent on last syllable?	*only one*

Since *keep* does not meet one of the requirements (it has *two* vowels preceding the final consonant), we do not double the *p* to form *keeping.*

walk + ed = walked

Can you tell why this word is not spelled *walkked?*

Exercise: Point 5

Form each of the following words by using the rules you have learned in Point 5.

1. control + ed = _____ *controlled* _____

2. admit + ing = _____

3. begin + ing = _____

4. small + est = _____

5. scream + ing = _____

6. develop + ed = _____

7. suffer + ing = _____

8. fish + ing = _____

9. puff + ed = _____

10. stir + ing = _____

Review Exercise: Points 1–5

All the following sentences contain spelling errors. Rewrite the sentences, correcting the errors, in the space provided.

1. This is a chapter about speling.

   This is a chapter about spelling.

2. I am admiting no fault whatsoever.

   _____

3. We visited Ripley's Beleive it or Not Museum.

   _____

4. Tomorrow we will go horseback rideing.

   _____

5. I have resistted greater temptations in the past.

   _____

6. Those bananas are roting!

   _____

7. Come to this office immediately!

   _____

8. This corner is the busyest one in Boston.

   _____

9. Everyone benefitted by his generosity.

   _____

10. All waiters should report to the dineing room.

HOW TO AVOID COMMON SPELLING ERRORS

1. Remember the rules for using *ie* or *ei*.
2. Keep in mind the rules for dropping final letters when you add an ending to a word.
3. Remember that you may need to change *y* to *i* or *ie* when adding an ending.
4. Be sure you know whether to add *-s* or *-es* to change a word from singular to plural, *and use your dictionary!*

Words Frequently Misspelled

1. absence	35. experience	68. performance
2. accept	36. extremely	69. possess
3. across	37. familiar	70. possible
4. address	38. finally	71. preferred
5. almost	39. foreign	72. prejudice
6. already	40. forty	73. preparation
7. always	41. friend	74. pressure
8. among	42. government	75. privilege
9. answer	43. guarantee	76. probably
10. athlete	44. immediately	77. professor
11. beginning	45. independence	78. realize
12. business	46. independent	79. recommend
13. college	47. intelligence	80. relieve
14. coming	48. interest	81. religious
15. committee	49. interfere	82. repetition
16. competition	50. judgment	83. rhythm
17. counselor	51. knowledge	84. ridiculous
18. criticism	52. laboratory	85. sacrifice
19. criticize	53. length	86. safety
20. decision	54. library	87. scene
21. definite	55. license	88. schedule
22. definition	56. marriage	89. science
23. describe	57. mathematics	90. separate
24. description	58. meant	91. similar
25. desperate	59. necessary	92. sophomore
26. discipline	60. ninety	93. straight
27. divide	61. ninth	94. succeed
28. eighth	62. occasionally	95. surprise
29. eliminate	63. occur	96. temperature
30. embarrassed	64. opinion	97. together
31. escape	65. opportunity	98. tragedy
32. etc.	66. paid	99. unusual
33. exaggerate	67. particular	100. Wednesday
34. excellent		

Chapter Review

I. Write *C* if the word is spelled correctly. If it is misspelled, rewrite it correctly in the space provided.

1. radioes _____

2. arrangeing _____

3. location _____

4. fortyeth _____

5. controllable _____

6. blotted _____

7. developed _____

8. recieve _____

9. unstoppable _____

10. bushs _____

11. paiing _____

12. greif _____

13. eightyeth _____

14. livly _____

15. trying _____

16. despairring _____

17. ladderes _____

18. associateion _____

19. liesure _____

20. entirety _____

II. Form the following words by using the rules you have learned in this chapter.

1. get + ing = _____

2. guide + ing = _____

3. satisfy + ed = _____

4. spy + s = _____

5. run + ing = _____

6. seize + ure = _____

7. party + ing = _____

8. relieve + ed = _____

9. like + ness = _____

10. hope + less = _____

11. pray + ing = _____

12. time + ed = _____

13. spite + ful = _____

14. toy + ing = _____

15. guide + ance = _____

16. manage + ed = _____

17. marry + ed = _____

18. pit + ed = _____

19. chop + ed = _____

20. pity + able = _____

III. Form the plurals of the following singular nouns:

1. goat _____

2. baby _____

3. guitar _____

4. envelope _____

5. woe _____

6. tree _____

7. history _____

8. taco _____

9. church _____

10. glass _____

IV. Circle the correctly spelled word given in the parentheses.

1. Can't you accept (criticism, critisism)?

2. She gets (embarassed, embarrassed) when she drops something.

3. Try to avoid (carless, careless) spelling errors.

4. It (pays, payes) to shop at Arthur's.

5. You are not a very (friendly, freindly) person.

6. His temper is (uncontrolable, uncontrollable).

7. It is your (privilige, privilege), not your right!

8. The students (seized, siezed) the administration building.

9. I enjoyed my (sophomore, sophmore) year best of all.

10. She is (emploied, employed) by Warren's Grocery.

V. All the following sentences contain spelling errors. Rewrite the sentences, correcting the errors, in the space provided.

1. Ken sliped on the ice and broke his ankle.

_____

2. My girlfriend spendes too much time studying.

_____

3. The lamp broke into hundreds of peices.

_____

4. Forget it; it is niether my business nor yours.

_____

5. I'll be fliing high if I get good news.

_____

6. The administration has adoptted a new policy on energy.

_____

7. Camping in Vermont was such a pleaseure.

_____

8. She is the fairest and lovliest child I know.

_____

9. The criminal was sentenced to ninty years in prison.

———————————————————————————————

10. You have embarased me with your remark.

———————————————————————————————

11. Church and state must be separated.

———————————————————————————————

12. "Discribe the man you saw," said the detective.

———————————————————————————————

13. This is your third abcence from class this week.

———————————————————————————————

14. I admited my secret passion.

———————————————————————————————

15. Welcome to the nieghborhood!

———————————————————————————————

16. The weather around here is so changable.

———————————————————————————————

17. We have gone to four partys allready this week.

———————————————————————————————

18. I can't stand shoping for shoes.

———————————————————————————————

19. The stringes are broken and have to be replaced.

———————————————————————————————

20. I am a very happyly married man.

———————————————————————————————

VI. Rewrite the following passages, correcting any misspelled words.

Late summer is truely a lovly time of the year. After being fryed by the heat and drenchhed by humidity, many people feel that it is a great releif to expirience the cool evenings that promise the comming of autumn. As the cool weather returnes, people seem to regain much of the energy that they had lost dureing the hot and stickey monthes of July and August. There are all kinds of outdoor activityes: baseball gams, barbecus, campfirs. It is as if the cool breezs bring with them a fresh and new feeling for life.

There is probaly no greater thrill or privelege than watching the birth of your own child. Manny of my freinds have acepted the responsability of takeing part in the proces, particularly by acting as an asistant to the doctor. These husbands have helped thier wifes with breathing and relaxashun techniques. Above all, they get the definate plesure of witnesing what is surly the most amazing act of all.

16

Possessives and Contractions

A useful little mark that handles two quite different chores in modern-day English is the *apostrophe* ('). It marks the place where letters have been dropped out of a word to form a *contraction*, and it also serves along with *s* to show *possession*. (A few centuries ago, these two uses were more closely related than they are now. We won't go into that, though.)

The value of both contractions and possessives is that they let us express things more quickly and in fewer words than we could without them. We say *I'll* instead of *I will*, *they haven't* instead of *they have not*, and *Ed's book* instead of *the book of Ed*.

There are a few things you need to keep in mind, however, in using these forms. One is that apostrophes are rather easily misplaced, and putting one in the wrong spot can sometimes change the meaning of the word. So can leaving out an apostrophe. *We'll* has quite another meaning than *well*. And if I write, *the boy's doughnut*, we have one boy and one doughnut—a reasonable situation. But if I write, *the boys' doughnut*, we have several boys and one doughnut. In this situation, there could be quite an argument if the boys are hungry!

The other thing to be careful about is that some contractions sound just like some possessive words, but they aren't spelled the same. So in writing, it's important to keep in mind what kind of a word you're using.

The rules about possessives and contractions are fairly simple. If you master them, you will be able to use these forms competently in your writing.

POINT 1   To determine ownership, ask, "Who owns what?"

> the radio of Cindy

To determine ownership, we ask *who owns what*. Cindy owns the radio.

the car of George

Who owns what? George owns the car.

friends of mine

Since one doesn't really *own* friends, we can ask, "Who has what?" The answer: "I have friends."

Do not get confused: The radio does not own Cindy; the car does not own George, friends do not have me.

Exercise: Point 1

For each of the following phrases, determine who owns what.

1. the house of mine _____ *I own the house.* _____

2. The whistle of the police officer _____

3. the leotard of the dancer _____

4. the headlights of the car _____

5. the newspaper of my father _____

6. the credit card of my mother _____

7. the ring of my wife _____

8. the power of the engine _____

9. the dolls of my baby sister _____

10. the fountain pen of Aretha _____

POINT 2 Use -'s to form the possessive of most singular nouns.

Cindy owns the radio.

Once we have determined that Cindy owns the radio, we can apply the *'s rule*. The sentence may be rewritten as follows:

It is Cindy's radio.

Cindy is a noun that does not end in *-s*. Therefore, we can add *-'s* to *Cindy*, making *Cindy's*. *Cindy's* is the possessive form of the noun.

The car belongs to George.

may be rewritten

It is George's car.

Here are some more examples:

> the hairstyle of my sister

becomes

> my sister's hairstyle

> the power of the engine

becomes

> the engine's power

Note: In these examples *Cindy, George, sister,* and *engine* are all singular nouns. For a review of the terms *singular* and *plural,* turn to Chapter 1, Point 1.

Exercise: Point 2

Change these phrases into possessives by using *-'s.*

1. the idea of my mother _____ *my mother's idea* _____

2. the plants of Judy _____

3. the copy machine of the library _____

4. the choice of the people _____

5. the job of the detective _____

6. the mail of the camper _____

7. the pants of Sam _____

8. the money of the bookie _____

9. the rattle of the baby _____

10. the paper route of the boy _____

POINT 3   Use only an apostrophe to form the possessive of plural nouns ending in -s.

> the boat of the boys

This phrase has a noun ending in *-s.* The boat belongs to the boys. To form the possessive, we need only add an apostrophe after the noun we wish to make possessive. The phrase may be rewritten as follows:

> the boys' boat

Note that the possessive is not written *boys's*. In this phrase, there is more than one boy.

It is *extremely important* to be able to distinguish the following:

boy
boy's (belonging to one boy)
boys
boys' (belonging to more than one boy)

Here are some more examples:

clothing for girls	girls' clothing
the noise of the cars	cars' noise
the sound of the bells	bells' sound

Note that all the preceding examples have words that end in *-s*. An exception to this rule is that if a *singular* word ending in *-s* has only *one syllable*, you should use *-'s* to form the possessive.

the dog of Charles	Charles' dog
the desk of the boss	the boss's desk

Be aware, also, of plural nouns that do not end in *-s*. These words, such as *men*, *women*, and *children*, are made possessive by adding *'s* to the end.

the center for children	the children's center
clothing for women	women's clothing

Exercise: Point 3

Change these phrases into possessives by adding an apostrophe.

1. the crying of the babies _____*the babies' crying*_____

2. the home town of my cousins _____

3. the chairs of the barbers _____

4. the slant of the rooftops _____

5. the smell of the cigars _____

6. the duration of the exhibits _____

7. the offices of the professors _____

8. the running shoes of the men _____

9. the salaries of the players _____

10. the legs of the tables _____

Review Exercise: Points 1–3

Rewrite the following sentences, adding apostrophes where necessary.

1. Johns mother belongs to the Professional Womens Club.

   John's mother belongs to the Professional Women's Club.

2. Have you read Marks essay on sexual freedom?

   _____

3. The womens marathon is the next event.

   _____

4. Is this Carlos raincoat?

   _____

5. Have you ever been to a worlds fair?

   _____

6. The publishers wanted to buy Marthas manuscript.

   _____

7. One of Bostons popular meeting places is the Common.

   _____

8. Mr. Dickens daughter will be married next week.

   _____

9. The managers lineup card was taped to the dugout wall.

   _____

10. The Yankees home field is Yankee Stadium.

   _____

Before going on, we might note a common kind of expression that is not exactly a possessive but behaves just like one:

> I will be there in less than an hour's time.

(that is, in time *of* less than an hour, or a time *lasting* less than an hour). Since *an hour* is singular, this expression behaves just like a singular possessive.

> She took a three weeks' vacation.

Three weeks is plural, so the expression behaves like a plural possessive.

| **POINT 4**   **Be sure to distinguish between plurals and possessives.**

Remember, plural refers to number, and specifically, to more than one. Plural words do not necessarily show ownership.

Possessives may, of course, be either singular or plural. Do not be tempted to "overcorrect" by adding apostrophes to plurals as well as possessives.

Plural	**Possessive**
boys (more than one boy)	boys' (belonging to more than one boy)
girls (more than one girl)	girls' (belonging to more than one girl)
boats (more than one boat)	boats' (belonging to more than one boat)

The following chart may help you understand the relationships among singular, plural, and possessive forms.

Singular	*Singular Possessive*	*Plural*	*Plural Possessive*
tree	tree's	trees	trees'
girl	girl's	girls	girls'
athlete	athlete's	athletes	athletes'
man	man's	men	men's
child	child's	children	children's
year	year's	years	years'

Can you use each of these different forms in a sentence?

Exercise: Point 4

Circle the correct word given in the parentheses.

1. Keep those (animals, animals') in their cages.

2. We visited both (senators, senators') offices.

3. What are the (titles, titles') of your courses?

4. What are your (courses, courses') titles?

5. Those rotted (trees, trees') will have to go.

6. They are my (parents, parents') parents.

7. The scientist clipped those (bugs, bugs') wings.

8. Two (candles, candles') provide all the light in this room.

9. They are the (stars, stars') of the show.

10. They are the (shows, show's) stars.

POINT 5   Do not use an apostrophe with possessive modifiers or pronouns.

Possessive *modifiers* come *before* a noun and describe it. They are

my	our	whose
your	your	
his, her, its	their	

Note that none of these words takes an apostrophe. Possession is built into them.

This is my dog.	*never*	This is my's dog.
This is your dog.	*never*	This is your's dog.
This is his dog.	*never*	This is his' dog.
This is her dog.	*never*	This is her's dog.
Whose dog is this?	*never*	Whose' dog is this?

Possessive *pronouns* are used when the possessive word is *separated from* the name of the thing possessed. They are

mine	ours	whose
yours	yours	
his, hers	theirs	

Note that these words are very similar to the possessive modifiers. Be careful not to get them confused. Again, none of them takes an apostrophe.

The magazine is ours.	*never*	The magazine is our's.
The magazine is yours.	*never*	The magazine is your's.
The magazine is hers.	*never*	The magazine is her's.
Whose is this magazine?	*never*	Whose' is this magazine?

Possessive words are used to take the place of possessives formed from nouns. Therefore, the sentence

> **Joe's** teacher is always late for class.

may be changed to

> **His** teacher is always late for class.

Likewise, the sentence

> I ran into a friend of Peggy's.

may be changed to

> I ran into a friend of hers.

Be very careful when using the possessive words *its, whose, your,* and *their*. Always remember that these words are used strictly to show possession.

> The stereo has lost **its** power.

The power "belongs" to the stereo.

> **Whose** apartment is this?

The apartment belongs to someone.

This is **your** life.

The life belongs to you.

The kids are brushing **their** teeth.

The teeth belong to them.

Exercise: Point 5

Fill in the blank with an appropriate possessive modifer or pronoun.

1. It is _____*his*_____ decision to make.

2. We will have to change _____ approach.

3. That sewing machine is _____ .

4. The storm had taken _____ toll.

5. _____ beautiful garden is this?

6. What can I do to make you change _____ mind?

7. They are taking _____ children to the ballet.

8. I bought it, so it is _____ .

9. I must be losing _____ mind.

10. I am sorry, sir, but that coat is not _____ ;

    it is _____ .

Review Exercise: Points 1–5

Rewrite the following sentences, correcting any errors with possessives.

1. The childrens play group meets once a week.
   The children's play group meets once a week.

2. Mr. Jones car needs to be washed.

   _____

3. Great writers messages are sometimes misunderstood.

   _____

4. That seat is not yours'; it is mine.

   _____

5. The superintendents apartment was vandalized last night.

_____

6. Now it is someone elses game to win or lose.

_____

7. Whose' ten-speed bicycle are you using?

_____

8. The teachers union supported the strike.

_____

9. Do you understand the reasons' for my decision?

_____

10. The river overflowed it's banks.

_____

POINT 6 **A contraction (two words condensed into one) is formed by replacing a letter (or group of letters) with an apostrophe.**

When forming a contraction, you should make sure that the apostrophe goes in the exact place where the letter would have been.

I am   I'm

Here the apostrophe takes the place of _a_.

you are	you're	I would	I'd
he is	he's	he would	he'd
she is	she's	they would	they'd
it is	it's	are not	aren't
we are	we're	cannot	can't
you are	you're	does not	doesn't
they are	they're	do not	don't
there is	there's	have not	haven't
he has	he's	should not	shouldn't
she has	she's	could not	couldn't
they have	they've	would not	wouldn't
I will	I'll	let us	let's
she will	she'll	where is	where's
he will	he'll	will not	won't
I had	I'd	they had	they'd
he had	he'd		

Remember *won't* in particular. It is an exception to the rule for forming contractions.

Contractions are used frequently in everyday speech. It is usually better *not* to use them in writing, unless you want to sound "chatty." Although they are little more than time and space savers, it is important to use them correctly if you use them at all.

Note: Ain't is sometimes heard as a contraction of several expressions—*am not, is not, are not, has not, have not.* It should *not* be used in writing, except in direct quotations.

Exercise: Point 6

Rewrite the following sentences, changing the underlined words into contractions.

1. He <u>has</u> never been to summer camp before.

   He's never been to summer camp before.

2. I <u>will</u> buy the chips if <u>you will</u> make the dip.

   _____

3. They <u>would</u> have arrived on time if they <u>did</u> <u>not</u> have a balky car.

   _____

4. I <u>am</u> sorry, but this time <u>it</u> <u>is</u> not my fault.

   _____

5. She <u>will</u> never know what hit her.

   _____

6. I <u>would</u> have chosen a different color.

   _____

7. Let <u>us</u> work together for a change.

   _____

8. He <u>would</u> <u>not</u> mind if you combed his hair with a rake.

   _____

9. I <u>have</u> <u>not</u> been to the dentist in three years.

   _____

10. Patti <u>does</u> <u>not</u> plan to be an Avon lady all her life.

   _____

POINT 7   Do not confuse contractions with possessives.

There is an important difference between

Possessive		Contraction
your	and	you're
its	and	it's
their	and	they're
whose	and	who's

your means *belonging to you*
you're means *you are*

its means *belonging to it*
it's means *it is*

their means *belonging to them*
they're means *they are*

whose means *belonging to whom*
who's means *who is*

These pairs of words look similar and sound exactly alike. Make sure you have a reason for using one or the other in a sentence. Always determine whether you want a contraction or a possessive.

Exercise: Point 7

Circle the correct word given in the parentheses.

1. (Its, (It's)) a beautiful day for a drive in the country.

2. (Whose, Who's) bright idea was that?

3. This is (your, you're) problem, not mine.

4. Do you approve of the way they raise (their, they're) children?

5. My soda has lost (it's, its) fizz.

6. (Whose, Who's) the leader of the local Democratic organization?

7. (Your, You're) a good man, Charlie Brown.

8. (Their, They're) never going to be able to straighten out (their, they're) finances.

9. (Its, It's) a sure bet!

10. (Whose, Who's) going to pay for all this damage?

Review Exercise: Points 1–7

Rewrite the following sentences, adding apostrophes where necessary.

1. Were hoping that shell pass her English exam.

   We're hoping that she'll pass her English exam.

2. Its Russ car, and hell be angry if you drive it.

   _____

3. The days work isnt done yet.

   _____

4. The orchestras performance wasnt up to par.

   _____

5. Is the responsibility yours or Tims?

   _____

6. Lately weve been keeping a hawks eye on our diets.

   _____

7. That actress lines should be rewritten.

   _____

8. Thats Ernies problem, not mine.

   _____

9. Rays motorcycle isnt running smoothly these days.

   _____

10. Its never too late to say youre sorry.

    _____

HOW TO AVOID MISTAKES IN POSSESSIVES

1. In forming a possessive from a noun, think of the rules for deciding whether to add -' or -'s
2. Never use an apostrophe with a possessive modifier or pronoun.

HOW TO AVOID MISTAKES IN CONTRACTIONS

> 1. Note where you have removed letters to form the contraction, and be sure to put the apostrophe exactly there.
> 2. Be careful not to confuse contractions with possessives that sound the same.

Chapter Review

I. Write *C* if the sentence is correct as it stands or *X* if it contains an error with possessives or contractions.

_____ 1. He'll never make it to the finals.

_____ 2. Its a hard rain that's going to fall.

_____ 3. The coachs' son is the star of the team.

_____ 4. That parrot is Marthas pride and joy.

_____ 5. Glenn's teacher is from India.

_____ 6. I saw it in my minds eye.

_____ 7. They'll be arriving any minute now.

_____ 8. We each danced with the other's wife.

_____ 9. Their never going to believe this!

_____ 10. Youll never guess whom I saw today.

II. Fill in the blank with a noun that shows possession.

1. It belongs to Sally; it is _____

2. It belongs to Mr. Ross; it is _____

3. It belongs to Bill; it is _____

4. It belongs to my mother; it is _____

5. It belongs to Aunt Betty; it is _____

6. It belongs to the company; it is _____

7. It belongs to my son; it is _____

8. It belongs to your friend; it is _____

9. It belongs to the team; it is _____

10. It belongs to Chris; it is _____

III. Fill in the blank with a possessive modifier or pronoun.

    1. It belongs to Shirley; it is _____

    2. It belongs to us; it is _____

    3. It belongs to me; it is _____

    4. It belongs to Sam; it is _____

    5. It belongs to you; it is _____

    6. It belongs to them; it is _____ property.

    7. It belongs to me; it is _____ property.

    8. It belongs to them; it is_____

    9. It belongs to you; it is _____ property.

    10. I don't know whom it belongs to; _____ is it?

IV. Circle the correct word given in the parentheses.

    1. (Its, It's) a sin to tell a lie.

    2. It is (their, they're) way of showing affection.

    3. (Your, You're) the most beautiful woman I've ever seen.

    4. I am the one (who's whose) paper you read.

    5. The airplane is in trouble; (its, it's) wing has caught fire.

    6. (Their, They're) never going to believe this back in Muncie.

    7. He has been imitating (your, you're) style for some time.

    8. Guess (whose, who's) coming to dinner.

    9. It is the (captains, captain's) decision to make.

    10. (Whose, Who's) going to clean it up?

V. Put apostrophes where necessary in the following sentences.

    1. Womens wear is on the second floor.

    2. Youre a very stylish dresser.

    3. My sisters makeup kit is overflowing.

    4. That artists style is certainly unique.

    5. Marcus friend is staying with him for the summer.

6. Those books are Bobbys and mine.

7. Youre so pretty that you could be anyones girlfriend.

8. Lately I've grown close to Mikes wife.

9. My fathers business takes him to the Orient twice a year.

10. Did you heed the gurus advice?

11. Were learning the basic skills of writing.

12. The horse trotted to the winners circle.

13. The fireworks display was very exciting.

14. Your brothers van has a flat tire.

15. Lenins ideas do not appeal to everyone.

16. Those babies are twins!

17. The doctors office is closed today.

18. What is Brians idea of a good time?

19. Whos going to pay the check?

20. Lets go to the movies.

VI. All the following sentences contain errors in the use of possessives or contractions. Rewrite the sentences, correcting the errors, in the space provided.

1. It's your's, so do with it as you please.

   _____

2. I think its never going to stop raining.

   _____

3. She's minding someone elses shop today.

   _____

4. It was my employers idea to give me a raise.

   _____

5. Weve visited Marjories beach house twice before.

   _____

6. I met you're brother at the station.

   _____

7. Our familys motto is "Live and let live."

   _____

8. The musicians trumpet has been stolen.

   _____

9. The banks new vault is burglar-proof.

   _____

10. Those criminals records show they're history.

    _____

11. Lead me to the mens room, please.

    _____

12. I borrowed my parents car.

    _____

13. Wheres the beef?

    _____

14. Josephs piano needs to be tuned.

    _____

15. The sisters husbands have lunch together every Monday.

    _____

16. Girls haircuts are generally quite attractive.

    _____

17. James new car has an AM-FM radio.

    _____

18. The employees lunchroom is located downstairs.

    _____

19. My aunts tapioca pudding is the best in the world.

    _____

20. Dont try telling me that you're way is better.

    _____

VII. Rewrite the following passages, correcting any errors in the use of possessives or contractions.

Ella Fitzgeralds style of singing is one of the most exciting I have ever heard. Without any formal training in music, shes managed to develop her voice to it's full potential. Whose ever going to dispute the statement that her scat singing makes her voice sound like a musical instrument? Ellas versions of Cole Porters songs are particularly moving and beautiful. She is able to understand the songs so well, and get so much feeling into Porters lyric's that listening to her performances becomes one of lifes great pleasures.

Ive never been one to keep New Years resolutions. Its always been easy enough for me to promise to give up mine bad habits, but I just dont seem to keep my promises. Once, the day after Id resolved never to smoke cigarettes again, my wife found a pack around and yelled, "Who's are these?" "Their mine," I answered sheepishly. Its a sure bet Ill resolve to quit again this year, but unless I get serious, Im sure my wifes advice "Your never serious about something until your serious about it" will once again prove true.

Summary of Points Covered

CHAPTER 1

Points

1. Identify the subject of the sentence by asking *who* or *what* is doing something (or being something).
2. A subject may be a *noun*.
3. A subject may be a *pronoun*.
4. A subject may be an *-ing* word.
5. A subject may consist of more than one word.
6. A subject may appear anywhere in the sentence.
7. The subject is never within a phrase that begins with such words as *on, in, of, before, behind, near*.

CHAPTER 2

Points

1. A *verb* is a word (or group of words) used to express action.
2. The *tense* of a verb shows the time when the action happened—past, present, or future. Many verbs can be changed from the present tense to the past tense by adding *-d* or *-ed* to the end.
3. A *linking verb* is used to link the subject to a descriptive word in the sentence or to another noun.
4. Verbs ending in *-ing* require another verb (often some form of the verb *to be*) before them.
5. Some verbs are *irregular*. They do not follow a set pattern when they change tenses.
6. The *to* form of a verb is incomplete, and needs another verb before it.
7. Be sure to identify the *complete verb* in a sentence.
8. A sentence may contain two or more verbs.

CHAPTER 3

Points

1. Use singular verbs with singular subjects, and plural verbs with plural subjects.
2. When it is used as a subject, a pronoun must agree with the verb.
3. When a subject is compound (includes two or more elements), make sure it agrees with the verb.
   a. Compound subjects joined by *and* take plural verbs.
   b. Compound subjects joined by *or* or *nor* take singular verbs when both subjects are singular.
   c. When a singular subject is joined to a plural subject by *or* or *nor*, the verb agrees with the subject closer to the verb.
4. Some indefinite pronouns are singular and take singular verbs.
5. Some indefinite pronouns are plural and take plural verbs.
6. Singular subjects followed by phrases that describe the subject take singular verbs; plural subjects take plural verbs. Subjects are sometimes followed by phrases beginning with *with, as well as, together with, including,* and so forth.
7. A collective noun (group word) takes a singular verb when the group is referred to as a single unit; it takes a plural verb when the members of the group are being considered as a set of individuals.
8. When the verb comes before the subject of the sentence, it is especially important to identify the subject and make the verb agree with it.
9. Words or names that are plural in form but singular in meaning take a singular verb.

CHAPTER 4

Points

1. Make sure every sentence has a subject and a verb.
2. Watch out for *-ing* words. No word ending in *-ing* can ever be the complete verb of a sentence.
3. A group of words containing a subject and a verb is called a *clause.*
4. When a dependent clause comes at the beginning of a sentence, it is followed by a *comma.* However, if the independent clause comes first, you may or may not need a comma.
5. Every sentence must have at least one independent clause.
6. Avoid other common types of fragments, such as the "list" type.

CHAPTER 5

Points

1. Connect two independent clauses with a comma *plus* one of the connecting words: *and, but, for, or, nor, yet, so.*
2. Separate two independent clauses with a semicolon. In addition, connecting words such as *however, therefore, consequently, nevertheless, likewise, besides, also, then,* and *furthermore* may be used after the semicolon.
3. Make the two independent clauses into two sentences by using a period, a question mark, or an exclamation point.
4. Change one of the independent clauses into a dependent clause.

CHAPTER 6

Points

1. A *modifier* is a word (or group of words) that describes or explains another word (or group of words) in a sentence.
2. Place a modifier as close as possible to the word it modifies.
3. When dealing with modifiers, ask yourself, *what goes with what?*
4. Be sure that words such as *almost, even, hardly, just, merely, only, nearly,* and *scarcely* refer clearly to the words they modify.
5. Avoid placing a modifier between two words when its explanation can apply to either word.

CHAPTER 7

Points

1. A modifier is said to be *dangling* when there is no word in the sentence for it to modify.
2. When a sentence begins with *a group of words introduced by an -ing word*, the person or thing performing the action (the subject) should be identified right after the *-ing* phrase.
3. Put the modifier as close as possible to the word it explains.
4. Sometimes you can turn a dangling modifier into a dependent clause.
5. A group of words that has an *-ing word somewhere* in it must refer clearly to the subject of the sentence.
6. Modifiers beginning with a *to* form of a verb must refer clearly to the word they modify.

CHAPTER 8

Points

1. A pronoun may be used as the subject of a sentence.
2. A pronoun may be used as the *object* of a verb in a sentence.
3. Often a sentence contains both a noun and a pronoun that refers to the noun. To decide whether to use a subject pronoun or an object pronoun, look at the pronoun's relation to *its own verb*.
4. When a sentence contains two or more nouns, place the pronoun as close as possible to the noun it refers to, and make sure the reference is clear.
5. Be sure that pronouns refer to a single noun and not to a whole idea.
6. Be sure that a pronoun has a word, and not an unexpressed idea, to refer to.

CHAPTER 9

Points

1. When elements are parallel in thought, use parallel forms to express them.
2. Balance a noun with a noun, a verb with a verb, a modifier with a modifier, and so on.
3. Use parallel constructions for words joined by such connectors as *and, but, nor, or.*
4. Use parallel structure with such constructions as *either . . . or, neither . . . nor, not . . . but, not only . . . but also, both . . . and.*
5. Make sure that *parallel groups of words* in a sentence have parallel structure.

CHAPTER 10

Points

1. *Number* refers to the number of units referred to. In English grammar, there are only two numbers: singular and plural.
2. Be sure to keep number consistent throughout a sentence.
3. There are only three *persons* in English grammar. Each person may be either singular or plural.
4. Be sure to keep person consistent throughout a sentence.
5. Be sure to keep *tense* consistent throughout a sentence.

CHAPTER 11

Points

1. Use a *period* at the end of a sentence that makes a statement.
2. Use a period after an abbreviation.
3. Use a *question mark* after a direct question.
4. Use an *exclamation point* after an expression or statement that shows strong feeling.
5. Use *quotation marks* to enclose the exact words of a speaker or writer.
6. a. Periods and commas are always placed *inside* quotation marks.
   b. Question marks and exclamation points are placed *outside* quotation marks except when the quotation itself is a direct question or an exclamation.
   c. Semicolons and colons are placed outside the closing quotation marks.
7. Use quotation marks to enclose the titles of short works such as a story, essay, short poem, or song. For longer works, such as novels, plays, movies, newspapers, full-length books, and magazines, use underlining instead of quotation marks.

CHAPTER 12

Points

1. Use a *semicolon* to separate two independent clauses.
2. Do not use a semicolon when two independent clauses are joined by such weak connecting words as *and, but, for, nor, or, so, yet*. However, if the clauses are joined by stronger connecting words such as *also, however, therefore, then, otherwise, nevertheless, moreover*, you should use a semicolon.
3. Use semicolons to separate items in a series when the items (a) have internal punctuation or (b) are long.
4. Use a *colon* to introduce a list following a noun that names the list.
5. Use a colon to set off a list or a statement that is introduced by the words *the following* or *as follows*.

CHAPTER 13

Points

1. Use *commas* to separate three or more items in a series.
2. Use a comma between two independent clauses if they are connected by such words as *and, but, for, or, nor, yet, so*.

3. Use a comma after a long introductory phrase or clause. Use a comma after a short introductory phrase if it is necessary to avoid unclear meaning.
4. Use commas on both sides of a word (or group of words) that interrupts the flow of the sentence.
5. Use commas to set off nonessential material.
6. Use a comma after every item in an address or date.

CHAPTER 14

Points

1. Capitalize the first, last, and important words in a title.
2. Capitalize the names of specific persons, places, languages, nations, and nationalities.
3. Capitalize names of days of the week, months, and holidays; do not capitalize names of the seasons.
4. Capitalize the first word of a direct quotation.
5. Capitalize words of family relationship when they are used as *names*.
6. Capitalize words such as *college, doctor, building*, when they are part of the names of specific people or things.
7. Capitalize events in history, movements, and periods.
8. Capitalize the names of specific school courses, but do not capitalize general words that refer to the courses.

CHAPTER 15

Points

1. Use *i* before *e*
   Except after *c*
   Or when sounded as *a*
   As in n*ei*ghbor or w*ei*gh.
2. In putting an additional ending on a word, drop a *final silent e* when the ending begins with a vowel; keep a final silent *e* when the ending begins with a consonant.
3. Change *y* to *i* when it is preceded by a consonant and followed by any letter other than *i*. Change *y* to *ie* when it is preceded by a consonant and followed by the ending *-s*. Do not change *y* when it is preceded by a vowel.
4. Add *-s* to form the plural of most nouns; add *-es* when the plural has an extra syllable, unless the singular ends in a silent *e*.
5. Double a *final single consonant* before an ending beginning with a vowel when *both* of the following occur: (a) a single vowel precedes the consonant, *and* (b) the accent is on the last syllable.

CHAPTER 16

Points

1. To determine ownership, ask, "Who owns what?"
2. Use *-'s* to form the possessive of *nouns that do not end in -s*.

3. Use only an apostrophe to form the possessive of *nouns ending in -s.*
4. Be sure to distinguish between plurals and possessives.
5. Do not use an apostrophe with possessive modifiers or pronouns.
6. A contraction (two words condensed into one) is formed by replacing a letter (or group of letters) with an apostrophe.
7. Do not confuse contractions with possessives.

Answers to Exercises

PRETEST

I
1. V	6. C	11. V	16. C
2. V	7. V	12. C	17. V
3. S	8. S	13. S	18. V
4. C	9. C	14. C	19. C
5. S	10. V	15. S	20. C

II
1. <u>Jamie</u> is going out for the track team.
2. <u>The Dodgers and the Mets</u> play tonight.
3. <u>Correct grammar</u> is an important aspect of good writing.
4. In the cabana is <u>the rowboat</u>.
5. <u>Jazz</u> is my favorite kind of music.
6. <u>Hans and Lisa</u> bought that car.
7. <u>Organic food</u> is healthful but expensive.
8. <u>Exercising</u> is part of my morning routine.
9. Around the corner fled <u>the stray dog</u>.
10. <u>That hibachi near the garage</u> is broken.

III
1. My father <u>is retiring</u> from business.
2. We <u>have</u> never <u>been</u> to Europe.
3. She <u>grew</u> more and more tired.
4. I never <u>promised</u> you a rose garden.
5. You <u>should be</u> sure to check the oil.
6. Holding down a job <u>is</u> never easy for Luke.
7. I <u>have tried</u> my hardest to succeed.

8. Woodworking <u>requires</u> skill and patience.
9. We <u>spent</u> our paychecks yesterday.
10. I always <u>visit</u> my parents on holidays.

CHAPTER 1

Exercise: Point 1

1. plumber	6. family
2. Doug	7. speakers
3. tree	8. brother
4. motorcycle	9. Fans
5. Lucy	10. store

Another Exercise: Point 1

1. S <u>Sally</u> ran after the bus.
2. S My <u>friend</u> built a new beach house.
3. P <u>Ducks</u> swim in that pond.
4. S The <u>airplane</u> needs to be refueled.
5. S Our <u>daughter</u> gave us a surprise party.
6. S <u>Sam</u> writes extremely well.
7. P The <u>clouds</u> obscured the sun.
8. S <u>Jason</u> sings in the choir.
9. S <u>Ms. Peterson</u> bought a moped.
10. S The <u>snowstorm</u> lasted for hours.

Exercise: Point 2

1. (California) joined the <u>Union</u> in 1850.
2. (Henry) runs a <u>mile</u> every day.
3. (Flowers) grow best in <u>sunlight.</u>
4. (Exercise) strengthens the <u>body.</u>
5. That (boy) joined our <u>club.</u>
6. My (watch) comes from <u>Japan.</u>
7. The (senators) voted on the <u>bill.</u>
8. (Sally) wrote a <u>letter</u> to her <u>member of Congress.</u>
9. (Starvation) worries <u>people</u> all over the <u>world.</u>
10. (Bills) are a <u>part</u> of <u>life.</u>

Review Exercise: Points 1 and 2

Answers to this exercise will vary. Check with your instructor if you need to.

1. Vermont is a state in New England.
2. My mother taught me everything I know.
3. Columbus discovered America.
4. Japan fought against America in World War II.
5. The explorer sailed around the world.
6. Jimmy Carter is a former president.
7. Michael Jackson appeared on television.
8. My uncle is my mother's brother.
9. White rats make good pets.
10. Ms. Kirkpatrick was my favorite teacher.

Exercise: Point 3

1. He is a shrewd businessman.
2. She has just completed college.
3. It does not bother me.
4. We are going to write a song.
5. They make a lot of money.
6. She is buried in Grant's Tomb.
7. It takes time.
8. He surely knows how to water-ski.
9. They sent me birthday cards.
10. They understood each other.

Exercise: Point 4

1. <u>Singing</u> is her chief talent.
2. <u>Driving</u> drives me crazy.
3. <u>Jogging</u> is good exercise.
4. <u>I</u> am losing my patience.
5. <u>I</u> don't like cleaning my apartment.
6. <u>You</u> are finding it difficult to concentrate.
7. <u>Sewing</u> was never her favorite activity.
8. <u>Advertising</u> is a good way to get votes.
9. <u>They</u> always go skiing in January.
10. <u>Cooking</u> is her favorite hobby.

Exercise: Point 5

1. <u>Collecting stamps</u> is my hobby.
2. <u>His sister</u> is an expert pianist.
3. <u>Looking for an apartment</u> is hard work.
4. <u>Herb and Everett</u> are starting a dynamic new business.
5. <u>Choosing a spouse</u> can be confusing.
6. <u>Using common sense</u> is important.
7. <u>Bowling on Wednesdays</u> keeps me sane.
8. <u>Clara's radio</u> needs to be repaired.
9. <u>Jack and Jill</u> went up the hill.
10. <u>A green light</u> means that we may go.

Review Exercise: Points 1–5

Answers to this exercise will vary. Check with your instructor if you need to.

1. Jogging is a good way to get exercise.
2. Cold beers go great with a barbecue.
3. Big cars use a lot of gasoline.
4. Bowling is more fun than watching television.
5. Frank Sinatra is a great singer.
6. Sky-diving is exciting but dangerous.
7. Christmas comes once a year.
8. Baking biscuits makes me remember the good old days.
9. Those players always beat us in tennis.
10. Germany fought against the Allies.

Another Review Exercise: Points 1–5

Answers to this exercise will vary. Check with your instructor if you need to.

1. Practical jokes can get you into trouble.
2. Ms. Murphy is running for mayor.

3. Collecting coins is my hobby.

4. Robert and Richard are twin brothers.

5. Shopping for shoes can give you tired feet.

Exercise: Point 6

1. Around the corner went the <u>motorcycle.</u>

2. In the box seats was the <u>commissioner</u> of baseball.

3. There was a long <u>line</u> at the ticket booth.

4. Here is one <u>way</u> to solve the problem.

5. There is <u>work</u> to be done.

6. Down the ladder came a <u>firefighter</u> with a baby in his arms.

7. There was no <u>way</u> out.

8. Through the train walked the <u>conductor.</u>

9. In town this week is a great new <u>show.</u>

10. There was a <u>sale</u> in the department store today.

Exercise: Point 7

1. program	6. dreaming
2. woman	7. fishermen
3. man	8. teachers
4. weeds	9. calm
5. problem	10. beers

Review Exercise: Points 1–7

1. <u>Melvin</u> wants to study law.

2. <u>Obeying the speed limit</u> helps conserve fuel.

3. <u>He and I</u> will do it together.

4. The <u>switch in the glove compartment</u> opens the trunk.

5. <u>Eating low-calorie foods</u> is one way to lose weight.

6. On the beach is a <u>lighthouse.</u>

7. <u>The stores on Third Street</u> are closed today.

8. There must be <u>something</u> wrong with you.

9. <u>The man in the bullpen</u> will soon come in to pitch.

10. Around the corner is <u>the mailbox.</u>

Chapter Review

I 1. X

2. S <u>Listening</u> to my stereo relaxes me in the evening.

3. S That <u>dog</u> with the floppy ears is mine.

4. X

5. S A <u>collection</u> of rare books is a real treasure.

6. S <u>Ms. Strauss</u> is coming to visit me.

7. X

8. S In the closet is a <u>pillow.</u>

9. S <u>Bob Dylan</u> was a cultural hero of the sixties.

10. S Spring <u>cleaning</u> is a necessary chore.

II 1. A <u>fear of dogs</u> is common to many people.

2. <u>Phyllis</u> travels to Japan with her husband.

3. <u>Going on a picnic</u> is a great way to spend an afternoon.

4. <u>One part of my idea</u> involves you.

5. <u>Home repair</u> might become a lost art.

6. <u>Juggling</u> required good eyesight and coordination.

7. There are three <u>gas stations</u> at that corner.

8. Of all my friends, <u>Chris</u> is the nicest.

9. <u>Blowing my nose</u> unclogs my ears.

10. <u>That leak in the radiator</u> should be fixed.

11. <u>Choosing courses</u> wisely is a student's responsibility.

12. <u>She</u> is the one for me.

13. <u>The filter of an air conditioner</u> should be cleaned regularly.

14. <u>Going to the dentist</u> was a painful experience for me.

15. <u>We</u> all believe his explanation.

16. <u>Repaving the road</u> takes time.

17. <u>Who</u> wrote the textbook?

18. List in space, <u>the astronaut</u> tried to radio Earth.

19. <u>He</u> got a job in the new shopping mall.

20. Over the river, <u>the exploding fireworks</u> shed light.

III Answers to this exercise will vary. Check with your instructor if you need to.

1. Her moped was parked illegally.

2. In the cupboard is a chocolate cake.

3. Insect repellent helps keep the bugs away.

4. Mexico is the country just south of the United States.

5. Her grandparents are coming to see us.

6. My sister is learning how to play tennis.

7. The rear-view mirror has to be adjusted.

8. Weightlifting is one way to stay in shape.

9. Rainy weather keeps people indoors.
10. Spareribs taste great when they are barbecued.
11. The windows were shattered during the storm.
12. Three young men were arrested for drunken driving.
13. Bats come out only at night.
14. Ronald Reagan is president of the United States.
15. In the sink was a huge stack of dirty dishes.
16. Politics can give me a headache.
17. I never want to see you again.
18. Trout fishing is my idea of fun.
19. Geraniums are beautiful house plants.
20. Through the city marched the high school band.

CHAPTER 2

Exercise: Point 1

1. <u>Paul</u> <u>mailed</u> the letter.
2. The <u>police officer</u> <u>directs</u> the traffic.
3. <u>I</u> <u>took</u> that exam yesterday.
4. The <u>dog</u> <u>chased</u> the cat around the yard.
5. <u>Arthur</u> <u>operated</u> the ice-cream maker.
6. The <u>cow</u> <u>slept</u> in the shade.
7. A good <u>investment</u> <u>pays</u> for itself.
8. A good <u>fan</u> <u>cools</u> a hot room.
9. The <u>firefighter</u> <u>rescued</u> the child from the burning building.
10. <u>She</u> <u>wrote</u> the lyrics to that song.

Exercise: Point 2

1. smiled	6. loved
2. laughed	7. exploded
3. agreed	8. adopted
4. fixed	9. rented
5. bounced	10. called

Review Exercise: Points 1 and 2

1. Pr Russ <u>smokes</u> a pack of cigarettes a day.
2. Pa The poet <u>imagined</u> a better world.
3. Pa He <u>confessed</u> his part in the practical joke.
4. Pr The candle <u>sheds</u> a soft light.
5. Pr The neighbors <u>play</u> bridge every Thursday.
6. Pa I <u>wandered</u> through the Public Garden.
7. Pa I <u>joined</u> the fraternity as a sophomore.

8. Pr I <u>cook</u> her breakfast every morning.
9. Pa Jack <u>watered</u> his bonsai.
10. Pr Our doctor <u>treats</u> his patients kindly.

Another Review Exercise: Points 1 and 2

Answers to this exercise will vary. Check with your instructor if you need to.
1. Yesterday Sam called his mother on the telephone.
2. I voted for the candidate from Maine.
3. She doubted if he would ever return.
4. We go to the mall twice a week.
5. Theresa grows tomatoes in her garden.
6. To avoid an accident the driver swerved to one side.
7. I promised to send her a card on her birthday.
8. In a thunderstorm lightning often strikes a tree.
9. Peanuts and beer go well together.
10. The baby cried all night long.

Exercise: Point 3

1. Michael <u>is</u> going.
2. You <u>seem</u> to read my mind.
3. This cigarette <u>tastes</u> stale.
4. The union members <u>are</u> ready to strike.
5. They <u>were</u> standing and applauding the runner.
6. The actor <u>appeared</u> to have forgotten his lines.
7. She <u>looked</u> angry as she spoke.
8. The steak <u>was</u> rare and juicy.
9. The sky <u>grew</u> dark before the thunderstorm.
10. He <u>sounded</u> furious.

Exercise: Point 4

1. Brian (is) washing his car.
2. The player (began) circling the bases.
3. Dogs (were) barking all night long.
4. Kevin (is) weeding the garden.
5. I (am) preparing for the worst.
6. Mr. Potts (is) running for a post on the city council.
7. They (keep) trying to resolve their problems.
8. Americans (are) choosing a new president.
9. Lucy (was) singing in the nightclub.
10. We (are) attempting to improve our performance.

Another Exercise: Point 4

1. We are going on a camping trip.
2. I was waiting for that bus for an hour.

3. You are trying too hard.
4. Janice was balancing her checkbook.
5. We were vacationing in Canada.
6. They are remodeling their basement.
7. The children were making all kinds of noise.
8. I am studying for an English exam.
9. Bobby is swatting flies.
10. The mayor was shaking everybody's hand.

Review Exercise: Points 1–4

1. Ted <u>was cleaning</u> his room.
2. She <u>seemed</u> elated about the news.
3. He <u>drives</u> like a maniac.
4. I <u>am vacuuming</u> the carpet.
5. The baby <u>grows</u> more interesting every day.
6. Debra <u>cut</u> slices of her birthday cake.
7. We <u>are developing</u> new habits.
8. The day <u>turned</u> cold and bleak.
9. They <u>started issuing</u> free passes to the amusement park.
10. He <u>remembered</u> his father's advice.

Exercise: Point 5

1. been	6. sunk
2. broken	7. dealt
3. lost	8. lain
4. swum	9. laid
5. grown	10. sung

Another Exercise: Point 5

Answers to this exercise will vary. Check with your instructor if you need to.

Exercise: Point 6

1. C The boys <u>plan to come</u> tomorrow.
2. I The boy <u>to shake</u> the apples from the tree.
3. C She <u>meant to take</u> a tour of New Orleans.
4. C My younger sister <u>is longing to have</u> a horse of her own.
5. I The leaves <u>to fall</u> in September.
6. C They <u>are hoping to go</u> on a picnic tomorrow.
7. I My mother <u>to go</u> back to college next year.
8. I The lake <u>to freeze</u> if the temperature drops.
9. C Larry's brother <u>tried to join</u> the navy at sixteen.
10. C Do you <u>expect to see</u> Dolores on your vacation?

Exercise: Point 7

1. She <u>should have been elected</u> class treasurer.
2. He <u>has</u> always <u>wanted</u> an outfit like that one.
3. They <u>should</u> never <u>have lost</u> that game.
4. Richard <u>was appointed</u> chairperson of the committee.
5. You <u>should have learned</u> from your mistakes.
6. Monica <u>is learning to build</u> cabinets.
7. He <u>has</u> just <u>purchased</u> a condominium.
8. Gretchen <u>had</u> never <u>experienced</u> that before.
9. We <u>had been hoping</u> for better news.
10. It <u>would</u> not <u>have alarmed</u> me.

Review Exercise: Points 1–7

1. <u>Joe</u> <u>would have been</u> the perfect candidate for the job.
2. <u>Moe, Larry, and Curly</u> <u>are acting</u> wildly.
3. The <u>pollution</u> <u>seems to be getting</u> worse.
4. The <u>caterpillars</u> <u>have eaten</u> the leaves.
5. <u>We</u> <u>are prepared to do</u> anything necessary.
6. <u>I</u> <u>am looking</u> for true love.
7. The <u>professor</u> <u>should</u> not <u>have assigned</u> so much homework.
8. <u>You</u> <u>will have to plug</u> it in.
9. <u>Joining the club</u> <u>will be</u> good for you.
10. <u>She</u> <u>was recalling</u> her childhood.

Exercise: Point 8

1. Mandy <u>washed</u> the dishes and then <u>dried</u> them.
2. Tourists <u>were swimming</u> in the ocean and <u>tanning</u> themselves on the beach.
3. We <u>stripped</u> the wallpaper and <u>painted</u> the walls.
4. The fans <u>were cheering</u> and <u>waving</u> banners.
5. Renata <u>took</u> the course and <u>learned</u> to speak Spanish.
6. He <u>was moaning and groaning</u> all night long.
7. In the summer, I <u>sneeze</u> a lot and <u>get</u> itchy eyes.
8. I <u>called</u> her and <u>told</u> her the news.
9. They <u>were</u> angry and <u>did</u> not <u>hesitate</u> to tell us so.
10. We <u>have</u> always <u>worked</u> hard, and now it <u>is paying</u> off.

Chapter Review

I 1. I   6. C
  2. C   7. I
  3. C   8. C
  4. I   9. I
  5. I   10. C

II 1. I should never have brought that dog home.

  2. Toni was talking with her professor.

  3. I was raising the flag.

  4. The bandits hid in the warehouse.

  5. Raoul was spreading the good news.

  6. Golf had never been so enjoyable.

  7. We preserve our own vegetables every year.

  8. The children want to play.

  9. Herb has been appointed chairperson of the committee.

  10. We have always spent our summers on Cape Cod.

  11. Pheobe had never before cooked spaghetti.

  12. Alex is going to the dump tomorrow.

  13. Mel appears to be making progress.

  14. Shirley is worrying.

  15. He was whining like a baby.

  16. Margaret is an editor at a big publishing company.

  17. He arrived late too often and lost his job.

  18. She looked in the mirror and saw that her hair was turning gray.

  19. The city lights look beautiful tonight.

  20. We have begun saving money and planning for the future.

III Answers to this exercise will vary. Check with your instructor if you need to.
  1. He was installing the storm windows.
  2. I should have bought it when it was on sale.
  3. Leslie looked lovely in that dress.
  4. Yesterday, I read and had a great time.
  5. We read and studied until class was over.
  6. My mother screamed when I fell.
  7. I like that magazine and buy it every month.
  8. She is working until midnight tonight.
  9. You should sweep and vacuum whenever you get the chance.

  10. I am ready, willing, and able.
  11. The job sounds interesting, but I have decided not to take it.
  12. I would have taken you there if you had asked me.
  13. Carrie is directing and appearing in the play.
  14. Stuart works hard, but he is failing the course.
  15. The teacher spent the entire class session explaining that poem.
  16. We strolled around, looking for a theater.
  17. The fireworks display was a sight to behold.
  18. I have chosen the best possible job.
  19. Donna is practicing scales on the piano.
  20. You are never going to get away with this.

MASTERY TEST

I 1. V   6. V   11. C   16. C
  2. S   7. S   12. S   17. V
  3. V   8. C   13. C   18. C
  4. C   9. V   14. C   19. S
  5. S   10. S   15. V   20. C

II 1. With the aid of a telescope, the class saw Jupiter.

  2. Betty and her friend arrived late.

  3. "Lover Baby" is what I call my wife.

  4. Breakdancing and moonwalking are my specialties.

  5. Into the stratosphere shot the space shuttle.

  6. The murmur of the ocean is music to my ears.

  7. By changing your mind, you ruined our plans.

  8. My dog is better than your dog.

  9. A volcano is a mountain that expels ashes and lava.

  10. Every sentence must have a subject.

III 1. Our plans include a trip to Niagara Falls.

  2. I might have known better than to trust him.

  3. Citronella candles keep the bugs away.

  4. Last night they told us of their plans.

  5. You are home!

  6. This case smells of foul play.

  7. He went out and had a great time.

  8. Sculpture has always been my hobby.

  9. We have been wondering where you were.

  10. I have just spent my week's salary.

CHAPTER 3

Exercise: Point 1

Answers to this exercise will vary. Check with your instructor if you need to.

1. S The detective <u>solves</u> the case.
2. P Trees <u>are</u> masterpieces of nature.
3. S The professor <u>is</u> a genius.
4. S A book <u>falls</u> off the shelf.
5. P Children <u>visit</u> the zoo.
6. P Motorcycles <u>speed</u> down the highway.
7. S My nephew <u>loves</u> his new chemistry set.
8. P Accidents <u>happen</u> to careless people.
9. S Karen <u>is playing</u> with her puppy.
10. P The apartments <u>have been</u> rented.

Exercise: Point 2

Answers to this exercise will vary. Check with your instructor if you need to.

1. (Mr. Small) He <u>is</u> a businessman.
2. (My sister) She <u>has</u> a new bicycle.
3. (All of us) We <u>need</u> to borrow a car.
4. (Cats) They <u>are chasing</u> a ball.
5. (The desk) It <u>has</u> a broken leg.
6. (Paul and I) We <u>wave</u> to our friends.
7. (The police officer) He <u>arrests</u> the suspect.
8. (Jogging) It <u>is</u> good exercise.
9. (Denver) It <u>is</u> the largest city in Colorado.
10. (The two women) They <u>are riding</u> horseback.

Exercise: Point 3

Answers to this exercise will vary. Check with your instructor if you need to.

1. The players and coaches sign autographs before the game.
2. My father or his friends are picking us up.
3. Mary and Joseph applied for an auto loan.
4. A gentleman and a scholar are having an argument.
5. Either my aunt or my uncle is going to tuck in the children.
6. Cars, boats, and trains carry passengers.
7. Spring and summer are my favorite seasons.
8. Salary and benefits depend on your qualifications for the job.
9. The owner and manager is Mr. James.

10. Pieces of wood and glue are used in constructing models.

Review Exercise: Points 1–3

Answers to this exercise will vary. Check with your instructor if you need to.

1. CP Jim and I are best friends.
2. S Beer is cooling in the refrigerator.
3. CP Neither my dog nor my cats behave very well.
4. P Traffic jams frustrate most motorists.
5. CP Jack and his gerbil understand each other.
6. CP Either staples or paper clips satisfy the need for a fastener.
7. CP Violins and cellos echoed through the concert hall.
8. CS The owner and captain sailed the boat himself.
9. P Millionaires contribute to political campaigns.
10. CP Stu, Alice, and I went to the beach.

Exercise: Point 4

Answers to this exercise will vary. Check with your instructor if you need to.

1. One of them (carries) a large suitcase.
2. Anyone (gets) angry once in awhile.
3. Everyone here (belongs) to the club.
4. Nothing (is) meaningful according to some philosophers.
5. Anybody (wants) to be best in the class.
6. Everything (counts) on your final record.
7. Somebody (is whistling) in the next room.
8. Nobody (wants) to take the blame.
9. No one (knows) who the stranger is.

Another Exercise: Point 4

1. Neither of us cares to attend.
2. Either of you gets the starring role.
3. Anything serves the purpose.
4. Neither one of them deserves the award.
5. Neither pair of pants fits correctly.
6. Either flavor tastes delicious.
7. Either seat is fine with me.
8. Each of the tools works.
9. Neither of those candles has a wick.
10. No one does the work properly.

Review Exercise: Points 1–4

1. The green car races through the street.
2. Neither of my friends calls me anymore.
3. No one bothers me anymore.
4. Neither of those batteries works.

5. Sears, Roebuck, & Co. is a big mail-order house.
6. Beautiful women and weightlifters are on the beach.
7. Phil and his wife buy lottery tickets every month.
8. One of you dies!
9. Never again will they hitchhike.
10. The boxer and his manager know their business.

Another Review Exercise: Points 1–4

Answers to this exercise will vary. Check with your instructor if you need to.

1. S   Anyone <u>is</u> welcome in my house.
2. S   Fishing is my favorite sport.
3. S   Everyone who is anyone is here.
4. CP   Buildings and grounds <u>need</u> a great deal of maintenance.
5. CP   You and I <u>have</u> a lot in common.
6. S   Either of those recipes produces a great cake.
7. S   Somebody <u>is parking</u> a green car.
8. S   Neither of those responses satisfies me.
9. P   They <u>cannot make</u> it tonight.
10. CP   Anne, Susan, and I <u>love</u> one another.

Exercise: Point 5

1. Both of us are packed and ready to go.
2. Many of us need a vacation.
3. Several phones are ringing.
4. Each of the canisters is empty.
5. Each of the citizens votes once.
6. Few people wish upon stars.
7. Others want to change jobs.
8. Both of them visit often.
9. Each of us minds his own business.
10. Both Alex and Marty work for the phone company.

Exercise: Point 6

1. The bus as well as the car was damaged in the accident.
2. The presentation of the trophies follows the game.
3. The theories of my professor are controversial.
4. John, along with thirty friends, was in attendance.
5. The moon as well as some stars is visible tonight.
6. The children together with their mother watch the movie.
7. The seasons of the year are all distinct.
8. The street singer with a crowd around him performs beautifully.
9. A pile of rocks has to be moved.
10. Sadie, in addition to her friends, is protesting the school board's decision.

Review Exercise: Points 5 and 6

Answers to this exercise will vary. Check with your instructor if you need to.

1. Both food and drink are necessities of life.
2. Each time is better than the time before.
3. Both notebooks and rulers are sold at this counter.
4. Both men as well as their wives are at the convention.
5. The captain, along with the other players, celebrated.
6. Everyone I care about is coming.
7. Both shoes and sneakers need laces.
8. Each of the Beatles has a special talent.
9. Part I together with Part II contains a review section.
10. The musicians, including the drummer, are on strike.

Review Exercise: Points 1–6

1. Both you and I together with Al want ice cream.
2. Neither of the sandwiches has onions.
3. Rakes and mowers are used by gardeners.
4. Each of the boys needs a haircut.
5. I will be glad to see anyone who wishes to come.
6. Neither of the boys was allowed to enter the race.
7. Chris, Maureen, and all their children visit us weekly.
8. Those cars, including the white Ford, are parked illegally.
9. Both women were hired.
10. A wild and woolly dog runs around our apartment.

Another Review Exercise: Points 1–6

Answers to this exercise will vary. Check with your instructor if you need to.

1. Neither of the appointments was convenient for me.
2. Coffee, as well as tea, upsets my stomach.
3. Both coffee and tea contain caffeine.
4. Either one of the movies appeals to me.
5. You and I have exams on the same day.
6. Each daughter of mine is beautiful.
7. Nobody who is anybody will miss the event.
8. Strolling through the park is a good way to relax.
9. My girlfriend calls me twice an hour.
10. The area including First and Second Streets has badly deteriorated.

Exercise: Point 7

1. A lot were trying out for the team.
2. My family is the most important thing in the world to me.
3. The band was louder than we expected.
4. A lot was accomplished at the last meeting.
5. The audience was booing and throwing tomatoes.
6. A number of items are missing.

7. A class is canceled almost every week.
8. One team is Pat and Mike.
9. Today our committee reaches a decision.
10. A dozen are prepared to strike.

Exercise: Point 8

1. There is a <u>way</u> to stop the leaking faucet.

2. There are <u>veterans</u> of the war here tonight.

3. Inside the shack is a stray <u>dog.</u>

4. Over there is the <u>governor</u> of our state.

5. Behind that door waits <u>danger.</u>

6. There is more than one <u>way</u> to skin a cat.

7. Under the rock are over a hundred <u>ants.</u>

8. In our system, there are two <u>senators</u> from each state.

9. Right behind me is <u>everyone</u> who supports me.

10. Beside the table was a <u>high chair.</u>

Exercise: Point 9

Answers to this exercise will vary. Check with your instructor if you need to.
1. P The Dodgers lead the league.
2. S The *Daily News* is our largest newspaper.
3. P Animals are my best friends.
4. S Benchley's *Jaws* was an imaginative picture.
5. P The five senses are not equally important to existence.
6. S Mathematics is the study of number theory.
7. P Shouts echoed through the halls.
8. P Games build competitive spirit.
9. S Economics is not my favorite subject.
10. S Business tends to ignore the rights of the consumer.

Review Exercise: Points 7–9

Answers to this exercise will vary. Check with your instructor if you need to.

1. There <u>are</u> twenty students in this class.

2. The *London Times* <u>is</u> an excellent newspaper.

3. Up the hill <u>ran</u> Jack and Jill.

4. There <u>is</u> danger involved in that plan.

5. <u>Have</u> you any spare change?

6. The public <u>has</u> the right to be informed.

7. Yesterday there <u>was</u> a terrible snowstorm.

8. *The Pickwick Papers* <u>is</u> a novel by Charles Dickens.

9. The Yankees <u>are</u> a baseball team.

10. There <u>is</u> a good audience tonight.

Another Review Exercise: Points 7—9

Answers to this exercise will vary. Check with your instructor if you need to.
1. The House of Representatives is part of the government.
2. My family prefers not to eat in fast-food restaurants.
3. Many of us were astonished.
4. There is no one here who can help us.
5. Here are my ideas for the project.
6. Liberal arts is the cornerstone of education.
7. Beside the field are the lost sheep.
8. Our English class is going to present a debate.
9. The members of our class are all about the same age.
10. A heap of trash was left after the parade.

Chapter Review

I 1. Almost everybody has some difficulty with writing.
2. Neither the chipmunk nor the squirrels are bothering us.
3. Both of us are voting in the next election.
4. Milo, Phoebe, and I were offering our help.
5. Neither of you jumps to conclusions.
6. Some say the Indians have been treated unfairly.
7. There were only two choices on the menu.
8. Rudy as well as his cat likes milk.
9. He is my boss and friend.
10. Sunbathing is my favorite form of exercise.
11. Either of us has to pay the fine.
12. The twins and their parents travel together.
13. Nobody believes your alibi.
14. America and Russia are the most powerful nations.
15. "Safe" and "out" are two calls in baseball.
16. Neither of them dances to disco music.
17. Each serves a different purpose.
18. The hammer as well as the saw makes work easier.
19. Jacques was working for his uncle last year.
20. Our team plays hard every night.
21. Neither of the boys has to shave.
22. The Johnsons, including their son Frank, ski.
23. The Seven Wonders of the World are extraordinary.
24. The Empire State Building and Macy's are in New York.
25. Time flies when you're enjoying yourself.
26. Either Cathy or the Millers cook dinner on Fridays.

27. Each of the brothers has been on a quiz show.
28. My wife and I were late for the movie.
29. There was no way out of the tunnel.
30. You are nobody until somebody loves you.

II Answers to this exercise will vary. Check with your instructor if you need to.

1. The enemy <u>was</u> captured late last night.

2. I <u>suppose</u> the men are safe now.

3. Nothing <u>excites</u> those two.

4. It <u>stands</u> as testimony to a great person.

5. One of us always <u>guesses</u> the right answer.

6. The Smiths <u>live</u> in the next apartment.

7. Amos and Andy <u>were</u> a great comedy team.

8. Someone <u>has</u> to take me to the station.

9. I <u>was</u> disappointed with their performance.

10. They <u>were</u> the best of times.

III Answers to this exercise will vary. Check with your instructor if you need to.

1. The <u>furnace</u> is not working today.

2. Paul and Paula are expecting their first child.

3. <u>Most of us</u> signed up for the event.

4. Neither of us cares much for caviar.

5. <u>Thunderstorms and hurricanes</u> are examples of foul weather.

6. <u>Jamie and Dave,</u> together with Mr. Powers, are going sailing.

7. <u>Mark, Bonnie, and Nancy</u> want more food.

8. <u>My parents</u> went shopping for a used car.

9. There are never enough <u>hours</u> in the day.

10. <u>Fishing</u> is a good way to pass the time.

IV 1. X Marge as well as Amy does not wish to register.
2. X Each assignment needs to be done carefully.
3. X One of you has to sit on my lap.
4. X Babies are innocent and adults are not.
5. X Neither of us is in the mood.
6. X Weddings are fun.
7. X Alfonso buys records and listens to them in his room.
8. X Both of them wish they were going.
9. X Grammar and spelling are being tested.
10. X Anyone who winks at me embarrasses me.

V Answers to this exercise will vary. Check with your instructor if you need to.

1. Each of the teams in the NFL plays half of its games at home.
2. Either of those latex paints covers beautifully.
3. Swimming in salt water does wonders for your hairstyle.
4. Charles Dickens was an English author.
5. There are six kittens in the litter.
6. Here is the man I've been talking about.
7. Rain and sleet are road hazards.
8. The group, including fifty women, had many interests in common.
9. Skydiving is too scary for me.
10. Charlotte and Mark attend the same school.

VI Answers to this exercise will vary. Check with your instructor if you need to.

Carpenters use many different tools in their work. When they are faced with jobs that are particularly difficult, they have to use their patience as well as their skills. Without patience, hammers, saws, or screwdrivers will do carpenters no good. They have to be able to understand their problems, and find the best ways to solve them. Sometimes, the quickest solutions are not the best ones. Their customers, or clients, have to be pleased with their work, or they lose their chances to be hired for other jobs. There are great pressures on carpenters to succeed. By no means are their jobs easy ones.

VII Answers to this exercise will vary. Check with your instructor if you need to.

People who grow up in the South get used to warm weather. There is never a major snowstorm there, although hurricanes are not entirely unusual. A northerner, on the other hand, has to learn to live with harsh weather for several months of each year. People who travel from one region of the country to another are almost always surprised at the change of climate. Although a southerner thinks that warm weather is nice all year round, a northerner may enjoy the change of seasons.

VIII Answers to this exercise will vary. Check with your instructor if you need to.

In John Steinbeck's *Of Mice and Men,* two men travel around California looking for work. George, the shorter and smarter of the two, wants to find a steady job so he can save enough money to buy his own place. George promises that when they have their farm, Lennie will be the only one who ever takes care of the rabbits. However, Lennie gets the men in trouble, and George is forced to shoot him. He wishes he did not have to do it, as losing his friend makes him very unhappy. Steinbeck's novel forces the reader to consider the qualities of a true friendship.

CHAPTER 4

Exercise: Point 1

1. Heating <u>costs</u> <u>are</u> on the upswing.
2. <u>We</u> <u>choose</u> the freshest fruit we can find.
3. There <u>is</u> a pickle in the refrigerator.
4. Many <u>people</u> <u>read</u> best-selling novels during the summer.
5. That <u>train</u> <u>is</u> late as always.
6. <u>Babies</u> <u>require</u> a great deal of attention.
7. A good <u>meal</u> <u>improves</u> my disposition.
8. <u>You</u> <u>are</u> a sight for sore eyes.
9. <u>Gardening</u> <u>is</u> therapeutic for some.
10. These <u>are</u> the best <u>years</u> of your life.

Another Exercise: Point 1

Answers to this exercise will vary. Check with your instructor if you need to.

1. C
2. F <u>We</u> <u>live</u> near the center of town.
3. F <u>We</u> <u>ate</u> at a famous restaurant.
4. C
5. C
6. F <u>We</u> <u>will done</u> at my grandparents' house.
7. C
8. F <u>I</u> <u>can't buy</u> a record with only fifty cents.
9. F <u>Susie</u> <u>attends</u> the University of Georgia.
10. C

Exercise: Point 2

Answers to this exercise will vary. Check with your instructor if you need to.
1. The customer was asking a question.
2. I hear the birds singing in the trees.
3. The man was trying to escape.
4. My neighbor is always working on his house.
5. The woman is beginning a new career.
6. I am practicing the piano.
7. The attendant was checking the tire pressure.
8. The convict was trying to evade the police.
9. She was smiling at me from across the room.
10. Mel was making his career plans.

Review Exercise: Points 1 and 2

Answers to this exercise will vary. Check with your instructor if you need to.

1. F The motorcyclist was racing wildly through the park.
2. F She was falling in love.
3. C
4. F Rockefeller, Carnegie, and Getty were all millionaires.
5. F The old man rarely displayed any emotion.
6. F The hail was dropping like stones from the sky.
7. C
8. He received the punishment that he deserved.
9. C
10. F I am choosing a new major.

Exercise: Point 3

1. D	6. D
2. D	7. D
3. I	8. D
4. D	9. D
5. D	10. D

Another Exercise: Point 3

Answers to this exercise will vary. Check with your instructor if you need to.
1. I We went to the movies.
2. D Let's sing while we are waiting.
3. I Abby and I are married.
4. D We got both kinds because some people prefer Coca-Cola.
5. D I can't make it although I promised otherwise.
6. D Listen to the sound effects before the song begins.
7. D I am willing to go there if it is a good place to shop.
8. I The Rockies are magnificent.
9. D I will quit unless you give me a raise.
10. D He had to drop out of the tournament after he sprained his ankle.

Exercise: Point 4

1. Because it is raining, we cannot go outside.
2. While you wait, you may read a magazine.
3. My life has changed since I met her.
4. If you want to go, you will have to buy a ticket.
5. If you go swimming, wear a swimcap.
6. Unless you chage your ways, you will lose your job.
7. When he left, the room was dark.
8. After this inning, the game will be over.
9. I want to try even if it is difficult.
10. After I swept the floor, I dusted.

Review Exercise: Points 1–4

Answers to this exercise will vary. Check with your instructor if you need to.
1. He hopes to go tonight even though he is tired.
2. I have been so happy since I fell for you.

3. You will be amazed if I decide to go along with your wishes.
4. Although he has been teaching for twenty years, he is boring.
5. Until they discover a cure for the common cold, I guess I'll just have to keep sneezing.
6. He met her while he was standing at the meat counter in the supermarket.
7. She will leave him unless he changes his vile ways.
8. We will go inside after the sun goes down.
9. As the world turns, I get dizzy.
10. We checked to be sure we had everything before we packed the car.

Exercise: Point 5

1. Even though there is enough time, <u>I feel rushed.</u>

2. Unless you work harder, <u>you will receive a poor grade.</u>

3. As long as you use suntan lotion, <u>you will not get burned.</u>

4. <u>The show begins</u> when the curtain rises.

5. <u>My paper was better</u> after I revised it.

6. If I am nominated, <u>I will not run.</u>

7. <u>I didn't like olives</u> until I had them on pizza.

8. <u>I am happy</u> when I am reading.

9. As soon as the match ends, <u>the winner will be crowned.</u>

10. <u>Lock the door</u> before you leave.

Another Exercise: Point 5

Answers to this exercise will vary. Check with your instructor if you need to.
1. Since we painted the house, we've gotten lots of compliments.
2. I'll call you back as soon as I finish the assignment.
3. He leafed quickly through the gift book before calling to say thank you.
4. Let's wait until the tide comes in.
5. You can count on me whenever you need a friend.
6. Even though we have known each other for years, there are still surprises in our relationship.
7. While working the night shift, I dozed off.
8. I will do it because there is no other choice.
9. Although there was little hope for recovery, we prayed for his health.
10. Whenever I'm feeling depressed, I take the dog out for a run.

Review Exercise: Points 1–6

Answers to this exercise will vary. Check with your instructor if you need to.
1. I invited everyone, including my friend Roger.
2. We can leave as soon as the mail arrives.
3. John wants to attempt to break the world record.
4. For example, baseball and football require great coordination.
5. Even though we used to be friends, now we can't stand each other.
6. After she finished the manuscript, she mailed it to the editor.
7. Everyone celebrated, including my parents and me.
8. Reference books such as the dictionary and the thesaurus are valuable.
9. It started to rain while I was weeding the garden.
10. The dog tried to find his way home.

Exercise: Point 7

1. C	6. C
2. C	7. C
3. C	8. F
4. F	9. F
5. C	10. C

Chapter Review

I
1. F
2. C They lost the battle.
3. F
4. F
5. C Come over for dinner.
6. C Never say die.
7. F
8. F
9. F
10. F

II
1. F
2. F
3. C Sports cars are fun.
4. F
5. F
6. C I was amazed at the performance.
7. F
8. C Bring it tomorrow.
9. F
10. F

III
1. <u>We played baseball</u> until it grew too dark.

2. Even though it was foggy, <u>we made a smooth landing.</u>

3. Because he hurt himself, <u>he could not play.</u>

4. <u>I should quit smoking</u> because it's unhealthy.

5. Although she has a quick temper, <u>Mary kept calm.</u>

6. While I'm here, <u>I should call my aunt.</u>

7. After you run, <u>take a shower.</u>

8. <u>We bought their album</u> after we heard them in concert.

9. <u>I brought my guitar</u> since I knew you would be here.

10. When you come to the third stop light, <u>turn left.</u>

IV Answers to this exercise will vary. Check with your instructor if you need to.

1. Because I want to know you better, I will encourage your honesty.

2. Even though I am broke, I can find a way to amuse myself.

3. Unless you change your mind, we're going.

4. When the times comes, I will have completed the project.

5. As long as you are away, I might as well visit some friends.

6. We will eat after we go for a swim.

7. I will peel the carrots while you chop the onions.

8. I'll send you a road map so that you can find your way.

9. I always get a wonderful dinner whenever I visit my grandparents.

10. She had a very prickly personality, although she was pretty.

V 1. C Call me if you need me.
2. F
3. F
4. F
5. F
6. F
7. F
8. C I know.
9. C It's okay with me.
10. F

VI Answers to this exercise will vary. Check with your instructor if you need to.

1. C The traffic was heavy.

2. F Everyone loves a gorgeous autumn afternoon.

3. F I am trying to make the Dean's List.

4. F We need to find a bigger apartment.

5. F I was exhausted after chasing my dog around the block.

6. F It was very crowded, with all the noise and confusion of a busy airport.

7. F She arrived at the last possible moment.

8. F She was laughing and crying at the same time.

9. F Let's go now before I change my mind.

10. F I enjoy soft drinks like root beer and ginger ale.

VII 1. As long as you're not lazy, I won't complain.

2. We're celebrating tonight because I gave up cigarettes.

3. If you want to play, change your clothes.

4. Having moved to the country, he leads a quieter life.

5. After all, we have known each other for a year.

6. We hated summer until we bought an air conditioner.

7. Since you left me, I am so lonely.

8. You have to fix the leak before you can go sailing.

9. As soon as we arrived in Miami, we ran out to the beach.

10. We are raising a family because we love children.

VIII Answers to this exercise will vary. Check with your instructor if you need to.

1. I worked hard to that I could get a promotion.

2. Although she enjoys painting, she doesn't take art courses.

3. We went to the circus, where we saw lions and clowns.

4. Tell me the truth if you know it.

5. There have been many improvements since he was elected senator.

6. I love facing danger wherever I can find it.

7. I am too tired to go for a walk.

8. He was arrested because he was speeding.

9. You will find the underwear in the drawer where I keep my socks.

10. Judging the distance and holding her breath, she jumped.

IX Answers to this exercise will vary. Check with your instructor if you need to.

Today, more and more people are becoming interested in discovering their roots. This is because of the popularity of a book by Alex Haley, called *Roots*. It tells the story of Haley's search for his ancestors, in Africa and other places. Before he wrote *Roots*, Haley worked on another book, *The Autobiography of Malcolm X*. After *Roots* was published, it became a bestseller. Then they made a movie for television based on it. Now, people of all backgrounds are interested in tracing their ancestry. *Roots* is a good book, and Haley is a great man.

Ten years ago there were not as many shopping malls as there are today. In a mall, many stores are gathered together under one roof. Shoppers appreciate the convenience a mall can offer, because they can make one stop and accomplilsh all their shopping in one place. On Saturday, malls are usually very crowded, with people walking, talking, eating, and buying all over the place. Malls are air-conditioned so that shoppers can browse comfortably. You can buy a birthday card, a mattress, a baseball mit, or a pizza, all under one roof. Shopping malls offer a great way to shop.

When we moved from an apartment to a house, we discovered that we had more belongings than we thought. So much stuff had to be packed, so we used boxes, suitcases, and even large garbage bags. We rented a truck from the local gas station so we could avoid spending the extra money to hire a mover. We certainly put in a full day's work that day. Although the process was long and hard, it was worth it.

CHAPTER 5

Exercise: Recognition

1. I like rock music|I don't like jazz.
2. The invitation was beautiful|it was hand-lettered.
3. The tide is high|it is a good time to swim.
4. Ben is a trucker|he is from Georgia.
5. It was a good film|I saw it twice.
6. Babies are cute|they cry a lot.
7. He is my friend|he understands me.
8. The trip was postponed|we had no sleeping bags.
9. The firefighters were called|they handled the blaze.
10. I raked the beach|there is no seaweed left.

Another Exercise: Recognition

1. RO	6. C
2. RO	7. RO
3. RO	8. RO
4. RO	9. RO
5. RO	10. RO

A Third Exercise: Recognition

1. RO	6. RO
2. RO	7. RO
3. C	8. RO
4. C	9. RO
5. RO	10. RO

Exercise: Point 1

Answers to this exercise will vary. Check with your instructor if you need to.
1. It was my mother's birthday, so I called her on the phone.
2. Going out to dinner is fun, but it is expensive.
3. I won't do it, and you can't make me.
4. We can usually see for miles, but today it is too cloudy.
5. I want that job, but I don't think I have enough experience.
6. We found some shells on the beach, and they were beautiful.
7. I never knew his name, yet I'll never forget him.
8. Tell me your problem, so I can help you.
9. Our daughter is in the third grade, and she is very bright.
10. I've never tried blueberry ice cream, but I bet I will like it.

Another Exercise: Point 1

One way to correct a run-on sentence is to connect two independent clauses with a comma *plus* one of these connecting words: *and, but, for, or, nor, yet, so.*

Exercise: Point 2

1. I received the most votes; therefore, I was elected.
2. The ship sails from North Wharf; it leaves at 2:00 P.M.
3. We lost; however, we still lead the league.
4. The play was a tragedy; we left the theater weeping.
5. You want your freedom; nevertheless, you will have to get a job.
6. I am running for office; furthermore, I intend to win.
7. She must be out of town; otherwise, she would be here.
8. First buy your ticket; then get in line.
9. Those shoes are comfortable; I'll take two pairs.
10. There was no heat; consequently, we froze all night.

Review Exercise: Points 1 and 2

Answers to this exercise will vary. Check with your instructor if you need to.
1. We rented a floor buffer, but it did not work.
2. Joe ran all the way home; consequently, he was tired.
3. I cooked a hamburger for dinner, but I forgot to buy a roll.
4. The horse I bet on came in second; nevertheless, I lost money.
5. The window was shattered, so we had to get a new one.

6. The candle burned for hours; therefore, we did not have to use the lamp.
7. Apple pie is delicious; however, it is fattening.
8. The show came on too late; besides, she wasn't really interested in seeing it.
9. Summers are hot and humid, but winters are cold and dry.
10. He was wealthy, so he could buy anything he wanted.

Another Review Exercise: Points 1 and 2

1. Connect two independent clauses with a comma plus one of these connecting words: *and, but, for, or, nor, yet, so.*
2. Separate two independent clauses with a semicolon.

Exercise: Point 3

1. She asked for a raise. She got it.
2. That is a new hall. The acoustics are fantastic.
3. He is a good father. He pays attention to his children.
4. The birds are chirping. They sound so happy.
5. The parade is beginning. Let's get a good spot.
6. Your paper is late. Therefore, it will lose a grade.
7. He failed the test. Consequently, he will have to take it again.
8. Why did you go partying? You were tired.
9. That suit fits. You should buy it.
10. Bowling is fun for the whole family. It is good exercise.

Review Exercise: Points 1–3

Answers to this exercise will vary. Check with your instructor if you need to.
1. The sun went down, and the mosquitoes came out.
   The sun went down; the mosquitoes came out.
   The sun went down. The mosquitoes came out.
2. Ben ran a good race, and he came in second.
   Ben ran a good race; he came in second.
   Ben ran a good race. He came in second.
3. We applauded the actress, so she came out for a second bow.
   We applauded the actress; therefore, she came out for a second bow.
   We applauded the actress. Therefore, she came out for a second bow.
4. I like Chaucer, but I like Shakespeare even better.
   I like Chaucer; however, I like Shakespeare even better.
   I like Chaucer. I like Shakespeare even better.
5. I am happy to be here, and I'm glad you are with me.
   I am happy to be here; I'm glad you are with me.
   I am happy to be here. I'm glad you are with me.

6. Turn right here, and park where you can.
   Turn right here; park where you can.
   Turn right here. Park where you can.
7. I quit smoking, so I feel much better.
   I quit smoking; consequently, I feel much better.
   I quit smoking. I feel much better.
8. I love visiting you, for you treat me so well.
   I love visiting you; you treat me so well.
   I love visiting you. You treat me so well.
9. I have hay fever, and I take allergy pills.
   I have hay fever; therefore, I take allergy pills.
   I have hay fever. Therefore, I take allergy pills.
10. I'm in my second childhood, and I feel young again.
   I'm in my second childhood; I feel young again.
   I'm in my second childhood. I feel young again.

Exercise: Point 4

Answers to this exercise will vary. Check with your instructor if you need to.
1. While we went to the museum, Bob went to the ball game.
2. Because you are my friend, I trust you.
3. Although I don't like crowds, I enjoy going to the beach.
4. The temperature dropped as soon as it started to rain.
5. When I answered the phone, the caller hung up.
6. The kids are building sand castles while the adults have a conversation.
7. Let's find our seats before the show begins.
8. Even though I locked the door, they still broke in.
9. Since you were fired, the place has not been the same.
10. While you were gone, the plumber came.

Review Exercise: Points 3 and 4

Answers to this exercise will vary. Check with your instructor if you need to.
1. We moved here. We have been very happy.
   Since we moved here, we have been very happy.
2. Trash is collected on Mondays. It is taken to the dump.
   After trash is collected on Mondays, it is taken to the dump.
3. There is no easy remedy. We must research the matter further.
   Since there is no easy remedy, we must research the matter further.
4. I started taking fiddle lessons. I improved my style.
   Since I started taking fiddle lessons, I improved my style.
5. That type of defense will never work. The other team is too good.
   That type of defense will never work because the other team is too good.

6. We go swimming every night during the summer. The pond is nearby.
   We go swimming every night during the summer, since the pond is nearby.
7. We drove cross-country. We had no idea how beautiful America is.
   Until we drove cross-country, we had no idea how beautiful America is.
8. You don't look well. Lie down for a while.
   Since you don't look well, you should lie down for a while.
9. The professor raised his voice. He was sure angry.
   Whenever the professor raised his voice, he was sure angry.
10. He looks grubby. He has not shaved for weeks.
    He looks grubby because he has not shaved for weeks.

Chapter Review

I 1. RO Shirts sometimes come with cardboard in them|it protects them from wrinkling.
   2. C You need matches to start a fire.
   3. RO Fred wears madras shirts|they have gone out of style.
   4. C Before you paint, you have to strip the surface.
   5. C She was hired because she was the best one for the job.
   6. RO There is a late show tonight|what time does it start?
   7. RO Al called last night|he is getting married.
   8. RO Rest is important|vitamins will help.
   9. RO It is your turn|roll the dice.
   10. RO Max takes flying lessons|he is getting a license.

II Answers to this exercise will vary. Check with your instructor if you need to.
   1. RO Guns are dangerous; they can cause a lot of trouble.
   2. C
   3. RO Lilacs are fragrant, so we should grow some.
   4. RO Construction workers wear hard hats because they need protection.
   5. RO Come outside if you want to see the stars.
   6. RO Poker is a great game, because it takes skill as well as luck.
   7. RO I read a great novel; you can borrow it.
   8. C
   9. RO I chose a button-down shirt because I like that style.
   10. RO I wrote a letter to the editor, and it was printed.

III 1. We want to buy a new car, but it is too expensive.
   2. She is a teacher; therefore, she has her summers off.
   3. I wrote my member of Congress. He replied with a form letter.
   4. He started slowly. Then he speeded up and won the race.
   5. Al went to the ball game; he ate peanuts and drank beer.
   6. Italy is a lovely country, and so is Spain.
   7. We had a picnic, and Marie played the guitar.
   8. Although we got lost, we arrived on time.
   9. Young people are often energetic; furthermore, they have great ambition.
   10. Since we bought the fan, it has been much cooler in here.

IV Answers to this exercise will vary. Check with your instructor if you need to.
   1. Bring me my slippers, and see if you can find my pipe.
   2. I've never been there, and I don't want to go.
   3. I would like to get a bird's-eye view of things, but I can't fly.
   4. You must do your homework, or you'll get a poor grade.
   5. I don't usually read that magazine, but I did see that article.
   6. The movie was hilarious, and I saw it twice.
   7. I like playing tennis, but I'm not very good at it.
   8. I take lessons, and I practice every day.
   9. She wears army boots, and she rides a motorcycle.
   10. I have hay fever, but it only bothers me in August.

V Answers to this exercise will vary. Check with your instructor if you need to.
   1. Farming is hard work, but it is satisfying.
   2. We listened to oldies on the radio; it was an evening of memories.
   3. Although some people say horse races are fixed, they are fun to watch.
   4. Avoid poison ivy. It can irritate your skin.
   5. A fireplace is romantic. Besides, it can keep you warm.
   6. My teacher was close to me. She was almost my best friend.
   7. I arrived late, so I missed the interview.
   8. Although I can balance my checkbook, I cannot complete my income tax forms.
   9. My sign is Libra. However, my wife is an Aquarian.
   10. Writing is an important skill, but it takes time to develop.

VI Connect two independent clauses with a comma *plus* one of these connecting words: *and, but, for, or, nor, yet, so.*

VII 1. Andy loves golf, so he plays a round every day.

Andy loves golf; he plays a round every day.

Andy loves golf. He plays a round every day.

Because Andy loves golf, he plays a round every day.

2. I built a desk, and I keep it in my bedroom.

I built a desk; I keep it in my bedroom.

I built a desk. I keep it in my bedroom.

Since I built a desk, I keep it in my bedroom.

3. We traveled to Europe, and we saw the Eiffel Tower.

We traveled to Europe; we saw the Eiffel Tower.

We traveled to Europe. We saw the Eiffel Tower.

When we traveled to Europe, we saw the Eiffel Tower.

4. English is my favorite subject, so I get good grades.

English is my favorite subject; therefore I get good grades.

English is my favorite subject. I get good grades.

Because English is my favorite subject, I get good grades.

5. I mixed the ingredients, and I put the batter in the oven.

I mixed the ingredients; then I put the batter in the oven.

I mixed the ingredients. Then I put the batter in the oven.

After I mixed the ingredients, I put the batter in the oven.

6. I love summer, but I don't like the humidity.

I love summer; I don't like the humidity.

I love summer. I don't like the humidity.

I love summer although I don't like the humidity.

7. The mail arrives late here, for the postman walks a long route.

The mail arrives late here; the postman walks a long route.

The mail arrives late here. The postman walks a long route.

The mail arrives late here because the postman walks a long route.

8. I enjoyed the dinner, but I feel a bit bloated now.

I enjoyed the dinner; however, I feel a bit bloated now.

I enjoyed the dinner. However, I feel a bit bloated now.

Although I enjoyed the dinner, I feel a bit bloated now.

9. I see moisture in the basement, so there must be a leak somewhere.

I see moisture in the basement; there must be a leak somewhere.

I see moisture in the basement. There must be a leak somewhere.

If I see moisture in the basement, there must be a leak somewhere.

10. The wine is imported from France, and it is very good.

The wine is imported from France; it is very good.

The wine is imported from France. It is very good.

Because the wine is imported from France, it is very good.

VIII Answers to this exercise will vary. Check with your instructor if you need to.

1. Mario is a whiz at photography, whereas Sally is an excellent painter.

2. Although Beethoven was deaf, he was a great composer.

3. Hamburgers are delicious, and cheeseburgers are absolutely scrumptious.

4. Tom is lazy, although he knows how important exercise is.

5. John wants to be a registered nurse, so he is going to school to get his degree.

IX Answers to this exercise will vary. Check with your instructor if you need to.

1. A summer breeze is lovely; it cools the body and the mind.

2. That dog is very smart; sometimes it seems he can communicate with us.

3. When she bought a Volkswagen, she traded in her Ford.

4. Backpacking is a great way to spend the day, but it requires a lot of stamina.

5. He is my best friend, but he has moved to Detroit.

X Answers to this exercise will vary. Check with your instructor if you need to.

The energy crisis affects us all. As the price of home-heating fuel keeps rising, it gets too expensive to stay warm. One way to solve the problem is to buy a wood-burning stove, which, in some cases, can heat a whole house. Wood is also costly unless you have access to a supply. Since it comes in many different styles, a stove can be a beautiful addition to a house or apartment. Each kind of stove suits a different purpose.

Cats make great pets, but you have to be affectionate with them. As they are rather independent animals, they do not always come when you call them. Many people prefer dogs, because you can train them to come, or sit, or fetch a bone. With cats, on the other hand, you have to be willing to let them live their own lives. If you attempt to train them, you may become discouraged. If you put two cats in the same room, you are in for quite a treat. They chase each other, usually all in fun. When one catches the other, the real show begins. Oftentimes they will cuddle and clean each other, but sometimes they will fight. The wise pet owner will know when to break up a fight and when to let it go, since it is only play for the cats. They can be great company if you understand them.

Tennis is a sport that has gained great popularity over the last ten years. Both men and women enjoy it. Tennis courts are being built all over; they can be found in cities, in the country, and in the suburbs. People of all ages can play. In fact, some of the greatest players in the world are in their teens or early twenties. The most important and prestigious tournament is held every summer at Wimbledon, a suburb of London. However, America's most important tournament is the U.S. Open; it is held at Flushing Meadows, New York. One does not have to be a star athlete to enjoy tennis. It is great fun even for those who just want some fresh air and exercise.

CHAPTER 6

Exercise: Point 1

1. sunken
2. silently through the room
3. picket
4. with all her charm
5. with some reluctance; away from her family
6. home-made
7. with grey shingles
8. lovingly with his niece
9. with three red stripes
10. handsome

Exercise: Point 2

1. A <u>man</u> in a sharkskin coat sold us a lottery ticket.
2. We <u>strolled</u> along the boardwalk until the sun set.
3. The crowd <u>cheered</u> excitedly when Yaz came to the plate.
4. The banana comes in its own natural yellow <u>wrapper</u>.
5. I saw my <u>grandmother</u> climbing the steps in her house.
6. As usual, he <u>spoke</u> only about himself.
7. We watched the <u>horses</u> approaching the finish line.
8. Alex <u>smiled</u> happily when he heard the news.
9. She <u>warned</u> me in a whisper never to do that again.
10. The elastic <u>man</u> in the circus is a sideshow attraction.

Review Exercise: Points 1 and 2

1. MM Amazingly, Rick got an A on the test.
2. MM The ugly monster waited in the cave.
3. C
4. MM The quarterback instantaneously made the decision to run.
5. MM We watched the motorcyclist heading for a crash.
6. MM The city council voted unanimously to fund the project.
7. MM Wearing only his underwear, Max was chasing the dog.
8. MM The panhandler without a cent to his name approached the millionaire.
9. MM The furnace exploded with a crash, but no one was hurt.
10. MM My father, who is bald, bought a toupee.

Exercise: Point 3

1. of the fifteenth century
2. riding her bicycle
3. dressed in many colors
4. in the basement
5. with the floppy ears
6. loudly
7. promising better times for all
8. for fifty dollars
9. with the creamy complexion
10. barking at the fire hydrant

Exercise: Point 4

Answers to this exercise will vary. Check with your instructor if you need to.

1. After almost an hour, she was ready to go.
2. She does not even know his name.
3. You are hardly the one I need for this job.
4. She had just finished painting when I touched the doorknob.
5. There are just three eggs left in the refrigerator.
6. I received the only passing grade on the exam.

7. I put on a last burst of speed and nearly won the race.
8. The host had provided scarcely enough food for all the guests.
9. The police officer merely informed us of our rights.
10. This time we nearly made it.

Review Exercise: Points 1–4

Answers to this exercise will vary. Check with your instructor if you need to.

1. The birds in the trees are singing their songs of love.
2. I heard on the radio about the big music festival.
3. I almost fell over from laughing so hard.
4. She sighed happily when the good news came.
5. Nearly everyone loves a barbecue.
6. Pete turned away bashfully when he saw the girl of his dreams.
7. He sat on the roof watching his neighbors below.
8. We badly needed someone to work overtime.
9. I am talking on the telephone and relaxing.
10. You are the only one for me.

Exercise: Point 5

Answers to this exercise will vary. Check with your instructor if you need to.

1. Every day she told him to change his socks.
   She told him to change his socks every day.
2. Clara said she felt better after her operation.
   After her operation, Clara said she felt better.
3. He always told me to be practical.
   He told me to be practical always.
4. At midnight we were told the show would begin.
   We were told the show would begin at midnight.
5. On her way out, Ruth promised to close the door.
   Ruth promised to close the door on her way out.

Chapter Review

I 1. MM The man in the blue sweater was stopped for speeding.
   2. MM I saw almost the whole movie, but I fell asleep around midnight.
   3. MM Joe left the door hanging on one hinge.
   4. MM The initials carved on the tree were those of the lovers.
   5. C
   6. MM The doctor told him to take a pill every four hours.
   7. C
   8. MM The woman with the high heels walked into the elevator.
   9. MM The jet carrying 155 passengers crashed into a cliff.
   10. C

II Answers to this exercise will vary. Check with your instructor if you need to.
   1. MM With admiration, I watched the mechanic fix the car.
   2. MM He barely made it in time.
   3. C
   4. MM We borrowed a mower that was broken from a neighbor.
   5. MM We saw a squirrel climbing up the telephone pole.
   6. C
   7. MM The cat was rescued by a firefighter after the building had been set on fire.
   8. MM We've found almost all the pieces to the puzzle.
   9. MM Vandals stole the sign from the corner.
   10. MM I badly need food.

III Answers to this exercise will vary. Check with your instructor if you need to.
   1. C
   2. MM I've seen hardly any of those films.
   3. C
   4. MM I read a new book by my favorite author.
   5. C
   6. MM The boy with a crewcut waved to the Queen.
   7. C
   8. MM She was happy, she said in an interview.
   9. MM We flew through a terrible storm in a plane with a faulty engine.
   10. MM Lucy was skiing down the slope when she broke her ankle.

IV 1. After the game, the coach treated the team to beers.
   2. We saw a cowboy wearing a ten-gallon hat in the street.
   3. She giggled happily when she saw him.
   4. We buy vegetables in the supermarket five miles from here.
   5. The principal stopped the students running down the hall.
   6. She gave the baby in the crib a bottle.
   7. I bought a red shirt to go with my yellow slacks.
   8. We bought a picture that had been painted by an artist from New Mexico.
   9. She used a shampoo which she bought yesterday and then her usual conditioner.
   10. I promised to kiss her when she reaches sixteen.

V 1. The criminal almost laughed when he was arrested.
   2. He bought a suit with brass buttons and treated himself to a fancy dinner.

3. Sammy loves to ride around town in his scooter.
4. The cat barely escaped before the blaze spread.
5. We put insulation down in the attic, and now we are cool.
6. There is a friendly teller in that bank.
7. There is a noisy dog in our neighborhood.
8. He occasionally surprised his wife with a rose.
9. She bought a tie clasp made of brass for her husband.
10. We are just about ready to leave.

VI 1. Susie fixed the pocket which had a hole in it with a needle and thread.
2. I said I would tell you about my trip when I got home.
3. The tire with the puncture went flat.
4. The hunter barely escaped from the bear's claws.
5. The judges watched the models in swimsuits parade on stage.
6. Robin brought her dog with an injured tail to the veterinarian.
7. On his wedding day, he vowed to love, honor, and cherish.
8. My mother-in-law snores loudly when she sleeps.
9. She bought a ring that was made of gold and enamel from the jeweler.
10. We first baked a cake in the new oven for our friends.
11. I ran barefooted into the street.
12. We sent invitations in blue envelopes to all our friends.
13. He left the clothing store with a new pair of socks and bought a newspaper.
14. That salesperson with a bow tie sold me a Pontiac.
15. From the car, I watched my sister jumping rope.
16. Sally said, "I will be a millionaire before I am twenty."
17. I would like a banana in my sundae and a glass of water.
18. The suit with the brass buttons is at the cleaners.
19. The hospital where I was born has been torn down.
20. I banged up a car that did not belong to me in an accident.

VII Answers to this exercise will vary. Check with your instructor if you need to.

I nearly forgot to send Christmas cards this year. All my relatives in different parts of the country would have been disappointed. It really is not that much of a strain since I need to send only ten cards. It is as easy as writing "Hi, how are you?" on a note, putting it in an envelope, and mailing it. I usually work from a list of my friends' and relatives' names, which I keep in my desk. Luckily, I remembered the cards three days before the holiday; I just hope I did not mail them too late.

Raising a family is really an easy task. Almost everyone thinks he knows the best way; scarcely anyone does it perfectly. Many people read Dr. Spock's book, which presents clearly one accepted method. Nearly everyone has heard of that book at least.

No matter what method they follow, parents constantly are advised to be kind and affectionate toward their children. After the baby is born, some parents say their lives are changed completely for the better. They don't even mind if the baby cries. Pacing the floor, they rock the baby back to sleep. They calmly accept the trouble, knowing the baby wil soon outgrow that stage. If they have prepared themselves as early and completely as they could for the new arrival, they are almost never really upset by the little problems that come up.

These days, many people in all parts of the country are trying health foods. The "back to nature" movement has affected nearly everyone in one way or another. Producers of health foods use no preservatives, which they claim are bad for the system, in their products. Cereals such as granola, a totally natural food, are especially popular. People are also eating unstarched rice, which is supposed to be particularly good for the digestive system. Even ice cream comes in new, natural flavors such as banana, which is made with fresh bananas, and coconut. Certainly, health food companies are trying hard to attract customers interested in better nutrition.

CHAPTER 7

Exercise: Point 1

1. Driving in heavy traffic
2. Seasoning meat
3. Crossing the border
4. Choosing a career
5. preparing my costume
6. Mowing the lawn
7. Examining philosophy
8. Thinking aloud
9. Getting a tan
10. Practicing the piano

Exercise: Point 2

1. C Billy	6. C Patty
2. DM	7. DM
3. C cat	8. DM
4. C I	9. C audience
5. DM	10. C pitcher

Review Exercise: Points 1 and 2

Answers to this exercise will vary. Check with your instructor if you need to.

1. Preparing to land, the pilot radioed the tower.
2. Making a decision, she pulled over to the curb and stopped.
3. Training for the marathon, Oliver ate no sweets.
4. Staring out the window, she recalled her past.
5. Adjusting her rear-view mirror, my mother checked her hairstyle.
6. Checking my shoe size, the salesperson noted that one foot was larger than the other.
7. Following close behind, I never lost sight of my friend's car.
8. Growing prematurely bald, Steve began wearing a hat.
9. Crying in the crib, the baby let everyone know she was hungry.
10. Finally breaking through the clouds, the sun warmed our bodies and spirits.

Another Review Exercise: Points 1 and 2

Answers to this exercise will vary. Check with your instructor if you need to.

1. When ready, the dinner will be served.
2. Although a stranger, he seemed very nice.
3. At my high school graduation, I bade farewell to my old friends.
4. While shopping for a home computer, Peter tested over twenty models.
5. From under the table, the dog watched his master's guest.
6. In her younger days, she was a well-known singer.
7. By the way you dress, I can tell you like the latest fashions.
8. On my stereo television, I can enjoy the latest videos.
9. If damaged in shipment, this appliance should be returned.
10. When used properly, the attachments make sewing a lot easier.

Exercise: Point 3

Answers to this exercise will vary. Check with your instructor if you need to.

1. Reaching the finals, the Tigers won the game.
2. Playing skillfully, the home team made a touchdown.

3. Shouting, Joe offered his opinion.
4. Painting the ceiling, she got white paint on her hair.
5. Speaking for the community, Mrs. Santos raised the issue.
6. Losing his temper, his father shouted.
7. Running frantically, the ball carrier tripped on a loose shoelace.
8. Being fond of romance, Julie liked late-night movies.
9. Endorsing the check and handing it to the teller, Alex received twenty dollars.
10. Lighting the candle, I got hot wax all over myself.

Exercise: Point 4

Answers to this exercise wil vary. Check with your instructor if you need to.

1. While we were fooling around, the lamps got broken.
2. As they were dashing through the snow, a stone upset the sleigh.
3. As I pedaled fiercely, my bicycle moved faster.
4. While we were eating dinner, the dishes got dirty.
5. As the crowd was leaving the stadium, a section of the bleachers collapsed.
6. As my brother was taking out the garbage, snow started to fall.
7. When I called her on the phone for the first time, my throat was dry.
8. As she was watching a horror movie, her palms started to sweat.
9. When I was going into the sixth grade, my father's company transferred him to a different town.
10. Because she was spending a lot of time partying, her grades slipped.

Review Exercise: Points 1–4

Answers to this exercise will vary. Check with your instructor if you need to.

1. Scoring in the final seconds, our team won the game.
2. Going to the supermarket, he bought food for dinner.
3. Traveling alone, Jan took the plane from Los Angeles to Boston.
4. Running for mayor, Ms. James shook hands with everyone.
5. His biceps bulged when he flexed his muscles.
6. After escaping from the prison, the convict was captured by the warden.
7. She was smiling broadly as her hair blew in the wind.

8. As she recalled the past, a memory of her friend came to mind.
9. Crying and kicking, the child was sent to his room.
10. Because he was smoking a cigar, the room started to stink.

Exercise: Point 5

Answers to this exercise will vary. Check with your instructor if you need to.

1. Since moving to Nebraska, I have learned to appreciate open land.
2. Before selecting a business partner, you should interview several candidates.
3. While waiting for the Sears man, she tried the machine again.
4. After getting a credit card, she went on a spending spree.
5. By having the oil filter changed, we saved money.
6. On hearing about your divorce, I was really distressed.
7. While installing a skylight in my house, I discovered my talent for building.
8. While riding my bicycle, I passed a group of people in strange costumes.
9. Since moving to the country, we have come to appreciate peace and quiet.
10. By choosing to live in the city, he decided to live dangerously.

Exercise: Point 6

Answers to this exercise will vary. Check with your instructor if you need to.

1. To appreciate the music, you should turn up the volume.
2. To clean the roof gutters, you will need a ladder and a pair of gloves.
3. To be a good friend, we should always be sincere.
4. To stay healthy, eat well and exercise daily.
5. To understand poetry, you need to read it closely.
6. To find the secret of life, turn left when you get to India.
7. To avoid trouble, mind your own business.
8. To play professional baseball, you need skill and luck.
9. To prepare lasagna, he always bought high-quality ingredients.
10. To finish a cabinet, you should use a good stain.

Review Exercise: Points 1–6

Answers to this exercise will vary. Check with your instructor if you need to.

1. While he was skating on the frozen pond, his ankles buckled.
2. To run for public office, a person must meet certain requirements.

3. After I put up a scarecrow, the birds tore it apart.
4. While Carl was marching in the parade, the drum he was playing broke.
5. Jumping rope, Andrea sprained her ankle.
6. To make a decision, you should first have firm convictions.
7. To go camping, you need a tent and a flashlight.
8. When I was reading the book, the character reminded me of you.
9. Singing in the rain, Gene Kelly carried an umbrella.
10. To pass this course, you need to write one paper each week.

Chapter Review

I
1. Making a pizza, the chef flipped the dough into the air.
2. To learn to play the violin, a fellow must have patience and neighbors who really like him.
3. To work up a sweat, Arnie jogs four miles.
4. Since starting college, Tracy has learned the meaning of hard work.
5. While filling the gas tank, the attendant told us about the new show in town.
6. Barking furiously, the puppy chased the cat.
7. Pretending to be asleep, she listened to the transistor radio.
8. Before finding a parking space, they had driven around the block three times.
9. Not paying attention, the students dozed off.
10. To relax, you can put your feet up and read a good book.

II Answers to this exercise will vary. Check with your instructor if you need to.

1. Barking and wagging his tail, the collie showed his affection for his master.
2. Swerving to the left, the truck hit a lamppost.
3. To be a movie star, you need good looks and talent.
4. When lost in a strange city, I always use my CB to get directions.
5. In New England, the winter is generally very cold, and there is always a lot of snow.
6. Playing his role, the actor persuaded the audience that he really was Hamlet.
7. After dialing the wrong number, my friend asked the operator for assistance.
8. When scrambled with cheese and onions, eggs are absolutely delicious.
9. At the age of sixty, Dr. Katz retired from her job.
10. Using his professional knowledge, the plumber repaired our leaky faucet.

III Answers to this exercise will vary. Check with your instructor if you need to.

1. By sending her children to camp, Mrs. Mullins made her whole family very happy.
2. To make a Spanish omelet, use tomatoes, peppers, onions, and eggs.
3. After realizing he had made the wrong turn, Alex turned around.
4. When Kitty voices her opinion, people pay close attention.
5. When feeling blue, listen to the music.
6. Thinking of you, I always get a chill up my spine.
7. On being appointed president of the club, Joan delivered an eloquent speech.
8. While working in that restaurant, I made a lot of money in tips.
9. To cancel your appointment, simply call twenty-four hours in advance.
10. During her career as a newscaster, Jane visited nine foreign countries.
11. Ordering everyone around, the bully quickly made enemies.
12. Scrubbing the kitchen floor, Gene gets down on his hands and knees.
13. To lend me a hand in this job, you can pass me the tools when I need them.
14. After vacationing in Canada, we decided to go back there next year.
15. At the age of twelve, Andrea had already read the *Complete Works* of Shakespeare.
16. Expecting to see her boyfriend, Ellen put on her sexiest dress.
17. To change engine oil, you will need a pan to catch the old stuff.
18. When looking up a word in the dictionary, one should always check the part of speech.
19. Seeing his arch rival, he ducked around the corner.
20. To show me that you love me, tell me that you love me five times a day.

IV
1. D the captain
2. D him
3. C
4. D winner
5. D
6. D
7. D
8. C
9. C
10. D chicken

V Answers to this exercise will vary. Check with your instructor if you need to.
1. Because he had forgotten his meal ticket, the student could not get lunch.
2. Before pruning the trees, I had to sharpen the blades.
3. To get the student rate, you must meet certain requirements.
4. When playing the guitar, many people use finger picks.
5. His vision was impaired when he drove at night.
6. The blender broke while I was making the frappe.
7. When I was six, I fractured my finger.
8. While she was sailing on the lake, her hat blew away.
9. To lose weight, you must follow a diet.
10. To play golf, you need a set of clubs.
11. Before hitting the jackpot, he performed a good-luck dance.
12. While I was in a cast, the nurse told me to take it easy.
13. Since I fired Ben, business has improved.
14. By considering the options, we made a decision.
15. Being a pirate, he covered his right eye with a patch.
16. The dogcatcher chased the rabid dog, which was foaming at the mouth.
17. The crowd watched the fireworks exploding in brilliant colors.
18. You have to use the stick shift to put the car in reverse.
19. When a person is tired and hungry, a ham and cheese sandwich really hits the spot.
20. In setting a table, you must place forks, knives, and spoons correctly.

VI Answers to this exercise will vary. Check with your instructor if you need to.

On arriving in America, Pierre was amazed by the sights and sounds. Since he had traveled alone, the sight of so many people hurrying around and shouting came as a jolt to him. Coming from a small village in the south of France, the young traveler had never before witnessed so much commotion. He was only eight years old and a bit nervous, and his luggage seemed to be his only companion. On this trip, his cousins in Philadelphia would be his hosts. Looking for them at the gate, he was not able to find them. Then an attendant took him to the information booth and paged his cousins over the loudspeaker. To locate them, the attendant had to make the announcement twice. Then Pierre recognized his relatives running through the terminal, from the other end of the building. Feeling relieved, Pierre ran to them and escaped the crazy crowds of America.

To throw a successful party, you must take several factors into consideration. When making up a list of people to invite, you should be sure they are compatible. After deciding on the guests, you must decide the amount of food and drink. If you are preparing a fruit punch, a large bowl and a ladle are necessary. If you want to save money, a fruit punch is often better than serving everyone individual cocktails. Preparing the food in advance is also a good idea. When you are planning the meal, you must, of course, consider the number of guests. By cooking ahead of time, you may avoid a lot of bother. I suggest making lasagna, which is always a favorite. When a host serves punch and lasagna, you can be almost certain that the party will be a success.

As a way of fighting the high cost of travel and of conserving fuel, more people are buying smaller automobiles. Both on the highway and in the city, a small car saves gas and gets better mileage. A driver should bring his small car in for a tuneup after he has driven about 10,000 miles. After receiving the proper care, the vehicle is ready for continued efficient use. When you think about it, the day of the big car is gone.

CHAPTER 8

Exercise: Point 1

1. They are going on a vacation.
2. We will haul this stuff to the dump.
3. She is learning how to water-ski.
4. It has been snapped in half.
5. They are planning a strike.
6. He served in Vietnam.
7. They are celebrating an anniversary.
8. We spent the day at the museum.
9. She is going for her Ph.D.
10. It gives Fritz great pleasure.

Exercise: Point 2

1. She hit him with it.
2. I wrote it about her.
3. They starred in it.
4. She bought it.
5. He paid for it.
6. He told them to move it right away.
7. They called us.
8. We called them.
9. Do you smoke it?
10. It is important to them.

Review Exercise: Points 1 and 2

1. We them
2. She him
3. It her
4. They it
5. He them
6. They it
7. She it him
8. It them
9. He it them
10. We it

Exercise: Point 3

1. boat (S) it (O)
2. dress (O) it (S)
3. Martha and I (S) us (O)
4. Tom and his friend (S) they (S)
5. she (S) Dolores (S)
6. skateboarding (O) it (O)
7. Willie (S) him (O) he (S)
8. Ted (S) flat tire (O) He (S) it (O) him (O)
9. test (O) it (O)
10. a notebook and some pens (O) them (O)

Exercise: Point 4

Answers to this exercise will vary. Check with your instructor if you need to.

1. Stan told Barbara, "You will be elected class president."
2. He added pepper, salt, and then, more pepper.
3. The White Sox won when they played the Red Sox.
4. Maria lived in an orphanage before Ms. Sanchez adopted her.
5. Bill felt great when he finally approached his father.
6. The car was damaged when it hit the telephone pole.
7. My mother was quite upset when she scolded my little sister.
8. Paul told his nephew, "You will be a great man some day."
9. The doctor told her patient, "You will have to take some time off."
10. The boys were embarrassed when they asked the girls to dance.

Review Exercise: Points 1–4

1. O him   one of the boys
2. S she   Lee
3. O it   The traffic
4. S he   The senator
   O it   bill
5. O me   Eddie
   S you   Ivan
6. O it   The vase
7. O her   Gail
8. S you   Dave and Sandy
9. S she   Carol
10. O it   The carton

Exercise: Point 5

1. F which   The class show was a great success
2. F which   He hadn't heard about the change in plans
3. C
4. F This   People continue to drive after drinking.
5. F This   Every American has the chance to be whatever he or she chooses.
6. F It   Buses never seem to keep to the schedules anymore.
7. F that   I miss my family,
8. F which   She takes a ballet lesson every Thursday,
9. F this   my mother always bugged me about keeping my room clean.
10. F which   He always carries a slide rule with him,

Exercise: Point 6

1. his nervousness
2. fish
3. a redhead
4. members of the fraternity
5. a home run
6. the students' laziness
7. the IRS *or* the government
8. the people who were given the concert
9. the fact that her sandwich was stale
10. the trip

Review Exercise: Points 1–6

Answers to this exercise will vary. Check with your instructor if you need to.

1. (5, 1) Everyone who worked on the class show was pleased that it was a great success.
2. (5, 2) Because he hadn't heard about the change in plans, he was late.
3. (5, 3) Correct.
4. (5, 4) It is ridiculous that people continue to drive after drinking.
5. (5, 5) One of the basic concepts of American democracy is that every person has the chance to be whatever he or she chooses.
6. (5, 6) Buses never seem to keep to the schedules anymore. The problem is really getting out of hand.
7. (5, 7) I go home for the holidays every year, because I miss my family.
8. (V, 8) To help strengthen her leg muscles, she takes a ballet lesson every Thursday.
9. (5, 9) When I was younger, my mother always bugged me about keeping my room clean. But she stopped doing it as I grew older and more mature.
10. (5, 10) He always carries a slide rule with him. Having it makes his work a lot easier.
11. (6, 1) Joseph is nervous about the upcoming exam, but his nervousness doesn't show.
12. (6, 2) Whenever I swim in that lake, the fish always nip at my feet.
13. (6, 3) Paula bought some red dye for her hair so she could become a redhead.
14. (6, 4) He joined the fraternity because its members enjoy the same things he does.
15. (6, 5) Although he made a home run, he was intimidated by all the home-run hitters in the lineup.
16. (6, 6) Some teachers feel that their students are lazy, and that the laziness is a result of too many hours spent watching television.
17. (6, 7) To avoid getting penalized for a late return, you have to send the IRS your income tax forms by April 15.
18. (6, 8) The concert was sold out, so we will have to see the group some other time.
19. (6, 9) Her sandwich was stale, because she had not wrapped it properly.
20. (6, 10) When we flew to Europe, I was surprised at how quickly the trip went.

Chapter Review

I

1. I
2. She me
3. him
4. her
5. him
6. us them
7. They us
8. them
9. him me
10. us
11. we us
12. her
13. They
14. him her
15. He I
16. she I he
17. We us
18. she
19. He
20. we they

II Answers to this exercise will vary. Check with your instructor if you need to.

1. she
2. it
3. they
4. them
5. her
6. he
7. we
8. you
9. her
10. it

III

1. F
2. F
3. F
4. F
5. F
6. C
7. F
8. F
9. F
10. C
11. C
12. F
13. F
14. F
15. F
16. F
17. F
18. C
19. F
20. C

IV Answers to this exercise will vary. Check with your instructor if you need to.

1. My wife was pleased that I changed my mind about buying a motorcycle.
2. The saw fell down when he put it on the shelf.
3. Betty said, "Jenny, you are the best cook in the world."
4. I bought a new pair of sneakers, but I always wear my old ones, which are still pretty good.
5. We were late because we could not find a parking space.
6. Gene moved there because he loves nature.
7. She told her sister, "I have found true love."
8. Because I did not know how to fix it, I brought the broken tool to the hardware store.
9. There is plenty of snow in New England.
10. As soon as I pumped up the tires, I went for a ride on my bike.
11. She made her debut in a Shakespearean play.
12. My wife went crazy when I used her coupon.
13. Vincent told Stephen, "You have been awarded a medal of honor."
14. Rudy said that he had heard I was moving to California. I am not.
15. He is a good father because he pays a great deal of attention to his children.

16. Although his happiness never shows, Oscar is happiest when he is working!

17. I got the job because I knew the president of the company.

18. Sally said that her mother's plans were outrageous.

19. When I went to the supermarket, I was happy to see that pork chops had gone down in price.

20. It is an elementary fact in mathematics that two plus two equals four.

V Answers to this exercise will vary. Check with your instructor if you need to.

Learning to drive a car was a harrowing experience. I took ten weeks of very helpful lessons at a driving school. But it was not until I was preparing for my road test that I found out how inexperienced I really was. Inexperience was really the problem.

In my last trial run, I backed the car out of my driveway and hit a lamppost. Fortunately, the car was not badly damaged. That incident was only the beginning. I finally got the car moving smoothly, and was nervous about running into something else, but I didn't let my nervousness show. I was cruising along at 25 miles per hour with the radio playing, since the radio always helped to calm me down. A police officer who was patrolling the neighborhood must have thought I was going too slowly and pulled me over. We talked for a few minutes, and the conversation turned out to be rather helpful: He suggested I use the headlights while driving at night.

I was excited when I heard about the rally. As soon as I heard about the demonstration, I got my shoes ready. They had shiny leather tops, brand-new laces, and thick rubber soles. Just looking at them put me into the right frame of mind for walking. I looked forward to the march because I really believed in the cause. Although I never let my weariness show, sometimes I get tired during a long walk. Besides, this was a truly important demonstration! This time when I slid into my shoes, my feet did not ache at all.

The nine-to-five workday, which millions of Americans experience five times a week, may be slowly dying out. Many people would be very happy if it did vanish. Employers are saying that their employees could use some extra time to themselves. A four-day work week may be with us shortly, and people are pleased to have the chance to spend more time with their families. Fathers and mothers will be able to take up new hobbies and pursue new interests, and the increase in free time will serve to improve the health of many people. Both physical and mental health will be improved. Working fewer hours would make millions of people very happy, but there would also have to be a promise of no drop in income. There are still some problems in setting up the shortened working schedule, but its promoters are confident that as the need for it becomes more apparent, it will come about.

CHAPTER 9

Exercise: Point 1

1. dancing, singing, laughing
2. to blend, to mix, to stir
3. pushed, pulled, shoved
4. have written, have stamped, have sent
5. fed, swallowed, digested
6. building, painting, whitewashing
7. rose, sank, reappeared
8. to love, to honor, to obey
9. drove, parked, paid
10. living, laughing, loving

Exercise: Point 2

Answers to this exercise will vary. Check with your instructor if you need to.
1. hungry, thirsty, tired
2. proud, brave, patriotic
3. brunette, brown-eyed, dark-complexioned
4. weaving, crocheting, sewing
5. bought, traded, sold
6. to replace, to repair, to restore
7. playing baseball, playing football, playing soccer
8. exciting, fantastic, thrilling
9. planting, reaping, storing
10. dreamed, desired, wished

Exercise: Point 3

Answers to this exercise will vary. Check with your instructor if you need to.

1. Eduardo has always enjoyed fishing and hunting.

2. You can see the moon and stars in the sky tonight.

3. As an accountant, Phyllis adds and multiplies figures all day long.

4. I will probably be washing the dishes or mopping the floor when you arrive.

5. He is old but alert.

6. Filling the gas tank and checking the oil are two of the responsibilities of a gas station attendant.

7. A teacher expects his students to do their <u>home-work, to attend classes regularly,</u> and to pay atten-tion to lectures.

8. Before she left, <u>she combed her hair, polished her fingernails,</u> and applied her makeup.

9. When customers are not satisfied, they <u>return the merchandise</u> or make a complaint.

10. The day is <u>sunny, hot,</u> and humid.

Review Exercise: Points 1–3

Answers to this exercise will vary. Check with your in-structor if you need to.

1. You put the cheese between two slices of bread and fry it in a pan.
2. He was a good lecturer, a kind man, and a hard worker.
3. A lifeguard supervises the beach, flirts with girls, and rescues swimmers who are having difficulty.
4. Lynn is preparing her résumé, reading the want ads, and going on interviews.
5. A good friend is thoughtful, truthful, and supportive.
6. I enjoy seeing shows, reading good books, and going to the movies.
7. To be a doctor, one must have ambition, persis-tence, and willingess to work long hours.
8. The cat purred, meowed, and cleaned itself.
9. He was forced to pawn his watch, sell his radio, and try to find a new job.
10. To be or not to be; that is the question.

Exercise: Point 4

1. P	6. P
2. X	7. P
3. P	8. P
4. X	9. X
5. P	10. P

Exercise: Point 5

Answers to this exercise will vary. Check with your in-structor if you need to.

1. Our house is located near the bus station, the laun-dromat, and the supermarket.
2. By taking lessons and practicing daily, Andrea has become a fine violinist.
3. My dream is to have a good job, a family, and a house in the country.
4. Washing my car, removing the rust, and getting a good finish takes time.
5. He said that he would stop by our house, deliver the package, and stay for dinner.
6. I bought a car with whitewall tires, leather seats, and an AM-FM radio.

7. She asked me where I went to school and what de-gree I earned.
8. Waiting for the bus and becoming a bit nervous, Hal started biting his nails.
9. I promise to dress properly and to arrive on time.
10. Doris wants to be a violinist, a music teacher, or a conductor.

Review Exercise: Points 1–5

Answers to this exercise will vary. Check with your in-structor if you need to.

1. He accepted the money, promised to spend it wisely, and went for a ride in his car.
2. Not only was she attractive, but her sense of humor was also good.
3. They went to Cape Cod on their vacation to camp and to have fun.
4. This book is boring and long.
5. Her coat has six brass buttons, flared sleeves, and a detachable hood.
6. Eating breakfast, eating lunch, and eating dinner are my three favorite activities of the day.
7. Debra was either angry or irritable.
8. The fullback is strong, big, and fast.
9. We went to the concert with Fred, Jane, and Zelda.
10. They were interested in buying the air conditioner, but were not willing to spend so much money.

Chapter Review

I 1. achieving a sense of satisfaction
2. escaping in the green Ford
3. having good luck
4. to comb his hair
5. his ability to keep cool
6. the piano player sang
7. by herself
8. charging at us
9. to do arithmetic
10. kind

II			
1. to cash a check		6. to get undressed	
2. looking out for bears		7. mowing the lawn	
3. with pimples		8. sturdy	
4. looking outside		9. on the sofa	
5. riding		10. to meet the neighbors	

III Answers to this exercise will vary. Check with your instructor if you need to.

1. It is my ambition <u>to be successful</u> and to be popular.
2. Rod can speak both <u>English</u> and German.

3. She said that she would be on either <u>the 7:00 bus</u> or the 9:15 bus.

4. The brown puppy was <u>wagging its tail</u> and licking my hand.

5. The cabinet he built is made of pine and is painted blue.

6. We strolled <u>under the boardwalk</u> and along the beach.

7. He wants <u>to move to Mexico</u> and to live there permanently.

8. Judy kept <u>a rabbit's foot, a four-leaf clover,</u> and a horseshoe in her drawer.

9. When we visited San Francisco, we <u>rode the cable cars, went to Fisherman's Wharf,</u> and attended the American Conservatory Theatre.

10. When left alone, he gets sad, lonely, and depressed.

IV Answers to this exercise will vary. Check with your instructor if you need to.

1. He admitted that he had committed the crime and that he deserved to get caught.

2. We were disappointed with our grades, but we understood them.

3. Batting, throwing, and fielding are important skills in baseball.

4. The dog dug up the bone and found it to his liking.

5. Ramon knows that he should work on his writing and should improve his spelling.

6. His lunch included soup, a roast beef sandwich, a peach, and dessert.

7. I respected his intelligence, his strength, and his humor.

8. It would make my day complete to see you, to go to a movie, and to have dinner with you.

9. That cigarette tastes harsh and is probably stale.

10. Marianne spends her day attending classes, studying, and listening to music.

11. The day was sunny, bright, and dry.

12. The dean told the teacher that classes were suspended and that the students could go home.

13. She could read on a bus, in an elevator, or in line at the bank.

14. The camper learned how to tie a knot, how to start a fire, and how to ride horseback.

15. That car with four-wheel drive can get out of mud, snow, and deep potholes.

16. There were news items about the rising price of coffee, the increasing crime rate, and the growing energy shortage.

17. The grass needed water and turned brown.

18. Going for a walk in the evening and meeting a friend on the street are both pleasant.

19. The movie starred Richard Burton, Elizabeth Taylor, George Segal, and Sandy Dennis.

20. Stupid questions make me angry and make me lose my temper.

V Answers to this exercise will vary. Check with your instructor if you need to.

1. I was watching the ball game and eating hot dogs.

2. We learned that we had won the lottery and also that we had become instant millionaires.

3. She was running, jumping, and trying to catch a butterfly.

4. We cooked our dinner, and then we cleaned the dishes.

5. I want to save money so I will be able to buy presents.

6. I enjoy going to a dance, choosing a partner, and dancing with her.

7. I like putting my feet up, listening to the radio, and relaxing.

8. He was sure that he could stand no more and that he would lose his temper.

9. That skirt is thin and flimsy.

10. Keeping good notes and using a tape recorder are valuable aids to study.

11. I went to the stadium with my buddies.

12. The first steps to finding work are applying for a job and scheduling an interview.

13. The face of the cliff was steep, dangerous, and slippery.

14. We have a family reunion on Mother's Day, on Father's Day, and on Thanksgiving.

15. When I am happy, I laugh.

16. You will find mothballs around the corner in aisle three.

17. If I got the job, when would I start working?

18. I enjoy building a fire and roasting marshmallows.

19. She told me that I was her best friend and that she wanted me to read her poetry.

20. I want both to have friends and to be free.

VI Answers to this exercise will vary. Check with your instructor if you need to.

A library is a good place to spend an afternoon and to relax. You can read the newspaper from any major city, look for a good novel, or listen to a record. Librarians can tell you where to find a particular book and can suggest a quiet place where you can read it. Many libraries have display halls where you can observe artwork or just stroll around.

People find many different things to do in the library. There is usually someone studying or writing a research paper; there are those who read periodicals and those who just chat with friends. All things considered, the library is an excellent place for meeting people, reading, or relaxing.

When we heard that we had won the lottery, we wanted to jump for joy, scream our lungs out, and pat each other on the back. We immediately made plans for renting a car, dining, and dancing. We went wild, spending the evening eating the best food we had ever tasted, drinking only the finest wines, ever tasted, drinking only the finest wines, and riding to the top of the Hancock Tower to get a dramatic view of Boston. Finally at around 3:00 A.M. we decided that we were pooped, that we had to go home, and that climbing into bed seemed just right.

Paul Newman is one of America's most popular actors. Not only is he a big drawing card, but he is also very talented. He has played in many pictures, including *The Hustler* and *The Sting*, and has starred most of the time. Many women feel he is handsome and has sex appeal; to many men he appears to be tough and strong-willed.

In *Butch Cassidy and the Sundance Kid*, he appeared with Robert Redford, another extremely popular American actor. In that movie, they robbed banks, dived off a steep cliff, and lived with a beautiful woman, who was played by Katherine Ross.

Paul Newman lives in Connecticut with his wife, Joanne Woodward. They live in a beautiful town, share a lovely house, and according to rumor, have a very happy marriage.

CHAPTER 10

Exercise: Point 1
1. S
2. S
3. P
4. S
5. P
6. S
7. P
8. S
9. P
10. P

Exercise: Point 2

1. <u>A reporter</u> should always write his stories objectively.
2. If <u>a driver</u> is careful, he will avoid accidents.
3. <u>A model</u> should always look his best when he is being photographed.
4. <u>Breakfast cereals</u> are tasty, and they supply vitamins and minerals.
5. <u>The headmaster</u> works in his office.
6. <u>A disc jockey</u> plays records; also, he reads commercials.
7. <u>A teacher</u> should be familiar with his material; moreover, he should be able to present it in a clear manner.
8. <u>Our boss</u> is vacationing in her trailer.
9. <u>My grandmother</u> is making her special soup.
10. <u>The fans</u> are waiting in line for their turn.

Review Exercise: Points 1 and 2
Answers to this exercise will vary. Check with your instructor if you need to.
1. A successful comedian tries to get a sense of his audience.
2. A person should try to understand his limitations.
3. I was looking for my hat, but I could not find it.
4. You have two chances, so use them wisely.
5. Teachers grade papers, and sometimes they also write comments.
6. A lawyer advises his clients, but his fees are often excessive.
7. Athletes often get their backs massaged.
8. The radio is broken, but it can be repaired.
9. Ms. Kanter is cooking her special pot roast.
10. A party can be a lot of fun, but it must be well planned.

Exercise: Point 3
1. 3
2. 1
3. 3
4. 3
5. 3
6. 2
7. 3
8. 1
9. 3
10. 3

Exercise: Point 4

1. A person can run for public office if he meets certain requirements.
2. If he were really my friend, he wouldn't have made that remark.
3. If one is running for office, he should always tell the truth.
4. One could ask her a question and he would never get a answer.
5. Anyone can quit smoking if he really puts his mind to it.
6. She sat in the sun for three hours, and one can't do that without getting a severe burn.

7. You can do it if you put your mind to it.
8. The bowler scored seven strikes in a row; one has to be skillful to do that.
9. After we left, we felt that we wanted to visit again.
10. A lawyer should advise his clients carefully.

Review Exercise: Points 1–4

Answers to this exercise will vary. Check with your instructor if you need to.
1. A good businessman is always helpful to his clients.
2. Students who study hard are sure to find satisfaction for themselves.
3. Roller coasters are exciting to ride, but some think they are dangerous.
4. She likes to watch television, but one should spend some of one's time reading.
5. A person should brush his teeth after every meal.
6. A son may sometimes try to take after his father.
7. Sherry always keeps her checkbook balanced.
8. A butcher must be careful not to back into his meat slicer, or he may get a little behind in his work.
9. A fool will soon part with his money.
10. Wise people look ahead to the future; they do not get themselves forever tied up in the past.

Exercise: Point 5

1. She <u>gave</u> him good advice, but he ignored her.
2. I <u>lost</u> my library card, so I got a new one.
3. I <u>could not find</u> my way, so I asked for help.
4. It <u>was</u> one of the weirdest experiences I ever had.
5. The police officer <u>stopped</u> him because he was jaywalking.
6. I <u>miss</u> you and want you.
7. When I <u>tell</u> her that I love her, she is happy.
8. She <u>asked</u>, "Are you coming?" and I said, "No."
9. We <u>stayed</u> for the entire show and then went out for ice cream.
10. The road <u>was</u> rocky, but because he was driving carefully, we arrived safely.

Review Exercise: Points 1–5

Answers to this exercise will vary. Check with your instructor if you need to.
1. We bought an air conditioner, so we stayed cool all last summer.
2. He was a man who always put his best foot forward.
3. A teacher must prepare his lesson plans every night.
4. She berates her brother and hits him, too.
5. A great chef will never tell you his secret recipes.
6. Everyone who was there had his fanciest clothes on.

7. I saw her at a distance, and then I ran to her.
8. A politician must know how to address his constituency.
9. If one intends to get an A in the course, he will have to work hard.
10. Man orbited the earth before he walked on the moon.

Chapter Review

I
1. A fashion designer has his work cut out for him.
2. When you know the answer, raise your hand.
3. She was hired yesterday and celebrated last evening.
4. Whenever he sneezes, he causes quite a ruckus.
5. Children should respect their parents.
6. The golfer measured the putt and tapped his ball in for a par.
7. A typewriter should be cleaned regularly or else it will not print clearly.
8. We went skiing, had drinks before a fireplace, and got to know each other better.
9. When a baby cries, it often means that he wants his mother.
10. Some people never get their car tuned.
11. Man's best friend is his dog.
12. Don't lose your cool!
13. We go for a ride, have a picnic, and then come home and have another party.
14. I came, I saw, I conquered.
15. A typewriter is useful to its owner.
16. The Beatles wrote most of their songs.
17. Food is very expensive today; also, heating costs are higher.
18. She ran out of the room and said, "I am leaving."
19. As Americans, we are supposed to have the opportunity to improve our future.
20. The singer signaled for her musicians to pick up the tempo.

II Answers to this exercise will vary. Check with your instructor if you need to.
1. A person may get his hair cut, or he may get it styled.
2. A doctor should be sympathetic with his patients.
3. We ate and drank until we were full.
4. A dog is man's best friend; it always comes when one calls.
5. I missed the bus, so I waited for another.
6. Children should respect their parents.
7. If you cross the street in the middle of the block, you have to be very careful.
8. A public official should heed the opinions of his constituents.

9. The building inspector expressed her opinion that the old house should be torn down.
10. The dog chased the man and bit his leg.
11. One should exercise his right to vote.
12. A student should try to hand in his papers on time.
13. The principal called the teachers in for a meeting and addressed them on methods of discipline.
14. The car swerved and hit a telephone pole.
15. A person should try to make his dreams come true.
16. People should try to make their dreams come true.
17. You are my best friend, for you always listen when I have problems.
18. The bus driver wanted the exact change, but we did not have it.
19. She wanted her boss to give her a raise.
20. Go tell Aunt Rodie that the old gray goose is dead.

III 1. they are
their number

2. decide tense

3. you present
your person

4. your person

5. got tense

6. his number

7. your person

8. your person

9. they are number

10. use tense

IV Answers to this exercise will vary. Check with your instructor if you need to.
1. First he read the novel; then he wrote the paper.
2. Sportscasters should be objective, but they always seem to root for the home team.
3. If a student studies regularly, he will not have to cram the night before a test.
4. She enjoys reading, but she dislikes writing.
5. One must participate in class discussion, or his grade will suffer.
6. Anyone can learn home repair if he concentrates.
7. Hansel and Gretel finally found their way home.
8. She counted to ten before she lost her temper.
9. Pilots always try to make their passengers feel at ease.
10. A person can educate himself if he puts his mind to it.
11. King Arthur ate with all of his knights at the Round Table.
12. Every morning she washes her face, brushes her teeth, and combs her hair.

13. If you want to see an enjoyable movie, you should see E.T.
14. A fisherman should always carry extra hooks with him.
15. He whines whenever he does not get his way.
16. Many taxpayers need an accountant to figure out their returns.
17. I don't enjoy shopping for clothes because I have to spend so much time in dressing rooms.
18. If one intends to quit his job, he should give two weeks' notice.
19. Pediatricians must like children, because they deal with them every day.
20. I went to the movies and saw *Fantasia*.

V Answers to this exercise will vary. Check with your instructor if you need to.

If one intends to be a writer, he must first learn the great task of self-discipline. Most novelists, or poets, or dramatists do not work in an office; they often work at home. If they are unable to rid themselves of distractions, they will probably find that they do very little work. There are always plenty of reasons or excuses not to write, but if the writer is able to set his mind to his work, they will not bother him. Some writers make schedules for themselves; others choose to work when they are inspired. Whatever the case, the point remains the same: If one wants to write, he writes; if one does not, he doesn't.

Today, news programs and magazines are quite the rage. Everywhere you look, you can see news of this strike or that tax increase. A newspaper should be objective, but its writers always seem to inject their own opinion into the stories. Because of the subjective nature of the news, more and more magazines find their way onto the newsstands. Moreover, these magazines often produce more in-depth accounts of the news. I suppose every form of the news media has its place.

I work in a bank, and when one has that type of job, he has to be willing to wake up at a very early hour. Each morning, I drive to work, park my car, and walk a block to work. I get a lunch break every day at noon, and I love to eat at the delicatessen around the corner. I worked at the bank for over a year, and decided that I had had enough. After looking around for a new job, I found one where I had to be at work by 6:00 A.M. This job was in a restaurant where I had to stand up all day, and after six months, I decided to go back to the bank. The manager was very nice to me and said, "You can have your old job back if you promise to stay at least two years." I took the job, and I enjoy an extra hour of sleep every morning.

CHAPTER 11

Exercise: Point 1

1. S They promised to arrive on time.
2. S The humidity bothers me.
3. X
4. S The repairman asked whether we had fooled around with the plug.
5. X
6. S Vote for me.
7. S I bought a new needle for my record player.
8. S Let's build a bonfire tonight.
9. S They danced the tango.
10. X

Review Exercise: Points 1 and 2

1. Dr. Mitchell canceled my appointment.
2. *Ms.* magazine is very popular reading these days.
3. A Ph.D is an advanced degree.
4. Combine two oz. butter with four oz. sugar.
5. Now I get it.
6. Mrs. Ames raised an objection.
7. I have been instructed to report on Sept. 30.
8. Sen. Rosser is a great man.
9. There are never enough hours in the day.
10. The room measured 20 sq. ft.

Exercise: Point 3

1. C	6. X
2. X	7. X
3. X	8. X
4. C	9. X
5. X	10. X

Exercise: Point 4

Answers to this exercise will vary. Check with your instructor if you need to.

The alarm clock was shrieking. I woke up with a start. When I looked at the clock, it said 8:30. Oh, no! I had meant to set it for 7:30. Now I'd never get to the bus stop on time! I jumped out of bed, yanked on my clothes, and grabbed a couple of doughnuts from last night's party. They would have to do for breakfast; I couldn't even take time to make coffee. With the doughnuts in one hand and my purse in the other, I dashed out the door and ran down the street. The bus was coming. I would never make it. Then, at the last minute, the traffic light turned red. The bus had to wait. I put on a last burst of speed and made it to the bus stop just as the bus rolled up. As I scrambled aboard, panting, the driver grinned. "I saw you coming," he said. "I would have waited for you." I ought to have thanked him, but the way he grinned made me want to hit him instead. I collapsed into the nearest seat, puffing like an overweight elephant. It didn't matter—I had caught the bus!

Review Exercise: Points 1–4

1. Working by candlelight can be inspiring.
2. Has the mail arrived yet?
3. She asked him if he would like to go out for dinner.
4. We do not take credit cards here.
5. I would like a corned beef sandwich.
6. Are you still taking violin lessons?
7. Good grief, he's having a heart attack!
8. Is there any reason to continue?
9. You had better comb your hair and straighten your tie.
10. I hope I don't have any cavities.

Exercise: Point 5

1. The teller said, "I'm sorry, but your check has bounced."
2. "I'll never lie again," he said. "I promise."
3. "This assignment is due Tuesday," the teacher announced.
4. I warned him to drive slowly on the icy roads.
5. "Do you know the answer?" the teacher asked.
6. The doctor said, "Take two aspirins and go to sleep."
7. Carol asked me if she could have a ride home.
8. "You can't get there from here," said the tour guide.
9. "I am telling the truth," he said. And then he added, "I know you won't believe me."
10. "Why don't you and Jane come for dinner?" she asked.

Exercise: Point 6

1. X Joyce said, "I think I have a cold."
2. X "Do you love me?" he asked.
3. X "Mend your ways!" I screamed.
4. X Billy asked, "Why is it always me?"
5. X I can't believe you actually said, "Fishing is for the birds"; you have a weird sense of humor.
6. X "Does this car need oil?" the attendant inquired.
7. X "Out, damn Spot!" she screamed, throwing her dog out the door.
8. C
9. X Did you shout, "Bargains galore"?
10. X Cries of "Help!" echoed through the building.

Exercise: Point 7

1. Last night we saw <u>Gone with the Wind</u> for the fifth time.

2. "Don't Think Twice" was written and sung by Bob Dylan.

3. "Grammar Review" is the first part of Trouble-shooting.

4. I read an article entitled "A Day with the President."

5. Harrison Ford starred in the film Indiana Jones and the Temple of Doom.

6. Great Expectations is one of Dickens' most enjoyable novels.

7. "The Star-Spangled Banner" is America's national anthem.

8. No Way to Treat a Lady is a frightening movie.

9. Coleridge wrote a poem entitled "Kubla Khan."

10. "Tradition" is the opening song in the musical Fiddler on the Roof.

Review Exercise: Points 5–7

1. Annie asked, "Are you going to sing that song again?"
2. I plan to read Moby Dick this summer.
3. "Are you my friend or aren't you?" she asked.
4. "The time is right," he said, "for us to move on."
5. Have you heard the Rolling Stones perform "Brown Sugar"?
6. She said that she would be studying all night.
7. John said, "Come visit us next weekend."
8. "Before I go," she said, "let me ask you one question."
9. "Do you read The New Yorker?" she asked.
10. "Get that car out of my driveway!" the man hollered.

Chapter Review

I   1. X   6. C
       2. X   7. X
       3. X   8. C
       4. X   9. X
       5. C   10. X

II   1. I am spending more time in the library these days.
       2. Have you ever eaten smelts?
       3. Don't try any funny business with me!
       4. I wonder why they say blondes have more fun.
       5. The show is on channel 5.
       6. He has a lighter with his initials on it.
       7. Did you say that you were driving to California this summer?
       8. The bellboy asked whether we needed any help with our bags.
       9. Dr. McCarthy is the new chairman.
     10. Debbie is working toward her Ph.D.
     11. What kind of fool am I?
     12. Get lost, Buster!
     13. Where were you on the night of June 3?
     14. Should I wait for her?
     15. Let's go, Mets!
     16. She asked whether she could expect a raise.
     17. Have you heard about Hugo and Kim?
     18. A rolling stone gathers no moss.
     19. Sgt. Anderson is an excellent detective.
     20. Should we call you Miss Burns or Mrs. Burns?

III   1. "I'm thinking. Give me some time!" Peter snapped.
       2. Rita asked, "Will there be an essay question on the test?"
       3. "We're late," she cried, "hurry up!"
       4. Have you seen The Big Chill?
       5. In the musical Oliver, Fagin sings a song called "Reviewing the Situation."
       6. "The metric system is too confusing," he complained.
       7. "Don't you get the joke?" she asked.
       8. "Block that kick!" the crowd chanted rhythmically.
       9. His mother pleaded, "Finish your vegetables. There are people starving in India."
     10. "Why don't you come up and see me some time?" she sang.
     11. "Get lost!" we screamed at the hoodlums.
     12. "Anything Goes" is one of Cole Porter's most popular songs.
     13. The doctor asked, "Are you feeling better?"
     14. "This won't hurt a bit," the nurse said as she stuck the needle into my arm.
     15. "What is your hurry?" asked the oldtimer.
     16. Stevie Wonder wrote "You Are the Sunshine of My Life."
     17. I heard her say, "This is the worst party I've ever been to!"
     18. "Hold it right there!" the police officer shouted
     19. "I hate peas!" wailed the child.
     20. "Run a mile a day," she advised, "and you're sure to feel better."

IV Answers to this exercise will vary. Check with your instructor if you need to.
       1. Earl asked, "Can I lend a hand?"
       2. The little boy cried when he hurt his leg.
       3. Inez asked her brother, "Did Mom say when she'd be back?"
       4. She wondered if he would ever ask her out.
       5. As I always say, "If you can't lick them, join them!"

6. Ms. Yee said, "The job is yours."
7. He responded by saying, "Sorry, lady. It's too risky."
8. Do you know that song called "Three Little Maids from School" from The Mikado?
9. My favorite movie is still High Noon..
10. The doctor warned us not to let him get up right away.

V 1. "I love scary movies," my sister informed us.
2. Dr. Gomez is an M.D.
3. "Where do you think you're going?" my mother asked.
4. "I wonder," he said, "if the economy will ever improve."
5. My sister said that she was going to run off to the Orient.
6. "Why must you always complain?" I asked her.
7. "A Child's Christmas in Wales" is a short story by Dylan Thomas.
8. "Full speed ahead!" shouted the captain.
9. "What's the deal?" he whispered.
10. The lyrics are, "Candy is dandy, but liquor is quicker."
11. "I'm working as a file clerk this summer," he said.
12. Was it you who asked that stupid question?
13. "There's no green cheese up here," said the astronaut.
14. "As Time Goes By" was a very popular love song.
15. "Get out of my life," she cried. "I've had enough!"
16. "While I'm away," he said, "please water my plants."
17. "Why are you so good to me?" she sighed.
18. "You fool!" screamed the man whose car I had just hit.
19. Al Jolson made a movie called The Jazz Singer.
20. "You will be a great writer," his teacher told him.

VI   "This is the third paper of the semester that you have turned in late," said Professor Martin, "and you are simply going to have to change your work habits."

"I know," said Bruce, "and I promise to change my ways."

Mr. Martin said, "Don't tell me your dog chewed up the paper. What happened?"

"I don't have a dog," replied Bruce, "but I do have a little brother."

"And he tore it up?" Mr. Martin asked.

"No," said Bruce, "but he wrote it for me, and since his spelling was so bad, it took me two whole days to correct it."

Three men were stationed in the farthest reaches of Alaska, and their supply of whiskey was running low. Two of the men felt that they could take advantage of the third, so they told him to go out into the blizzard and buy some more whiskey in the nearest town. The third man said, "I will go only if you promise to save the last drop of this remaining whiskey for me."

"Don't worry," the others said, "we promise."

"I will definitely not go if you drink that last drop," the third man said.

"We promise, we promise," the others assured him.

With that, the third man left. A day went by. Two days went by. A week and then two weeks went by. The two men figured that the third must have died in the blizzard and decided to drink the last bit of whiskey. They took the bottle down from the shelf, said, "Cheers," and were about to indulge when the third man flung the door open.

"I told you," he announced, "I wasn't going to go if you drank that last drop!"

CHAPTER 12

Exercise: Point 1

1. My family vacationed in Canada; we visited Toronto and Montreal.
2. The baseball game was exciting; it went into extra innings.
3. We always see the latest horror films; we like being scared.
4. Mary lost her I.D. card; she couldn't get the student rate.
5. The lawn was overgrown; Dave volunteered to mow it.
6. Firefighters have to be brave; they risk their lives almost every day.
7. We got the mortgage; we bought the house.
8. I will use a road map; I will not lose my way.
9. The concert was given outdoors; it was free of charge.
10. He talks to his house plants; they just don't want to grow.

Exercise: Point 2

1. X	6. C
2. C	7. C
3. C	8. X
4. X	9. C
5. X	10. X

Review Exercise: Points 1 and 2

1. The weather was miserable; it rained all day.
2. The cabinet is handcrafted; it is made of oak.
3. Mr. Ryan got a new job; however, he is not very happy in it.
4. We went skiing last weekend; the snow was perfectly packed.
5. I witnessed the accident; therefore, I will testify in court.
6. Alice missed a week of class; nevertheless, she passed the exam.
7. I enjoy reading novels of the occult; however, I find the movies boring.
8. Reporters have strict deadlines; they work under great pressure.
9. Raking leaves is spiritually rewarding; it is also exhausting.
10. I have planted a garden; I expect tomatoes by the end of the summer.

Exercise: Point 3

1. I read in the newspaper about the governor's efforts to lower automobile insurance rates; the latest troubles in the Middle East; and a new program for providing hot meals for the elderly on holidays.
2. In my refrigerator are the remains of a bacon, lettuce, and tomato sandwich, which I made two weeks ago; some cheddar cheese, which could probably be used for penicillin; a fried egg; and two bottles of beer, which I should probably drink to forget about the sad state of my refrigerator.
3. Nancy has lived at three different addresses: 505 South Street, Miami, Florida; 71 Granite Avenue, Atlanta, Georgia; and 12-47 Maxwell Boulevard, Charlotte, North Carolina.
4. Our neighborhood council has resolved that street lights will be turned on every evening at 7:30; that parents should keep a close watch on their children to see that vandalism declines; and that a recycling dropoff point will be established at the corner of Northend and Pleasant Streets.
5. The terms of the contract stated that the work must be finished by August 15; that payment would be made in two installments, one by September 30, the other by December 30; and that all work must be presented in a manner judged acceptable by the employer.

Exercise: Point 4

1. C records
2. X
3. C talents
4. X
5. X
6. C uses
7. C vices
8. X
9. X
10. C types

Chapter Review

I
1. X
2. X
3. X
4. C
5. C
6. C
7. X
8. X
9. C
10. X

II
1. The car has a flat tire; there is a spare in the trunk.
2. I didn't finish the assignment; I was too busy.
3. That dress comes in three colors: red, blue, and yellow.
4. We've never traveled so much; it's fun.
5. He told me the following: that he was fed up with the city and that he was moving to the country.
6. I'm exhausted; moreover, I still have more to study.
7. Carl has only two desires: to be rich and to be famous.
8. Linda had two boyfriends before she met me: Jack and Frankie.
9. Russian dressing is good; nevertheless, I prefer Italian.
10. We were late for the concert; the usher made us wait until the first number had been completed.
11. President Kennedy once said, "Ask not what your country can do for you; ask what you can do for your country."
12. They drove through three states: Oregon, Idaho, and Washington.
13. You cook with love; therefore, your dinners are wonderful.
14. We went horseback riding in the afternoon; then we settled down to an evening of food and good talk.
15. Human needs: food, clothing, and shelter.
16. I don't enjoy flying; nevertheless, we flew to Europe last summer.
17. Norm used to smoke cigarettes; now he smokes a pipe.
18. Intramural sports are great; they give you a chance to exercise without high-pressure competition.
19. Ingredients for a salad: lettuce, tomatoes, carrots, and peppers.
20. You have been given three wishes; make them carefully.

III
1. We bought tickets well in advance; therefore, we got good seats.
2. I would love to go; however, I am too tired.

3. <u>Choose one essay question</u>; <u>answer it in 500 words or less.</u>

4. <u>I keep losing my ball-point pens</u>; <u>I should get one with a clip.</u>

5. <u>Our team won the championship</u>; <u>we were awarded a trophy.</u>

6. <u>You must learn to control your temper</u>; <u>it can get you into trouble.</u>

7. <u>Robert Redford starred in the movie</u>; <u>he gave a great performance.</u>

8. <u>A calendar watch can be a great convenience</u>; however, <u>it has to be reset once a month.</u>

9. <u>A sense of humor is important</u>; <u>try to develop one.</u>

10. <u>I get hay fever attacks every August</u>; however, <u>they do not bother me much with my new allergy pills.</u>

IV 1. I have two <u>reasons</u> to be depressed: my girl-friend left me, and I'm developing dandruff.

2. Shakespeare wrote plays in different <u>styles</u>: comedy, tragedy, and history.

3. We had a great <u>dinner</u>: veal, spaghetti, green beans, and wine.

4. <u>Aspects</u> of a novel: plot, character, setting, theme, and tone.

5. Our teacher stressed two <u>points</u>: that we should attend class regularly and that we should hand assignments in on time.

6. Hank has two <u>pairs</u> of sneakers: one for tennis and one for basketball.

7. You will receive the <u>following</u>: a demonstration lesson and a free career brochure.

8. We learned two new dance <u>steps</u>: the tango and the hustle.

9. We saw two <u>movies</u> last weekend: *Ghostbusters* and *The Karate Kid*.

10. Choose one main <u>dish</u>: chicken chow mein or chop suey.

V Answers to this exercise will vary. Check with your instructor if you need to.

VI Answers to this exercise will vary. Check with your instructor if you need to.

1. Janet works in the library; she is a page.
2. You don't understand; I apologize for my thoughtlessness.
3. That store sells jeans, jeans, and more jeans.
4. I have been to that part of town once, but I will never go back.
5. He was arrested on the following charges: assault and battery and armed robbery.
6. Beatrice exercises daily, and it shows in her fine physique.
7. Call me anytime; I'm here when you need me.
8. Birds fly, fish swim, and snakes crawl.
9. He sang as follows: off-key and very loud.
10. The cast rehearsed for weeks; still, they were nervous on opening night.
11. There's no business like show business; I should know.
12. She appeared calm; on the inside, though, she was scared.
13. It was Melvin's fault; he is such a klutz.
14. Tomorrow is her birthday; she'll be twenty-five.
15. We watch the news and the *Tonight Show* every night.
16. He is responsible for the following: tending the garden, painting the house, and washing the car.
17. The jury announced its verdict as follows: guilty of first-degree murder.
18. First the leaves turn colors; then they fall.
19. I want bigger muscles; therefore, I lift weights.
20. Ralph doesn't take care of his teeth; consequently, he gets at least six cavities a year.

VII Answers to this exercise will vary. Check with your instructor if you need to.

The team was in trouble; it had dropped from first place to last in three weeks. The manager called a meeting of the players at which the following issues were discussed: the importance of developing a winning attitude, whereby the players would place the goals of the team over their individual achievements; the imposition of a strict curfew so that the players would be well rested for the games; the problem of teammates competing among themselves for higher salaries and greater coverage in the newspapers; and last but not least, the general lack of hustle and determination on the part of the team's stars.

My friends and I recently spent a day driving around New England trying to hit as many hamburger joints as we could in sixteen hours. Our travels took us to the following places: Burlington, Massachusetts, where we prepared out stomachs with thick shakes and French fries; Concord, New Hampshire, where we indulged in double cheeseburgers; Canaan, New Hampshire, were we settled for soft drinks; Woodstock, Vermont, where we each downed a filet of fish; and finally to Worcester, Massachusetts, where we celebrated with chicken sandwiches. We ate dessert at the quick lunch bar at Boston University, Boston, Massachusetts.

CHAPTER 13

Exercise: Point 1

1. She was lonely, depressed, and nostalgic.
2. Kathy planted tulips, daffodils, and roses.
3. It is hot and muggy today.
4. He stormed out of the house, went for a walk, and came back the next morning.
5. I've been to South America, Central America, and Canada.
6. Bend me, shake me, break me; do anything you want.
7. The letter was signed, sealed, and delivered.
8. We strolled along the beach and gathered shells.
9. This library has books, books, and more books.
10. For lunch we had soup, salad, and a sandwich.

Exercise: Point 2

1. He thinks he should be a star, but he really isn't very talented.
2. I can type very fast, but I make a lot of mistakes.
3. That's the way it goes, and you will have to accept it.
4. My wife tries to rush me, yet I always take my time.
5. She had a cold, so she stayed in bed all day.
6. I'm taking flying lessons, but I can't seem to get the hang of making turns.
7. Randy will graduate this year, and he hopes to get a job in the clothing industry.
8. Friendship is simple yet complex.
9. Be truthful with me, or I will leave you.
10. He is very bright but can't seem to get his head together.

Review Exercise: Points 1 and 2

1. Joe, Sue, and Anne were invited to the party.
2. We hoped the humidity would end, but it didn't.
3. There were cows and horses roaming around the field.
4. I ate pizza, and she ate a grinder.
5. We spoke seriously yet insincerely.
6. She used parsley, garlic, and tarragon in the sauce.
7. She is superstitious, and her husband is a nervous wreck.

8. We got to the show on time, but we left at the intermission.
9. Reading, writing, and arithmetic are the basics of education.
10. We sang, laughed, and drank all night long.

Exercise: Point 3

1. After the party ended, we cleaned the apartment.
2. Yes, we have no bananas.
3. As I said before, the lecture is canceled.
4. Not wanting to go, I said I wasn't feeling well.
5. Since you wanted popsicles, I bought some.
6. By the way, you have been promoted.
7. Whenever I hear that album, I feel better.
8. As I feared, the end is near.
9. Thinking about the past, I always get melancholy.
10. Unfortunately, your plan will never work.

Another Exercise: Point 3

Answers to this exercise will vary. Check with your instructor if you need to.

Exercise: Point 4

1. I told you once, Margie, and I will not tell you again.
2. Shakespeare, for example, wrote beautiful sonnets.
3. I think, therefore, that we should adjourn immediately.
4. My grandmother, strangely enough, bought a motorcycle.
5. Watch out, Hubert!
6. I believe, on the other hand, that there is too much violence on television.
7. Her illness, of course, is the reason for her absence.
8. Jogging, as it turns out, has helped me lose weight.
9. Your theory, I am certain, is worthy of more consideration.
10. A car, if it is not tuned regularly, is likely to break down.

Review Exercise: Points 1–4

1. At the barbecue, we had hamburgers, hot dogs, and chicken.
2. We saw the game at the ballpark, and we watched the highlights on television.
3. After we finished eating, Harry and Gail went for a walk.
4. I am asking you, Mr. Maxwell, to give me a direct answer.
5. A bagel with cream cheese makes a great snack.
6. The manager, however, refused to listen to the demands of the employees.
7. During her road test, Trudy had to parallel park, back up, make a U-turn, and park the car on a hill.

8. He made copies of the article and circulated them among the students.
9. Without taking much time, Pat answered all the questions on the test.
10. A parent, if he wants his child to do well in school, should encourage him to work his hardest.

Another Review Exercise: Points 1–4

1. The anthropologist spoke to the audience and answered questions.
2. Before making up her mind, Linda asked her counselor for advice.
3. We cast our votes, as usual, just before the polls closed.
4. By the way, Mom, Happy Mother's Day.
5. Reading *Sports Illustrated* is my favorite way to relax.
6. In addition to mastering the use of commas, you have improved your vocabulary.
7. I am, have always been, and always will be your best friend.
8. Those wind chimes are lovely, but they are too expensive.
9. Never before in my life have I met such a man.
10. That puppy with the floppy ears is mine.

Exercise: Point 5

1. His car, which had been repaired at Moe's Garage, broke down again.
2. My sister, an Aquarian, was born in January.
3. Mr. Thomas, the coach of our football team, called practice off for today.
4. Her suggestion that we feed the cats was reinforced by a chorus of meows.
5. This cottage, which was built in 1901, is our favorite vacation spot.
6. The teakettle that I bought at the bazaar is an antique.
7. Tomorrow, June 20, is our wedding anniversary.
8. Joey, smiling like a fool, looked ridiculous.
9. The kerosene lamp, which we always use in an emergency, came in very handy.
10. The job that you applied for has been filled.

Another Exercise: Point 5

Answers to this exercise will vary. Check with your instructor if you need to.

Review Exercise: Points 1–5

1. A fool and his money are soon parted.
2. It is, I think, the best way to solve the problem.
3. Chicken soup, which some people believe can cure diseases, is delicious.
4. He can play the flute, the clarinet, the oboe, and the trumpet.

5. After a while, even the most exciting entertainment can become boring.
6. That, in fact, is exactly the reason I am here.
7. As sure as I'm breathing, you're a double for my brother.
8. Backgammon, a game which involves gambling, is very popular.
9. Nuclear plants, which some people feel are destructive to the environment, are being built in many states.
10. We browsed in the bookstore for an hour.

Exercise: Point 6

Answers to the last question in this exercise will vary. Check with your instructor if you need to.

1. Paul was born on September 3, 1953.
2. Renee works at State Hospital, 600 Washington Street, Evanstown, Kansas.
3. The paper is due on Monday, May 15.
4. The play opens on September 1, 1985, at the Stoner Theater, 50 Broad Street, Fresno, California.
5. We celebrated our anniversary July 19 in Charleston, South Carolina.

Review Exercise: Points 1–6

1. There were no runs, two hits, and two men left on base.
2. That guy in the blue suede shoes is really wild.
3. After deliberating for two hours, the jury reached a verdict.
4. Toby, Al, and Dave have moved to Palo Alto, California.
5. Biology, the study of living things, is my favorite subject.
6. I have, after much thought, reached a decision.
7. We walked and talked all night long.
8. I'm afraid it will rain, although I hope it doesn't.
9. I have, up until now, handed in my assignments on time.
10. Are you sure, pal, that you want to come along?

Chapter Review

I
1. X	6. X
2. C	7. C
3. X	8. X
4. X	9. C
5. C	10. X

II
1. This section, therefore, will be closed.
2. Hey, wait!
3. While waiting for the bus, we told each other jokes.
4. Why, Mr. Carl, must you be so rude?
5. The television set, which was stolen last week, was found in the basement of a warehouse.

6. The store is located at 520 Elm Street, Lewistown, Michigan.
7. We must, if we are ever to change our ways, begin today.
8. I'd love to go, but she won't let me.
9. Sometimes, when I am feeling blue, a good record can lift my spirits.
10. You know, of course, that our television is broken.
11. In a sense, you are right.
12. We plan, if the weather is good, to go swimming tomorrow.
13. He had always wanted to participate in the Olympics, but he had never trained properly for the trials.
14. The recipe directs you to mix the batter with one egg, add the premeasured packet of chocolate chips, and bake the mixture for forty-five minutes in an oven set at 350°.
15. Time, as it always does, has a way of changing things.
16. While showering, I sing to myself.
17. That novel, which, by the way, I have never read, is supposed to be excellent.
18. A sandwich, if made with whole wheat bread, is delicious and healthful.
19. There has never been, as far as I can remember, such a destructive storm.
20. Well, how do you like that!

III
1. (4)	6. (4)	11. (2)	16. (3)
2. (4)	7. (3)	12. (4)	17. (4)
3. (1)	8. (4)	13. (4)	18. (4)
4. (2)	9. (4)	14. (1)	19. (4)
5. (3)	10. (1)	15. (4)	20. (1)

IV Answers to this exercise will vary. Check with your instructor if you need to.

V
1. Waving her wand, the princess performed some magic.
2. Never, never will you get away with that.
3. I had a bacon, lettuce, and tomato sandwich for lunch.
4. Who, in your opinion, is the world's greatest athlete?
5. Her latest poem is superb.
6. As of next week, the prisoner will be a free man.
7. His answer, which was wrong, made the class laugh.
8. That dog barking at the tree is mine.
9. We were wed on April 17, 1977.
10. When our guests arrived, we greeted them at the door.
11. Once upon a time, there was a dog who could fly.

12. We met, as usual, at the corner of Hollywood and Vine.
13. I waited for nearly a month for your letter.
14. It is my choice, however, to travel alone.
15. For once, try studying.
16. You are mine, and I am yours.
17. Write to me at 65 Market Street, Portland, Maine.
18. You are all prepared, I'm sure, for the test.
19. Ice cream, if it is made at home, is very good.
20. As long as I live, I will love to dance.

VI When we spent the day at my grandmother's cottage on the beach, we had a great time. My wife and I, together with two friends, drove about sixty miles from our home to the small two-room beach house, which had been built over a hundred years ago. We stopped at a small market to pick up some food for sandwiches and ate as soon as we arrived at the cottage. We spent the rest of the day eating, drinking, sunning ourselves, going for walks, and swimming. By the time the sun went down, we were thoroughly exhausted. Isn't it strange, I ask you, that doing nothing can make someone so tired?

Liberal arts, contrary to what some people think, provides a good basis for an education. It is important, I believe, for every student to be well grounded in such subjects as art, history, science, politics, and English. These subjects give students a good idea of what has been accomplished in the history of the world, and of what is yet to be accomplished. By the time one completes a full program in liberal arts, he or she will be ready to live with vigor and vitality.

CHAPTER 14

Exercise: Point 1

1. Have you ever seen *The Agony and the Ecstasy?*
2. I read an article entitled "The History of Jazz."
3. One of Freud's most important books is called *The Interpretation of Dreams.*
4. We saw a production of Shakespeare's *The Taming of the Shrew.*
5. I have a book called *How to Grow Beautiful House Plants.*

Another Exercise: Point 1

Answers to this exercise will vary. Check with your instructor if you need to.

Exercise: Point 2

1. The Fowlers always spend their vacation in the Caribbean.

2. Mel gave up his United States citizenship when he moved to Canada.
3. Joe Perry has moved to Los Angeles, California.
4. Does Lorie know how to speak German?
5. Venezuela, Argentina, Mexico, and most of Latin America have been free countries since they rebelled against Spain.
6. Lou takes great pride in his Italian-American heritage.
7. The school is going to offer a course in black history next semester.

Another Exercise: Point 2

Answers to this exercise will vary. Check with your instructor if you need to.

Another Exercise: Point 3

1. September 21 is the first day of autumn.
2. I am on the road on Monday and Thursday.
3. Independence Day falls on July 4.
4. We visit my family on the first Sunday of every month.
5. September and October are the loveliest months of the year.

Another Exercise: Point 3

Answers to this exercise will vary. Check with your instructor if you need to.

Review Exercise: Points 1–3

1. I read *The Boys from Brazil* last spring.
2. Barry Smith works in New York, but he lives on Long Island.
3. On Monday we will discuss Ibsen's play entitled *A Doll's House*.
4. I travel to the mountains every autumn.
5. Marcia was born in Canada, but she lives in Kansas and considers herself an American.
6. The police found the stolen car in Norfolk County.
7. Have you read the article "A Way to Understand the Universe"?
8. Be careful on April Fool's Day.
9. She is reading a book about American Indians.
10. Last summer we visited Texas, Oklahoma, and Nevada.

Exercise: Point 4

1. John asked Lucy, "Will you come to the dance with me?"
2. The pharmacist said, "Here is your prescription."
3. "When will we get our tests back?" I asked.
4. "You are all invited to the victory party," the candidate announced.
5. "Please pick up some tomatoes," she said.

Another Exercise: Point 4

Answers to this exercise will vary. Check with your instructor if you need to.

Exercise: Point 5

1. Happy Birthday, Sister.
2. I'm not eating these lima beans, Mom.
3. My aunt is a champion at poker.
4. Have you heard from Uncle Ebenezer?
5. My brother is also my best friend.
6. I heard that Ed's father used to play professional baseball.
7. My grandmother married a man half her age.
8. Is it true that Father knows best?
9. I visited Grandpa Mac in his office.
10. Abby's cousin Lisa is very pretty.

Exercise: Point 6

1. We took a boat ride on the Colorado River.
2. The ice cream shop is located on Franklin Drive.
3. She teaches literature at Thomas University.
4. He has been our senator for twelve years.
5. Mr. Michaels is our professor.
6. He expects us to call him Professor Michaels.
7. She was the architect for the Wilson County Courthouse.
8. Have you ever visited Phoenix Park in Dublin?
9. They went swimming in the pond.
10. They went swimming in Walden Pond.

Review Exercise: Points 1–6

1. Dr. Meyer's office is on State Street.
2. On the first night of Chanukah, we visited Grandma and Grandpa.
3. We went to Time Square on New Year's Eve.
4. Our teacher is from the Iberian Peninsula.
5. "When will you hand in that paper?" the professor asked.
6. I answered, "I will hand it in next Tuesday."
7. Have you seen *Terms of Endearment*?
8. I liked *An Officer and a Gentleman* even better.
9. Does your brother still work at the plant?
10. In the fall we will go camping at Bear Mountain.

Another Review Exercise: Points 1–6

Answers to this exercise will vary. Check with your instructor if you need to.

Exercise: Point 7

1. The Declaration of Independence was signed in 1776.
2. Life was exciting in the Frontier Age.
3. The Vietnam War was thought by many to be a tragedy.

4. Leonardo da Vinci was an important figure during the Renaissance.
5. The Gettysburg Address was delivered by Abraham Lincoln.

Another Exercise: Point 7

Answers to this exercise will vary. Check with your instructor if you need to.

Exercise: Point 8

1. She is studying English with Professor Ross.
2. Do you expect to take German 101 next semester?
3. Esther plans to major in anthropology.
4. I wanted to take English 2a, but my advisor suggested I take Basic Composition.
5. He got an A on his physics final.

Another Exercise: Point 8

Answers to this exercise will vary. Check with your instructor if you need to.

Review Exercise: Points 1–8

1. Who was responsible for the break-in at Watergate?
2. Aunt Tilly is preparing her annual Christmas dinner.
3. Next winter we will ski in the Alps.
4. "Why didn't you fill that prescription?" Dr. Cohen asked.
5. Do you refer to Taj Mahal the singer or to Taj Mahal the building?
6. Chrissy got a B in Biology 2a last term.
7. So, Mom, do you think I should buy a Ford or a Chevy?
8. The United States entered World War II after the attack on Pearl Harbor.
9. Can we try that new French restaurant?
10. Peter Sellers is the star of *The Return of the Pink Panther*.

Chapter Review

I

1. X	6. X
2. X	7. X
3. X	8. X
4. C	9. X
5. X	10. X

II
1. He is my uncle from Las Vegas.
2. The professor asked, "Who knows the answer to this question?"
3. I always buy the newspaper on Sunday.
4. Jefferson City is the capital of Missouri.
5. The boutique is located on Willis Avenue.
6. Don't capitalize every letter you see!
7. I just finished reading *The Double Helix*.
8. Did you see the football game on New Year's Day?
9. When, Dad, will you ever understand me?
10. Zelda lives a zesty life in Zanzibar.
11. Mr. Fisher, our biology teacher, is also coach of the basketball team.
12. I will play basketball for the Detroit Pistons.
13. You can find the book you want at the Atlanta Public Library.
14. For the second time, I flunked Economics 101.
15. "I live near the Charles River," he said.
16. Richard plans to join the Peace Corps.
17. In October the leaves begin to fall.
18. When we were in California, we visited the La Brea Tar Pits.
19. She teaches Spanish at Billings High School.
20. He was born in Mexico City, and he lives in San Antonio, Texas.

III Answers to this exercise will vary. Check with your instructor if you need to.

IV

1. summer	11. *in*
2. father	12. weekend
3. *Story*	13. do
4. Why	14. time
5. Doctor	15. bagpipes
6. Latin	16. Winter
7. aunt	17. Ages
8. teacher	18. sister, school
9. Yankees	19. Greek
10. River	20. whether

V
1. "Lucy in the Sky with Diamonds" is a Beatles' song.
2. He was born in Mexico, and he has lived there all his life.
3. I would like to drive a Rolls Royce.
4. I'm only asking you, Dad, to give me another chance.
5. The babysitter pleaded, "Behave yourself."
6. My grandfather will be ninety years old next month.
7. The Chicago Cubs are in the National League.
8. Let's see the fireworks on Independence Day.
9. Albert's Aunt Alberta has arrived!
10. We ate dinner in the restaurant at the top of the building.
11. Is there a doctor in the house?
12. When you are in New York, visit Macy's.
13. Come on, Horatio, you're holding us up.
14. I asked Dr. Simmons if I could change my appointment.
15. Mario is the manager of a big department store.
16. Mail the form to John Doe, Anytown, U.S.A.
17. I read the bestseller called *Sophie's Choice*.

18. Everyone wants to know when the stock market will improve.
19. My brother exclaimed, "So this is your apartment!"
20. Martin Luther King headed the civil rights movement.

VI Many people think of baseball as the Great American Game. And why not? Fans get to sit in beautiful parks such as Yankee Stadium, eat hot dogs, watch an exciting event, and yell their lungs out. All the fun and excitement typifies the spirit of America. A great writer, Roger Angell, has examined the intricacies of the sport, and of the event, in his collection of essays entitled *Five Seasons: A Baseball Companion.* It makes great reading for the serious and even the not-so-serious fan.

If you need someone to fix something in your apartment or house, don't call me! I have read *The Book of Home Repair*, and still cannot manage to hang a picture or fix a leaky faucet. Whenever something goes wrong in my home, I always call my uncle, who is a whiz at such things. Last fall—I believe it was around Thanksgiving—our garbage disposal overflowed. As usual, I called my uncle, who said, "This is getting a bit out of hand. You can't expect me to drive all the way from Cleveland to fix your garbage disposal!" Seeing as we lived in Chicago, he was right. I called a plumber instead, who charged me fifty dollars for the job; the lake on the kitchen floor vanished, but I vowed I would either learn something about home repair or move to Cleveland.

CHAPTER 15

Exercise: Point 1

1. priest	6. C
2. C	7. piece
3. receipt	8. feign
4. weight	9. sleigh
5. retrieve	10. C

Exercise: Point 2

1. entirely	6. smoked
2. coming	7. safety
3. improvement	8. likable
4. guidance	9. useful
5. loveless	10. completion

Review Exercise: Points 1 and 2

1. Fernando weighs 165 pounds.
2. You will need a stepladder to paint that ceiling.
3. Your pleasure is my pleasure.
4. Gail bears a great likeness to her mother.

5. We expressed our condolences at the funeral.
6. The hobo scrambled aboard the freight train.
7. She always speaks sincerely about the most delicate of issues.
8. This is one weird party!
9. I was truly amazed at the feats the sword-swallower performed.
10. One pays a price for being famous.

Exercise: Point 3

1. gullies	6. strayed
2. worried	7. frying
3. happiness	8. necessarily
4. repaying	9. applied
5. attorneys	10. loneliest

Exercise: Point 4

1. girls	6. apartments
2. typewriters	7. porches
3. churches	8. buses
4. traces	9. aches
5. cigars	10. taxes

Review Exercise: Points 1–4

1. Norman was cursing his fate.
2. I have already applied to three graduate schools.
3. I'm looking for a piece of the action.
4. His whole apartment is lighted by gas lamps.
5. There are three different styles of couches to choose from.
6. That is a great weight off my shoulders.
7. We are looking ahead hopefully to the next election.
8. Richard is pursuing a new career.
9. Honey, you are my shining star.
10. This sandwich is just awful.

Exercise: Point 5

controlled	6. developed
2. admitting	7. suffering
3. beginning	8. fishing
4. smallest	9. puffed
5. screaming	10. stirring

Review Exercise: Points 1–5

1. This is a chapter about spelling.
2. I am admitting no fault whatsoever.
3. We visited Ripley's Believe It or Not Museum.
4. Tomorrow we will go horseback riding.
5. I have resisted greater temptations in the past.
6. Those bananas are rotting!
7. Come to this office immediately!
8. This corner is the busiest one in Boston.
9. Everyone benefited by his generosity.
10. All waiters should report to the dining room.

Chapter Review

I
1. radios
2. arranging
3. C
4. fortieth
5. C
6. C
7. developed
8. receive
9. C
10. bushes
11. paying
12. grief
13. eightieth
14. lively
15. C
16. despairing
17. ladders
18. association
19. leisure
20. C

II
1. getting
2. guiding
3. satisfied
4. spies
5. running
6. seizure
7. partying
8. relieved
9. likeness
10. hopeless
11. praying
12. timed
13. spiteful
14. toying
15. guidance
16. managed
17. married
18. pitted
19. chopped
20. pitiable

III
1. goats
2. babies
3. guitars
4. envelopes
5. woes
6. trees
7. histories
8. tacos
9. churches
10. glasses

IV
1. criticism
2. embarrassed
3. careless
4. pays
5. friendly
6. uncontrollable
7. privilege
8. seized
9. sophomore
10. employed

V
1. Ken slipped on the ice and broke his ankle.
2. My girlfriend spends too much time studying.
3. The lamp broke into hundreds of pieces.
4. Forget it; it is neither my business nor yours.
5. I'll be flying high if I get good news.
6. The administration has adopted a new policy on energy.
7. Camping in Vermont was such a pleasure.
8. She is the fairest and loveliest child I know.
9. The criminal was sentenced to ninety years in prison.
10. You have embarrassed me with your remark.
11. Church and state must be separated.
12. "Describe the man you saw," said the detective.
13. This is your third absence from class this week.
14. I admitted my secret passion.
15. Welcome to the neighborhood!
16. The weather around here is so changeable.
17. We have gone to four parties already this week.
18. I can't stand shopping for shoes.
19. The strings are broken and have to be replaced.
20. I am a very happily married man.

VI   Late summer is truly a lovely time of the year. After being fried by the heat and drenched by the humidity, many people feel that it is a great relief to experience the cool evenings that promise the coming of autumn. As the cool weather returns, people seem to regain much of the energy that they had lost during the hot and sticky months of July and August. There are all kinds of outdoor activities: baseball games, barbecues, campfires. It is as if the cool breezes bring with them a fresh and new feeling for life.

There is probably no greater thrill or privilege than watching the birth of your own child. Many of my friends have accepted the responsibility of taking part in the process, particularly by acting as an assistant to the doctor. These husbands have helped their wives with breathing and relaxation techniques. Above all, they get the definite pleasure of witnessing what is surely the most amazing act of all.

CHAPTER 16

Exercise: Point 1

1. I own the house.
2. The police officer owns the whistle.
3. The dancer owns the leotard.
4. The car has the headlights.
5. My father owns the newspaper.
6. My mother has the credit card.
7. My wife owns the ring.
8. The engine has the power.
9. My baby sister owns the dolls.
10. Aretha owns the fountain pen.

Exercise: Point 2

1. my mother's idea.
2. Judy's plants
3. the library's copy machine.
4. the people's choice
5. the detective's job
6. the camper's mail
7. Sam's pants
8. the bookie's money
9. the baby's rattle
10. the boy's paper route

Exercise: Point 3

1. the babies' crying
2. my cousins' home town
3. the barbers' chairs
4. the rooftops' slant
5. the cigars' smell
6. the exhibits' duration

7. the professors' offices
8. the men's running shoes
9. the players' salaries
10. the tables' legs

Review Exercise: Points 1–3

1. John's mother belongs to the Women's Club.
2. Have you read Mark's essay on sexual freedom?
3. The women's marathon is the next event.
4. Is this Carlos' raincoat?
5. Have you ever been to a world's fair?
6. The publishers wanted to buy Martha's manuscript.
7. One of Boston's popular meeting places is the Common.
8. Mr. Dickens' daughter will be married next week.
9. The manager's lineup card was taped to the dugout wall.
10. The Yankees' home field is Yankee Stadium.

Exercise: Point 4

1. animals
2. senators'
3. titles
4. courses'
5. trees
6. parents'
7. bugs'
8. candles
9. stars
10. show's

Exercise: Point 5

Answers to this exercise will vary. Check with your instructor if you need to.
1. It is his decision to make.
2. We will have to change our approach.
3. That sewing machine is hers.
4. The storm had taken its toll.
5. Whose beautiful garden is this?
6. What can I do to make you change your mind?
7. They are taking their children to the ballet.
8. I bought it, so it is mine.
9. I must be losing my mind.
10. I am sorry, sir, but that coat is not yours; it is his.

Review Exercise: Points 1–5

1. The children's play group meets once a week.
2. Mr. Jones's car needs to be washed.
3. Great writers' messages are sometimes misunderstood.
4. That seat is not yours, it is mine.
5. The superintendent's apartment was vandalized last night.
6. Now it is someone else's game to win or lose.
7. Whose ten-speed bicycle are you using?
8. The teachers' union supported the strike.
9. Do you understand the reasons for my decision?
10. The river overflowed its banks.

Exercise: Point 6

1. He's never been to summer camp before.
2. I'll buy the chips if you'll make the dip.
3. They'd have arrived on time if they didn't have a balky car.
4. I'm sorry, but this time it's not my fault.
5. She'll never know what hit her.
6. I'd have chosen a different color.
7. Let's work together for a change.
8. He wouldn't mind if you combed his hair with a rake.
9. I haven't been to the dentist in three years.
10. Patti doesn't plan to be an Avon lady all her life.

Exercise: Point 7

1. It's a beautiful day for a drive in the country.
2. Whose bright idea was that?
3. This is your problem, not mine.
4. Do you approve of the way they raise their children?
5. My soda has lost its fizz.
6. Who's the leader of the local Democratic organization?
7. You're good man, Charlie Brown.
8. They're never going to be able to straighten out their finances.
9. It's a sure bet!
10. Who's going to pay for all this damage?

Review Exercise: Points 1–7

1. We're hoping that she'll pass her English exam.
2. It's Russ's car, and he'll be angry if you drive it.
3. The day's work isn't done yet.
4. The orchestra's performance wasn't up to par.
5. Is the responsibility yours or Tim's?
6. Lately we've been keeping a hawk's eye on our diets.
7. That actress's lines should be rewritten.
8. That's Ernie's problem, not mine.
9. Ray's motorcycle isn't running smoothly these days.
10. It's never too late to say you're sorry.

Chapter Review

I
1. C
2. X
3. X
4. X
5. C
6. X
7. C
8. C
9. X
10. X

II
1. Sally's
2. Mr. Ross's
3. Bill's
4. my mother's
5. Aunt Betty's
6. the company's
7. my son's
8. your friend's
9. the team's
10. Chris's

III
1. hers
2. ours
3. mine
4. his
5. yours
6. their
7. my
8. theirs
9. your
10. whose

IV
1. It's a sin to tell a lie.
2. It is their way of showing affection.
3. You're the most beautiful woman I've ever seen.
4. I am the one whose paper you read.
5. The airplane is in trouble; its wing has caught fire.
6. They're never going to believe this back in Muncie.
7. He has been imitating your style for some time.
8. Guess who's coming to dinner.
9. It is the captain's decision to make.
10. Who's going to clean it up?

V
1. Womens' wear is on the second floor.
2. You're a very stylish dresser.
3. My sister's makeup kit is overflowing.
4. That artist's style is certainly unique.
5. Marcus' friend is staying with him for the summer.
6. Those books are Bobby's and mine.
7. You're so pretty that you could be anyone's girlfriend.
8. Lately I've grown close to Mike's wife.
9. My father's business takes him to the Orient twice a year.
10. Did you heed the guru's advice?
11. We're learning the basic skills of writing.
12. The horse trotted to the winner's circle.
13. The fireworks display was very exciting.
14. Your brother's van has a flat tire.
15. Lenin's ideas do not appeal to everyone.
16. Those babies are twins!
17. The doctor's office is closed today.
18. What is Brian's idea of a good time?
19. Who's going to pay the check?
20. Let's go to the movies.

VI
1. It's yours, so do with it as you please.
2. I think it's never going to stop raining.
3. She's minding someone else's shop today.
4. It was my employer's idea to give me a raise.
5. We've visited Majorie's beach house twice before.
6. I met your brother at the station.
7. Our family's motto is "Live and let live."
8. The musician's trumpet has been stolen.
9. The bank's new vault is burglar-proof.
10. Those criminals' records show their history.
11. Lead me to the men's room, please.
12. I borrowed my parents' car.
13. Where's the beef?
14. Joseph's piano needs to be tuned.
15. The sisters' husbands have lunch together every Monday.
16. Girls' haircuts are generally quite attractive.
17. James's new car has an AM-FM radio.
18. The employees' lunchroom is located downstairs.
19. My aunt's tapioca pudding is the best in the world.
20. Don't try telling me that your way is better.

VII
    Ella Fitzgerald's style of singing is one of the most exciting I have ever heard. Without any formal training in music, she's managed to develop her voice to its full potential. Who's ever going to dispute the statement that her scat singing makes her voice sound like a musical instrument? Ella's versions of Cole Porter's songs are particularly moving and beautiful. She is able to understand the songs so well, and get so much feeling into Porter's lyrics, that listening to her performances becomes one of life's great pleasures.

    I've never been one to keep New Year's resolutions. It's always been easy enough for me to promise to give up my bad habits, but I just don't seem to keep my promises. Once, the day after I'd resolved never to smoke cigarettes again, my wife found a pack around and yelled, "Whose are these?" "They're mine," I answered sheepishly. It's a sure bet I'll resolve to quit again this year, but unless I get serious, I'm sure my wife's advice, "You're never serious about something until you're serious about it" will once again prove true.

Student Questionnaire

In preparing the fourth edition of TROU-BLESHOOTING, we would appreciate your evaluation of the present edition. Your suggestions will definitely affect the contents of the fourth edition. Please return this questionnaire to the English Editor, College Department, Holt, Rinehart and Winston, 383 Madison Avenue, New York, N.Y. 10017

Name _____   Date _____

School _____   Course title _____

Instructor _____

1. Did you find this book too easy? _____ too difficult? _____

   about right? _____

2. Which chapters did you find most helpful? Which chapters did you find least helpful?

   _____

	Helpful	Not Helpful
Grammar Review		
Subjects	_____	_____
Verbs	_____	_____
Writing Better Sentences		
Subject-Verb Agreement	_____	_____
Fragments	_____	_____
Run-ons	_____	_____
Misplaced Modifiers	_____	_____
Dangling Modifiers	_____	_____
Pronouns and Faulty Pronoun Reference	_____	_____
Faulty Parallelism	_____	_____
Shifts in Number, Person, and Tense	_____	_____
Punctuation		
Period, Question Mark, Exclamation Point, Quotation Marks	_____	_____
Semicolon and Colon	_____	_____
Comma	_____	_____
Mechanics		
Capital Letters	_____	_____
Spelling	_____	_____
Possessives and Contractions	_____	_____

3. Did this book help you to write better? Yes _____ No _____

4. Do you intend to keep this book? Yes _____ No _____

5. What changes should we make in the next edition? _____